The Conce

Jorge Larrain is Lecturer in Sociology in the University of Birmingham. He was born in 1942 in Santiago, Chile. After taking a degree in Theology and another in Sociology (1971) at the Catholic University of Chile, he taught and researched at an interdisciplinary Centre (CEREN) in the same University. In 1973 he came to England, and at the University of Sussex took an MA in 1974 and a Ph.D in 1977. Since that year he has taught at the University of Birmingham, mainly in the fields of the sociology of knowledge and the sociology of development. He has published various articles on the Chilean experience before the military coup of 1973, both in Santiago and Madrid.

The Concept of Ideology

Jorge Larrain

Lecturer in Sociology
University of Birmingham

Hutchinson
London Melbourne Sydney Auckland Johannesburg

Hutchinson & Co. (Publishers) Ltd

An imprint of the Hutchinson Publishing Group

17-21 Conway Street, London W1P 6JD

Hutchinson Publishing Group (Australia) Pty Ltd
PO Box 496, 16-22 Church Street,
Hawthorne, Melbourne, Victoria 3122

Hutchinson Group (NZ) Ltd
32-34 View Road, PO Box 40-086, Glenfield, Auckland 10

Hutchinson Group (SA) (Pty) Ltd
PO Box 337, Bergvlei 2012, South Africa

First published 1979
Reprinted 1980, 1984

© Jorge Larrain 1979

Set in Monotype Times New Roman

Printed and bound in Great Britain by
Anchor Brendon Ltd, Tiptree, Essex

Larrain, Jorge
    The concept of ideology
    1. Ideology
    I. Title
    145   B823.3

ISBN 0 09 138950 x cased
        0 09 138951 8 paper

To Mercedes

Contents

Acknowledgements

I would like to thank very specially Professor T. B. Bottomore for his constant encouragement and inspiration, without which this book would have never been written. I am also greatly indebted to Steven Lukes and Stuart Hall for their patience in reading an early version of the manuscript and their useful suggestions. There are no adequate words to express my gratitude to F. Castillo and R. Echeverría, friends and former colleagues, with whom I held long discussions on the subject of this book and who greatly helped me to clarify my ideas. I owe a particular debt to J. Krige and Chris Chippindale for their useful criticisms and corrections of my primitive English. The responsibility for both the imperfections and the final views remains, of course, my own. I also want to thank Mrs B. Dodson and Ms D. Taylor for their help in typing the manuscript. The book owes much to the intellectual stimulus received at the Graduate School of Arts and Social Studies in the University of Sussex, the Sociology Department and the Centre for Contemporary Cultural Studies in the University of Birmingham. I am also indebted to the institutions which have made possible my life in England for the past six years, during which this book was conceived and written: the British Council, the Ford Foundation, World University Service, and the University of Birmingham. Finally, I owe to Mercedes, my wife, more than to anyone. Without her support and encouragement during the uncertainties of the past six years nothing would have been possible.

Foreword

by Tom Bottomore

Since that brief, scarcely remembered, interlude in the 1950s, when a few sociologists claimed to discern an approaching 'end of ideology', a notable resurgence of ideological disputation has occurred in many societies – capitalist and socialist, industrial and non-industrial – during the past two decades; and this movement, naturally enough, has reawakened the interest of social scientists in the nature and bases of ideology. For the most part, however, those who have dealt with the subject have confined themselves to examining, critically or otherwise, specific ideologies, or to analysing the concept of ideology, in rather summary fashion, from a particular theoretical perspective.

There has long been a need for a more comprehensive study, and this need is now handsomely satisfied by Dr Larrain in the present book. He provides, in the first place, a clear and well-documented account of the historical development of the concept through diverse formulations, in terms of four basic questions: namely, whether ideology is conceived negatively (as 'false consciousness') or positively (as a 'world-view' expressing the values of a particular social group); whether it is regarded as a subjective, psychological phenomenon or an objective, social one; whether it is seen as a specific element in the 'superstructure' of society or as identical with the whole sphere of culture; and, finally, how ideology is related to, and differentiated from, science.

But the book offers a great deal more than a well-ordered intellectual history, admirably though that aspect is handled. Within his historical framework Dr Larrain examines, in a thorough and searching manner, the coherence and value of some of the most important conceptions of ideology, from Mannheim to the modern structuralists. The chapter which he devotes to the structural analysis of myth and ideology demonstrates especially well his ability to expound complex theoretical views with exemplary clarity, and his skill in uncovering their problematic features.

This work will become, I believe, an indispensable source of reference for all those concerned with the problem of ideology. Still more, Dr Larrain's discussion in the concluding chapter, where he takes up the vexed question of the demarcation of science from ideology, and considers more general aspects of the social location of science, will suggest some new directions in the analysis of cultural phenomena.

Introduction

Ideology is perhaps one of the most equivocal and elusive concepts one can find in the social sciences; not only because of the variety of theoretical approaches which assign different meanings and functions to it, but also because it is a concept heavily charged with political connotations and widely used in everyday life with the most diverse significations. The purpose of this book is to introduce the reader to the concept of ideology by elucidating its most relevant meanings, functions and relationships, and by showing some of its methodological and political implications within the context of its various formulations.

The book is not intended to be either a merely descriptive and detailed historical review of the various conceptions or a search for a syncretic version. It aims rather at discussing analytically the basis upon which diverse schools of thought build up their theories. In doing this, it does not only try to throw light upon theoretical options, but also takes a position with respect to some of the central issues and questions which stem from them. Although the book cannot claim to be an exhaustive historical account of all the theories and interpretations concerned with ideology, I have tried to cover the most important contributions to the concept by emphasizing a critical and analytical approach within a loose historical framework. The very scope of the task has demanded a discussion pitched at a certain level of generality which necessarily precludes the development of too detailed and complicated arguments.

The main questions which this book sets out to clarify are concerned with the character, origin, scope and relationships of the concept of ideology. These questions present alternative solutions and although they overlap in some of their features, each one highlights a particular aspect which is worthwhile distinguishing.

First, the question arises as to whether ideology has a negative or positive meaning. On the one hand, ideology may be conceived in eminently negative terms as a critical concept which means a form of false consciousness or necessary deception which somehow distorts men's understanding of social reality: the cognitive value of ideas affected by ideology is called in question. On the other hand, the concept of ideology may be conceived in positive terms as the expression of the world-view of a class. To this extent one can talk of 'ideologies', in plural, as the opinions, theories and attitudes formed within a class in order to defend and promote its interests. The cognitive value of ideological ideas is, therefore, set aside as a different problem.

Secondly, the question can be raised as to whether ideology has an eminently subjective and psychological character or is, on the contrary, entirely dependent upon objective factors. If subjective, ideology is conceived of as a deformation of consciousness, which somehow is unable to grasp reality as it is. If objective, ideology appears as a deception induced by reality itself: it is not the subject that distorts reality but reality itself which deceives the subject. While the subjective view emphasizes the role of individuals, classes and parties in the production of ideology, the objective view sees ideology as impregnating the basic structure of society.

A further question arises as to whether ideology should be considered as a particular kind of phenomenon within the vast range of superstructural phenomena, or whether ideology is equivalent to and co-extensive with the whole cultural sphere usually called the 'ideological superstructure'. The first of these alternatives relies upon a restrictive concept of ideology since not all cultural objects would be 'ideological'. Conversely, the second identifies ideology with an objective level of society which includes all forms of social consciousness.

Finally, the question arises as to how one is to tackle the relationships between ideology and science. Ideology may be conceived of as the antithesis of science; that is to say, it may be equated with preconceptions or irrational elements which disturb reason, thus preventing it from reaching the truth. So when scientific method is correctly applied, ideology is supposed to vanish. On the other hand, it is possible to stress the common features between science and ideology, rather than their differences, so ideology and science would have a common basis in the world-view of the originating class. On this view, ideology cannot be overcome by science, and science itself may become ideological.

These four basic questions are tackled under different forms and in various contexts within the six chapters of this book.

Chapter 1 sets out, in a quick historical survey, how the concept of ideology came to be produced and which traditions and authors contributed to its formation from the sixteenth century to the nineteenth century. The concept of ideology is shown to have emerged from the new scientific and philosophical approach of the modern times and in close connection with the critique of religion. However, at first the term ideology was not widely used, and was first applied to designate a science of ideas. It is in Marx that the critical tradition and the term ideology fuse themselves into a new concept. Chapter 2 deals with this encounter by presenting Marx's concept of ideology in the context of his intellectual development. With Marx the concept loses its former psychological overtones and becomes connected with the historical evolution of social contradictions. The concept of ideology is born as a critical notion which accounts for a misrepresentation rooted in material reality.

Chapter 3 is concerned with the debates and contributions to the concept by the turn of the century. A number of new developments emerge. First and foremost is the evolution from a negative to a positive concept of ideology which Lenin institutionalized within Marxist theory. Second, the beginnings of a dual interpretation of Marx are apparent in the opposition between a historicist approach (Lukács, Gramsci) and a more positivist understanding which stems from Engels. Third, beyond the Marxist debate Pareto and Freud re-introduce a psychological concept of ideology while Durkheim, in the Baconian tradition, lays the foundation of a positivist conception of ideology. Chapter 4 tackles the development of the historicist tradition in Mannheim and Goldmann, who introduce the sociological analysis of literature and cultural phenomena using the concept of *Weltanschauung*. Ideology acquires a more definite subjective character as the world-view or 'perspective' of a class and is universalized to a point where its usefulness as an analytical and critical notion can be doubted.

Chapter 5 explores structuralism in its most important manifestations: the anthropological line of Lévi-Strauss and Godelier, the structural linguistic approach of Barthes and Greimas, the semiological line of *Tel Quel* and the Althusserian transposition of structuralist elements into Marxism. Structuralism originates, both within and without Marxism, new and forceful propositions for the understanding of ideology. Cultural phenomena are no longer understood as genetic products of a subject but rather as subjectless, synchronic, underlying structures. Hence the importance of linguistics and semiology, some of whose representatives rediscover in Freud a new source of insights into the concept of ideology. Finally, chapter 6 tackles the complex problem of the relationship between ideology and science in a global manner by reviewing and confronting three possible attitudes at the bottom of the contemporary debate on science and ideology, namely, positivism, historicism and Marxism.

1 Historical origins of the concept of ideology

The forerunners

The term ideology was first used by Destutt de Tracy at the end of the eighteenth century and was fully developed as a concept during the nineteenth century; but the preoccupation with some of the problems covered by this notion began much earlier. There have been phenomena related to the intellectual legitimation of social domination and to other sources of mental distortions in the knowledge of reality as long as there have been class societies. In this sense ideology is not a new phenomenon in the history of mankind. Yet the interest in analysing and systematically studying this kind of phenomenon only appeared in modern times following the disintegration of medieval society.[1]*

In effect, the emergence of the problematic, later associated with the concept of ideology, is closely related to the liberation struggles of the bourgeoisie from feudal fetters and to the new critical attitude of modern thought. The political opposition to the landed aristocracy was accompanied by a critique of its scholastic justifications for the exercise of power. To the new bourgeois ethics of labour, which opposed the medieval serf-holding society, there corresponded a new scientific and critical outlook which emphasized the practical knowledge of nature. Contemplation was replaced by cognition as production, the hierarchical and theocentric order of essences, passively accepted, was superseded by a critical approach which sought in man's own reason and in its dominion of nature the new criterion of truth. From the beginning, therefore, the problematic of ideology emerged in close connection with both political practice and the development of science.

N. Machiavelli (1469–1527), a representative of the early bourgeoisie,[2] is perhaps the first author who dealt with matters directly connected with ideological phenomena. His acute observations on

*Superior figures refer to the notes on pages 213–50.

the political practice of princes, and, in general, on human behaviour in politics, anticipate later developments of the concept, although he did not use the term 'ideology' at all. Some elements of the concept appear, for instance, when he relates the bias of human judgements to appetites and interests. Wondering why men are often partial in criticizing the present, he contends that

as men's appetites change, even though their circumstances remain the same, it is impossible that things should look the same to them seeing that they have other appetites, other interests, other standpoints . . . instead of blaming the times, they should lay the blame on their own judgement.[3]

Another important point made by Machiavelli is the way he links religion to power and domination. With great clarity he anticipates a recurrent theme of the concept of ideology, namely, the critique of the social functions of religious thought. Machiavelli wonders why earlier peoples were more fond of liberty than his contemporaries. His answer is that the difference lies in the education which is based upon a different conception of religion:

Our religion has glorified humble and contemplative men, rather than men of action. It has assigned as man's highest good humility, abnegation, and contempt for mundane things. . . . This pattern of life, therefore, appears to have made the world weak, and to have handed it over as a prey to the wicked, who run it successfully and securely since they are well aware that the generality of men, with paradise for their goal, consider how best to bear, rather than how best to avenge, their injuries.[4]

A third aspect of Machiavelli's ideas which can be related to ideology are his considerations on the use of force and fraud in order to get and maintain power. According to Machiavelli, princes must learn to practise deceit since force never suffices. While there is hardly a case of a humble man who acquires vast power 'simply by the use of open and undisguised force', this 'can quite well be done by using only fraud'.[5] While the exercise of power requires such good qualities as the honouring of one's word, compassion and devoutness, the prince need not have all of them, 'but he should certainly appear to have them'. Even more, 'his disposition should be such that, if he needs to be the opposite, he knows how'. The reason this could be successfully done is the fact that 'everyone sees what you appear to be, few experience what you really are'.[6] This distinction between appearance and reality was later developed in a new sense and acquired foremost importance in Marx's conception of ideology. Machiavelli's repeated attempts to strike a balance

between the use of force and the capture of the people's friendship
and goodwill (including here the use of deceit) might also be considered a forerunner of Gramsci's distinction between hegemony
and coercion.

Machiavelli's contributions to political practice are complemented
by other developments in the field of science. With the disintegration
of medieval society, a new scientific approach to the knowledge of
nature receives impulse and begins to supersede scholastic philosophy. Theoretical contemplation of a hierarchical and sacred world
is replaced by a conception which values the practical function of
thought. The development of commerce, money exchange, secular-
ized education, cities, and so forth, leads to a new consideration of
knowledge in its social and historical perspective. A precise and
unbiased knowledge of nature is needed for it to be practically
mastered, and this becomes the overwhelming preoccupation of
intellectuals. The new trends arise in opposition to the feudal system
and its theological view of the world. The development of an accurate
knowledge of nature has been so far limited, not because men are
essentially incapable of knowing the world, but because some artificial obstacles have prevented it. This is why, together with the
appearance of science, the concern for those factors which perturb
its development is born. In other words, the begetting of science is
necessarily accompanied by a critique of former methods of cognition.

Here is the origin of the question about the obstacles to real knowledge, about those irrational elements which crop up in the mind
and make it difficult fully to grasp reality. Bacon's *Novum Organon*
(1620), like Descartes' *Discourse de la méthode* (1637), is among the
first methodological writings which begin systematically to doubt
the traditional approaches to science. Both are concerned with the
need for a new methodology which could overcome the shortcomings of the Aristotelian–medieval thought. Yet while Descartes
remains at a more philosophical and deductive level, Bacon emphasizes the role of positive science and its observational character. He
wants to supersede Aristotle's *Organon* by a *New Organon* which no
longer insists on a deductive formal logic in the approach to reality
but replaces it by an inductive approach.

For Bacon the observational knowledge of nature cannot succeed
unless it is rid of certain irrational factors which beset the human
mind, the idols or false notions which obstruct human understanding

and prevent it from reaching the truth. These are four classes of idols; the idols of the tribe, the idols of the cave, the idols of the market-place, and the idols of the theatre. The first two are innate; they cannot be eliminated, only recognized. They operate spontaneously in the process of cognition in such a way that human understanding resembles a warped mirror 'whose shape and curvature change the rays of objects', distorting and disfiguring them.[7] The distortion brought by the idols of the tribe has its foundation in human nature itself, these idols therefore being common to the human species; the source of the errors brought by the idols of the cave is the idiosyncrasy of each individual as determined by his character, education and general predisposition.

Among the idols of the tribe, two are of particular interest. The first is the natural trend to accept those propositions which have been once laid down and established themselves, without making any critical examination. Although this idol is most seductive in science and philosophy, it is also the mechanism of superstition.[8] Even before he came up with his theory of idols, Bacon had been concerned with the corrupting effect of superstition upon science and philosophy. Superstition was the source of harmful distortions for scientific knowledge in so far as it subjected the mind to uncontrollable forces and sacrificed rational discussion for the sake of arbitrary whims.[9] More generally, Bacon thought that the scholastic confusion between philosophy and theology was especially damaging for science; he advocated a clear-cut separation between religious knowledge and philosophy. So Machiavelli's concern with the social effects of religion was extended by Bacon from the field of political practice to the field of science.

The other idol of the tribe worth mentioning is the influence of passions. For Bacon the human understanding cannot be reduced to its intellectual components – it is not a 'dry light' he would say – but it is also determined by feelings and passions which corrupt it.[10] This negative assessment of the effects which feelings and emotions, as well as religious representations and superstitions, have on the human understanding had a strong influence over the conception of science which positivism later developed. It also conveys a notion of ideology as those irrational aspects of man's mind which interfere with scientific knowledge. Hence, the opposition between ideology and rational knowledge becomes crucial.

The idols of the market-place are significant for a concept of ideology in a different and perhaps opposite manner. In effect, they are formed 'by the intercourse and association of men with each other' and receive the name of the market-place 'on account of the commerce and consort of men there'. Such idols arise in relation to language, 'for it is by discourse that men associate'.[11] Men learn the linguistic signs of things before they come to know them by their own experience; through the appropriation of these signs, which are often badly formed, an obstruction to the mind arises. Bacon's identification of those idols which originate in men's reciprocal intercourse by means of language is, implicitly, one of the first acknowledgements of ideology as a socially determined distortion; and it raises, more generally, the question about the social determination of knowledge.

The idols of the theatre, in turn, arise from the authoritative and dogmatic character of traditional theories. Men tend to see the world through the eyes of former philosophical systems, full of dogmas and false rules, which like plays create fictitious worlds. Bacon wants to liberate knowledge from blind obedience to the opinions of former authorities. All experience which does not come from reason itself should be rejected. When the idols operate, men apprehend reality '*ex analogia hominis*'. The true interpretation of nature, on the contrary, should explain the world '*ex analogia universi*'. Men can only master nature by obeying its laws; to achieve that, a proper understanding of them is required. This is why science must purge the mind of idols so that it can reach the truth. Then science may appear as a reflection of reality unhindered by ancient prejudices, superstitions, feelings and passions.

There are certain elements of contradiction in Bacon's thought.[12] How are the innate idols to be disposed of if they are not mere accidental psychological interferences but inherent in human nature or peculiar to each individual? If the mind is like a mirror which distorts the rays of objects, surely the intellect is constitutionally unsuited for the comprehension of nature. None the less, Bacon is clear enough in the sense that science could reach the truth despite the action of idols. This indicates that for him there is no logical necessity for the operation of idols and that, having the correct method, men can get rid of them. The mere recognition of the existence of idols is already a form of rendering them harmless.

Yet a problem which still remains is how to understand and reconcile the operation of innate idols and of external idols. The difficulty is at the bottom of later polemics concerning the concept of ideology. In a way, the dilemma which bedevilled the construction of the concept is already implicitly posed in Bacon's work: should ideology be conceived in the main as a phenomenon rooted in men's social relations and therefore as historically changing in relation to man's material practice; or should it rather be construed as a phenomenon derived from the universal presence of irrational and emotive elements, inherent in human nature, which recurrently assail and perturb science? The first option underlines the social determination of ideology, whereas the second emphasizes its opposition to science. Nor are the two options necessarily contradictory. Bacon is interested in the idols of the market-place only in so far as they also constitute an obstacle to science. Yet the important difference he overlooks is that while the innate idols may be logically dealt with at the level of human cognition, the idols dependent upon human intercourse cannot be easily got rid of without altering that intercourse. The reference to innate idols necessarily underlines the opposition to science, whereas the reference to social intercourse rather points towards the alteration of material circumstances.

Bacon does not discuss the relationships between the two classes of idols, nor does he see the difficulty in dealing with idols originated in social intercourse by means of an intellectual exercise. His overwhelming preoccupation is how to safeguard rational knowledge from any interference. The assumption is implicitly established that this could be done at the level of knowledge itself, even for the idols of the market-place. In fact Bacon separates progress in science from changes in civil society. While the former is welcomed, the latter are seen as dangerous. He prefers to emphasize the opposition of idols and science, so in his writings can be found the seeds of a concept of ideology which emphasizes more its opposition to science than its social referent. However, his contemplation of some idols which originated in language and social intercourse is, at the same time, the forerunner of an entirely different line of thought which culminated in Karl Marx.

The influence of Bacon upon the philosophy of the seventeenth and eighteenth centuries is decisive. Marx later acknowledged Bacon as the father of modern science and of English materialism.[13] Philosophers like Hobbes, Locke, Condillac, Helvetius, Holbach, Diderot and so forth, bear the marks of his theory. Bacon's idols became Condillac's 'prejudices', a concept also used by Holbach and Helvetius, and indeed, by almost every philosopher of the French Enlightenment.[14] But these authors concentrate now upon a particular source of irrational prejudices, namely, traditional religious representations. While Bacon's materialism had been compatible with the existence of God and His revelation and had only sought a clear-cut demarcation of fields between theology and philosophy, the Enlightenment became increasingly critical of religion itself.

A qualitative change is already noticeable in Hobbes (1588–1679), Bacon's successor and systematizer. For him men can only conceive what has been perceived first by sense. Consequently, only material and finite things are intelligible to the human intellect; there cannot possibly exist an idea or conception of anything infinite. In other words, men can know nothing about the existence of God.[15] Inquiring into the origins of religion Hobbes asserts that 'ignorance of natural causes disposes a man to credulity'. When man 'cannot assure himself of the true causes of things . . . he supposes causes of them, either such as his own fancy suggests or trusts to the authority of other men. . . .' Men make

little, or no inquiry into the natural causes of things, yet from the fear that proceeds from the ignorance itself, of what it is that has the power to do them much good or harm, are inclined to suppose, and feign unto themselves, several kinds of Power Invisible; and to stand in awe of their own imaginations. . . . And this fear of things invisible, is the natural seed of that, which everyone in himself calls religion. . . .[16]

Fear and ignorance are, therefore, the roots of any religious faith. So, Hobbes draws more radical conclusions from empiricism than Bacon ever did. This is why Marx later commented that Hobbes 'shattered the *theistic* prejudices of Baconian materialism'.[17] None the less, Hobbes, in his overwhelming concern with averting civil war and sedition and with finding theoretical bases for the absolute obedience to the Sovereign, does not fail to see the significance of religion for the peace and stability of the commonwealth. He is aware that legislators want to keep the people in obedience by instilling in their minds the belief that religious precepts proceed from the gods and by making them believe that the same things are displeasing to the gods which are forbidden by the laws.[18] But then the consequences of not having a strong power are 'perpetual war of every man against his neighbour'. So in the end Hobbes, like Machiavelli before him, believes that men need religion and autocratic monarchs so that common happiness and peace could be achieved through ignorance and fear. This is why he endeavours to show that absolute power is not only reasonable but also justified by scripture.[19]

The French Enlightenment: from the priestly deceit to the emergence of ideology

Whilst Hobbes's conception of religion as based in fear and ignorance was widely shared by the philosophers of the eighteenth century they completely abandoned his view that it is somehow necessary for the common good and for holding society together. The French Enlightenment proclaims, on the contrary, the right of free thinking.[20] Religious representations, whose origins had already been recognized by Machiavelli and Hobbes, become a real danger for human happiness as ideological prejudices. Religion is no longer seen as an integrating force, but, on the contrary, as the source of all superstitions, false notions and preconceptions. Helvetius (1715–71), and Holbach (1723–89) forcefully put forward this version in their theories about the priestly deceit. In their view, priests are interested in keeping people in ignorance so that they can maintain their power and riches. There is a sort of conspiracy against the people which is led by priests and which can only be destroyed by education.

Holbach starts his main work by arguing that man is unhappy

because he misunderstands nature. His mind is so infected by prejudices that one may think of him as forever condemned to error. . . . Reason, guided by experience, must attack at their source the prejudices of which mankind has been the victim for so long. . . . Truth is one and necessary for man . . . it is necessary to unveil it to mortals. . . . The chains which tyrants and priests forge are due to error . . . ignorance and uncertainty are due to errors consecrated by religion. . . .[21]

Helvetius, in his turn, speaks of the 'virtues of prejudice' as opposed to true virtues. The former do not contribute to the common good and belong to the fakirs, magicians and priests. Unfortunately, the virtues of prejudice are more honoured than true virtues in the majority of nations. The priests of false religions are interested in keeping people blind and persecute all those who may enlighten them. This also happens in the case of the true religion, whose ministers often resort to the same cruelties against great men.[22]

Hobbes recognized the origin of religion in fear and ignorance, but he still thought that the common interest represented by the Commonwealth was superior to individual interests. Holbach and Helvetius, on the contrary, try to reconcile individual and common interests. As Helvetius puts it, 'it seems therefore, that it is solely upon conciliation or opposition between particular interests and the general interest that public happiness or unhappiness depend. . . .'[23]

In order for the prejudices to be overcome, man ought to recognize his own interest. The connections between this position and the emergence of the bourgeoisie are quite plain. Man was to be liberated from all oppressive chains in his economic life as much as in his beliefs. In this sense the critique of the priestly deceit was a part of the bourgeois struggle against the remnants of the medieval order. Religion and the church, still closely linked to the old regime, began to be seen as the legitimation of political domination. The theory of the priestly conspiracy wanted to make it clear that behind religious representations, power interests were hidden.

Machiavelli and Hobbes had already noticed the legitimating social function of religion, and yet they had justified it for the sake of the prince or sovereign. Now, the emphasis on the connection between religion and politics is expanded, but acquires a negative and critical slant. Thus Holbach writes:

The dogma of the future life, accompanied by rewards and punishments, is looked at, after many centuries, as the most powerful, or even as the only motive capable of restraining men's passions. . . . Little by little this dogma has become the basis of almost every political and religious system, and today it seems as though one could not attack this prejudice without breaking absolutely the bonds of society. The founders of religions have used it for getting credule sectarian members; legislators have looked at it as a restraint capable of keeping their subjects under the yoke. . . . Nobody can deny that this dogma has been most useful for those who gave religion to the nations . . . it is the foundation of their power, the source of their riches, and the permanent cause of the blindness and terrors in which their interest wanted mankind to be nourished. It is because of it that the priest became emulous and master of kings. . . .[24]

Against this kind of ideological deception Holback and Helvetius propound the virtues of education, which men will find a remedy to their problems. Men raised by education will no longer need celestial rewards in order to know the prize of virtue. It is thus that education will form the citizen of the state. 'A vigilant, virtuous, enlightened and just government which seeks the public good with good faith, has no need of fables, or lies for governing reasonable subjects.'[25] Helvetius' dictum became famous: '*L'éducation peut tout*'. Man is beset by prejudices because he is the product of circumstances. This could be changed by educating him. As Barth has pointed out, this belief in the omnipotence of education had political consequences: 'Since education is everywhere closely related to the prevailing form of government, its principles cannot be reformed without also changing the constitution of the state.'[26] However, this unlimited confidence in education later provoked Marx's criticism: these authors have forgotten, Marx says, 'that circumstances are changed by men and that it is essential to educate the educator himself. This doctrine must, therefore, divide society into two parts, one of which is superior to society.'[27]

The sense of this criticism is that these philosophers, unable to discover the real causes of men's problems and the real solutions to them, resort to external agents in order both to understand an undesirable state of affairs, and to find a way out. Thus they blame the priests and make of educators and enlightened men a new kind of saviour. But in doing this they divide the passive majority of the people from the active chosen few who either mislead them or save them.[28] This is why Marx says that this doctrine divides society into two parts, forgetting that the active superior section need also be educated.

However, the French Enlightenment receives Marx's praise, not only for its struggle against religion and political institutions, but also for its open struggle against the metaphysics of the seventeenth century and the development of materialism which finally led to socialism.[29] While Helvetius and Holbach emphasize the critique of religion, Condillac deals mainly with the metaphysical prejudices of Descartes, Leibniz, Spinoza and Malebranche.[30] Helvetius' and Holbach's critique of religion was particularly relevant for the formation of the concept of ideology and had great influence upon Hegel, Bauer, Feuerbach and Marx himself.[31] Yet the conception of ideology which implicitly emerges from this critique is still very limited. It has not yet found meaningful connection either with man's nature or with man's social relations. Religion remains a conspiracy, an almost groundless deceit propagated by certain harmful agents who are its only support. To a great extent, this opposition between religion and education is a more specific version of the Baconian opposition between idols and science. Ideology, as much as its cure, is still merely conceived at the level of human cognition. But whilst in Bacon ideology and its cure was somehow internal to the process of knowledge of anyone, the French Enlightenment propounds priests and educators as the external agents of ideology and its cure.

This tradition of thought served as a background for Destutt de Tracy (1754–1836), the first author who uses the term ideology. Yet there is no straight connection between Bacon's idols or the Enlightenment's religious prejudices and the first use of the term ideology. In effect, Destutt de Tracy is concerned with systematizing a new science, the science of ideas which he calls 'Ideology'.[32] This science has as its object the establishment of the origin of ideas; in this task, it must set aside metaphysical and religious prejudices. Scientific progress is possible only if false ideas can be avoided. To this extent, Bacon's theory of idols and in particular Condillac's struggle against prejudices have a decisive influence upon de Tracy's science of ideas. But then ideology emerges as the opposite to those idols or prejudices; it emerges as a science.

Destutt de Tracy recognizes in Locke the first attempt to describe the human intelligence in scientific, observational terms. After Locke, Condillac perfected and enlarged his ideas, so that he can be said to be the real author of ideology as a science.[33] But neither is exempt from error. De Tracy wants to remedy those errors and propounds a science which would be able to achieve a precision comparable with that of the natural sciences. Like Condillac, Destutt de Tracy derives ideas from sensations. In successive chapters of his *Éléments d'idéologie* he argues that to think is to feel something, that memory is a particular kind of sensation which re-enacts a past sensation, and that the faculty of judgement is also a kind of sensation in so far as it is the faculty of feeling the relationships between perceptions.[34] For him ideology is a part of zoology, and in the case of human intellect, a part that is important and deserves to be explored in depth.[35]

Like the knowledge of any other aspect of nature, the science of ideas, based upon observations and free from prejudices, is considered the basis for education and the moral order. De Tracy's school of '*idéologues*' follows the tradition of the French Enlightenment in its belief that reason is the main instrument of happiness. After the years of revolution it wants to educate the French people and, above all, the young people, so that a just and happy society can be established. De Tracy himself wants his book to become a study programme for youngsters and explicitly acknowledges that a motive for writing it has been the new law introducing public education, to which he expects to contribute with this text.[36] So the '*idéologues*' share the enthusiasm and optimism about education of Holbach and Helvetius.

In this, its origin, the term ideology has a positive connotation: it is the rigorous science of ideas which, by overcoming religious and

metaphysical prejudices, may serve as a new basis for public education. At the beginning there was a divergence between this first
meaning of the term ideology and that concept of ideology which
had been foreshadowed in idols and prejudices and was later to
prevail. Curiously enough, Napoleon, who at the beginning had
shared the objectives and goals of the Institute of France[37] and of the
'*idéologues*', was the first to use the term ideology in a negative sense.
In effect, Napoleon disillusioned with his former friends, who could
not accept his despotic excesses, turned against them and labelled
them 'ideologists', with the derogatory meaning that they were unrealistic and doctrinaire intellectuals ignorant of political practice. As
Lichtheim points out, their attitude was thought to be ideological
'in the twofold sense of being concerned with ideas, and of placing
the satisfaction of ideal aims (their own) ahead of the material
interests on which the post-revolutionary society rested'.[38]

Ideology and critical thought: a difficult encounter

During the nineteenth century the convergence between the term
ideology and its negative content was completed. Yet this was not a
straightforward process. For a long time the term ideology continued
to have little significance either as the science of ideas or as a doctrinaire and unrealistic theory. Hegel mentions ideology in the first
sense, only to dismiss it as a 'reduction of thought to sensation'.[39]
Ideology as a science had not established itself. At the same time,
the critique of religion and metaphysics, the most important antecedent of the negative concept of ideology, continued to develop
without having any formal connection with the term ideology. In
effect, the two major lines of thought which follow the critical
tradition of the modern times, namely, French positivism and
German idealism still do not relate their critique to the concept of
ideology.

Auguste Comte (1798–1857), one of the founders of positivism,
develops his critique along the lines which Bacon had set up two
centuries before. Just as Bacon struggled against idols and wanted
to create a science based upon empirical observation, Comte seeks
to rid science of imagination so it can discover the invariable
natural laws of all phenomena. Thus Comte affirms that

the theological and metaphysical states of any science possess one characteristic in common – the predominance of imagination over observation.

The only difference that exists between them under this point of view is that in the first the imagination occupies itself with supernatural beings and in the second, with personified abstractions.[40]

Comte thinks that from the historical study of human intelligence he has discovered a fundamental law: our conceptions and theories pass through three different theoretical stages – the theological or fictitious, the metaphysical or abstract, and the scientific or positive.[41] This law announces the end of the metaphysical period and the beginning of a new stage in which the speculative conceptions will be replaced by a science of facts. Although this has already happened to natural science, social science has not yet entered the domain of positive philosophy and remains in the grip of theological and metaphysical methods. Its transformation into a 'social physics' is the aim which Comte sets himself in his main work.

Comte is also aware of the practical consequences of ideas. Against the theological and metaphysical philosophies which have failed to secure permanent social welfare, he propounds positive philosophy as the only possible agent in the reorganization of modern society. This practical and political application derives from his belief 'that ideas govern the world, or throw it into chaos – in other words, that all social mechanism rests upon opinions'.[42] Positive philosophy is the only way a rational social order can be established. While Bacon had drawn a distinction between progress in science and innovations in civil society (his theory of idols applying only to the former), Comte unifies both aspects so that his critique of metaphysical and theological philosophy has also a political character.

However, Comte's position is not more radical than Bacon's. On the contrary, just as Bacon thought that innovating popular movements were dangerous, Comte's aim in reorganizing modern society seeks to remedy its alleged anarchic and disorderly state. In this he is implicitly in line with Hobbes's main preoccupation with the stability of the commonwealth. In Comte's view

the positive philosophy befriends public order by bringing back men's understandings to a normal state through the influence of its method alone. . . . It dissipates disorder at once by imposing a series of indisputable scientific conditions of the study of political questions.[43]

The meaning of this assertion is soon made crystal clear:

As it is the inevitable lot of the majority of men to live on the more or less precarious fruits of daily labour, the great social problem is to ameliorate the condition of this majority, without destroying its classification, and disturbing the general economy; and this is the function of the positive polity, regarded as regulating the final classification of modern society.[44]

Comte has no inkling of the metaphysical character which this very statement may have. His main assumptions about the 'inevitable' lot of the majority of men and the need for the class structure in order to avoid disturbing the economy are not scientifically verified truths, even according to his own standards. Hence a doubt arises: is not his positive critique of theological and metaphysical philosophies in itself metaphysical? In terms of the forthcoming concept of ideology this would mean that his critique of ideology is itself ideological. Be that as it may, Comte's critique of religion and metaphysics follows in Bacon's steps and inaugurates a positivist tradition which later culminated in the Vienna Circle. The opposition between positive science and metaphysical propositions becomes paramount and foreshadows a concept of ideology understood as meaningless imagination, arbitrary metaphysical speculations which, like Baconian idols, obstruct the knowledge of reality. If for the French Enlightenment ideology amounted to a priestly lie, for positivism ideology has an imaginary and irrational character. In either case ideology appears an autonomous phenomenon which misleads man's cognition of reality.

Science, in turn, assumes a crucial role as an independent force which can get rid of these irrational imaginations in order to produce meaningful and indisputably truthful propositions about reality which are, simultaneously, the basis of progress and proper organization of society. Yet, as is already clear, Comte's fetishization of science and progress reintroduces through the back door the very metaphysical principles that he wants to overcome. Durkheim, himself a positivist, will later criticize Comte for having abandoned the positivist principles in his conception of progress.[45] Engels had already noted this contradiction when he asserted that one of the three characteristics of Comte's system was 'a hierarchically organised religious constitution, whose source is definitely Saint-Simonian but divested of all mysticism and turned into something extremely sober, with a regular pope at the head, so that Huxley could say of Comtism that it was Catholicism without Christianity'.[46] Marx was also critical of his synthesis and thought it was wretched in comparison with Hegel's.[47] At any rate, Comte's critique of metaphysics exercised considerable influence upon the development of positivism and is the unquestionable forerunner of Durkheim's concept of ideology.

Although in an entirely different direction, German idealism, too, continues the critique of religion without using the term ideology. Hegel's concern with the relationship between philosophy and religion, which lasted throughout his life (1770–1831), set the premises for a more radical and profound criticism, despite its inherent ambiguity. On the one hand he thinks the subject of both philosophy and theology is the same, namely, the Absolute, or rather, the relationship between the infinite and the finite. On the other, he is aware of the negative character which concrete and historical forms of religion acquire. Thus, the transformation of Christianity into an authoritarian and dogmatic system is for the first time described as responsible for the alienation of man from his true self. But the opposition is not insoluble. Philosophy must come to the rescue of Christianity, not by supporting its outmoded historical form, but by explaining the dialectical evolution of the opposition between the infinite and the finite, thus providing rational proof of its principles. The truth of religion has to be expressed as the truth of the concept.[48]

The ambiguities apparent in Hegel were resolved in a radical critique of religion by a number of his followers, the so-called left-wing Hegelians. The most important and influential of them, Ludwig Feuerbach (1804–1872) conceives the idea of God as a projection of man's essence, a product of objectivization of the human being. 'Man – this is the mystery of religion – projects his being into objectivity, and then again makes himself an object to this projected image of himself thus converted into a subject. . . .'[49] This is the origin of man's alienation from himself. He is separated from all that is good in him, which is projected into a new being; and his own imperfection and nothingness remain his basic identity. Therefore, in religion man reduces and alienates himself. This is why religion must be overcome. Yet the process is not arbitrary, subject to man's will. Religion has been the product of a necessary stage in man's process of self-awareness. Before man can recognize his true essence as his own, he has to objectify it into the idea of God, and this process of objectivation has reached its maximum development with Christianity, thus making it possible for man to recuperate himself. For at this moment man can understand that God is nothing more than his own idealized essence projected into a different being; in doing so, he can liberate himself from alienation.

In Feuerbach one can find the somehow naïve conception, which Comte also shared, that God corresponds to the infantile stage of mankind:

> Religion is the child-like condition of humanity; but the child sees his nature – man – out of himself; in childhood a man is an object to himself, under the form of another man. Hence the historical progress of religion consists in this: that what by an earlier religion was regarded as objective, is now recognized as subjective; that is, what was formerly contemplated and worshipped as God is now perceived to be something *human*.[50]

According to Feuerbach, therefore, religion will be surpassed when men's energies are devoted to earthly happiness. If on the one hand God is not a pure appearance but a reflection of the human essence, on the other hand there is no longer a need for this projection once philosophy has discovered its real nature.

Feuerbach's critique of religion goes much deeper than the theory of the priestly deceit. While the latter struggled against religious prejudices as if they were externally imposed upon the people, the former finds a much more profound connection between religion and the human essence. Religion is no longer conceived as an arbitrary and independent phenomenon which could explain people's ignorance and unhappiness. Feuerbach inverts the relationship and explains religion by the essence of man. So religion has a real basis; it is not an arbitrary invention of wicked priests who try to deceive the people, nor is it a totally irrational belief. This is a most important landmark in the critique of religion, for it inverts the order of determination, and allows religion itself to be explained in terms other than lies, deceit or fantastic imagination. To this extent it has enormous consequences for the emergence of the concept of ideology. Feuerbach's approach can be seen as the last mediating link between the traditional critique of religion and the concept of ideology. However, it is also fraught with problems. Marx criticized this conception because it abstracts from the historical process and fixes 'the religious sentiment as something by itself'. Feuerbach 'does not see that the "religious sentiment" is itself a social product, and that the abstract individual whom he analyses belongs to a particular form of society'.[51]

With Marx the term ideology finally catches up with and surpasses the critique of religion, thus asserting its negative and critical character. The importance of the critique of religion for Marx is not to be underrated, and is shown in his early statement that 'the criticism

of religion is the prerequisite of all criticism'.[52] Yet at the time he
wrote this Marx was still basically Feuerbachian and had not
produced his own concept of ideology. When Marx finally came up
with a general concept of ideology which subsumes not only religion
but all forms of distorted consciousness within itself, he not only
emphasized a negative connotation but also added to its critical
force by introducing a new crucial element in its definition – the
reference to historical contradictions in society.

From Machiavelli and Bacon, via Holbach, Helvetius, de Tracy
and Napoleon, to Comte and Feuerbach, the phenomenon analysed
under the name of idol, prejudice, religion or ideology, was almost
always considered a psychological distortion, a problem at the level
of cognition. The connection between mental distortions and the
historical development of men's social relations had not been
envisaged. Ideological distortions were accounted for by passions,
superstitions, individual interests, religious prejudices or man's
necessary self-alienation, but were never related to historically
necessary social contradictions. The theory of the priestly deceit
propounded an extreme form of this psychologism by insisting upon
the conscious lies and the conspiracies of priests. This theory could
explain man's misfortune by the existence of religion, but could not
explain religion except as a fabrication. This is why Lenk has pointed
out that it was more a theory of the lie than a theory of the necessary
false consciousness.[53]

Feuerbach went further than that, and explained religion as based
on human essence. His achievement permitted Marx to affirm that
'the foundation of irreligious criticism is: *Man makes religion*,
religion does not make man',[54] and also supported Marx's criticism
of Bauer, who 'explains the *real* Jews by the *Jewish religion*, instead
of explaining the mystery of the Jewish religion by the *real Jews*'.[55]
Yet when Marx produced his concept of ideology he went even further than this Feuerbachian anthropology and understood religion
as a social product. Feuerbach remained trapped in the main static
assumptions of the French Enlightenment.

In effect, the materialist critique of religious representations had
not studied them with a historical perspective. Ideology and reason
thus appeared as unhistorical phenomena which struggled with one
another in the theoretical field. This is why education was the remedy
for ideological distortions. In fact the struggle between reason and
religious prejudices was thought to correspond to a universal character or essence of human nature. Up to the Enlightenment prejudices

were supposed to have had the upper hand. From then onward reason, by liberating itself from prejudices, would bring progress and happiness. Indeed, the conception of man and society was still static. As Marx later analysed, history was conceived of as a succession of stages, its institutions artificial fetters which reason finally managed to get rid of. Thus history was supposed to have arrived at its plenitude. It is Marx's crucial contribution to have shown the precariousness and historical relativity of bourgeois society and hence the connection between ideology and the social contradictions inherent in that society.[56] The concept of ideology received a new forceful formulation and lost all vestiges of psychologism. This is why it can be said that with Marx the concept of ideology came of age.

2 Marx's theory of ideology

The methodological approach

The thought of Marx (1818–83) can certainly be located within the tradition of the Enlightenment, but it is also an attempt to surpass its limitations. The two main lines of thought developing since the seventeenth century and leading to Marx – the philosophy of consciousness and the new scientific rationality – had a common origin in the modern idea that man and his reason were the measure of all things and that objects should not dominate man. However, with regard to society, they had grown increasingly apart, the philosophy of consciousness becoming an ontological idealism, and the scientific rationality a mechanical materialism. Marx's thought integrates elements from both currents, but purposefully tries to overcome their shortcomings.

From the philosophy of consciousness Marx draws the idea of the active subject, but this subject becomes historically concrete. The Kantian consciousness as such and the Hegelian 'folk spirit' are replaced by the historical class and its practice. From the new scientific rationality Marx takes the concern for material reality as the real starting-point of science and the critique of religion, but this material reality is conceived as historically made by men and, therefore, susceptible to be changed by their practice. If on the one hand the subject is no longer the idea which produces reality, on the other hand Marx is interested not only in the scientific apprehension of reality as it is, but also in changing that reality by means of revolutionary practice.[1]

A system of thought which brings together idealism and materialism, philosophy and economy, science and revolution, is bound to present problems of interpretation.[2] The task is made complicated and hazardous not only by the integration of elements from heterogeneous sources but also by the historical changes of emphasis as Marx's thought develops and the lack of further theoretical elaboration of some points. Small wonder that there are so many different interpretations of his thought. The concept of ideology is no exception.

In effect, the question arises whether a uniform 'theory of ideology' underlies the whole of Marx's writings. Even if the answer is affirmative, one has to acknowledge that the concept of ideology is not clearly defined; it must be theoretically worked out from what little Marx wrote of it. The analytical precision and systematic treatment of concepts like surplus-value, capital or labour contrast with the sometimes sketchy remarks about the concept of ideology.

This is why the concept of ideology is particularly sensitive to the various methodological positions which may be taken in order to understand Marx. On the one hand is a tradition normally associated with German historicism and idealism, which strongly emphasizes the philosophical Marx and relies upon the works of his youth. The concept of ideology, consequently, is mainly worked out in the context of *The German Ideology*, and Marx's economic works are either disregarded as irrelevant for the concept or considered a dangerous reversal of former philosophical achievements.[3]

On the other hand, a tradition of positivist origin, to which some forms of structuralism can be associated, emphasizes Marx as a scientist and economist and relies upon the works of his maturity. It maintains the existence of an 'epistemological break' in Marx's intellectual evolution which distinguishes a pre-Marxist problematic up to 1845 from a new, scientific problematic from then onwards. Because *The German Ideology* was written in the period of the break, it is necessarily ambiguous and should not be taken as the best example of Marx's scientific achievement. The concept of ideology, therefore, cannot be entirely worked out upon the basis of that text. In many respects, it is claimed, Marx's idea of the origin of ideology is much changed in his later writings.[4]

It seems to me that one has to accept the existence of an intellectual development in Marx; consequently, the treatment of the concept of ideology is subject to an evolution in which new perspectives are introduced and new insights are gained. Marx's thought is not static. Both the refining of the method and the specificity of the subject-matters he progressively tackles, account for progress and new dimensions in his thought. Nevertheless, I contend that a basic nucleus of the concept of ideology is maintained throughout this evolution without any dramatic rupture. If Marx had not completed his thought on ideology in 1845, neither did he subsequently break with its essentials either.

As far as the theory of ideology is concerned, there are two main periods in Marx's development. The first one is inaugurated with the *Theses on Feuerbach* and *The German Ideology*, and lasts until 1858. Here the basis of the concept of ideology is laid down. The context in which this is done is the resolution of the opposition between subject and object. Marx, at this stage, clarifies his concepts of society and history in general. A second period could be said to begin with the *Grundrisse* which is characterized by the concrete study of capitalist social relations. The term ideology itself almost disappears, but could be said to be implicitly operating. A new context is developed which is relevant for the theory of ideology – the resolution of the opposition between essence and appearance. The important thing is the continuity between these two phases.

Notwithstanding the argument for a basic continuity in Marx's thought, the above-mentioned evolution poses very serious problems; some of Marx's formulations are not always successful in conveying a well-integrated and balanced conception. In arguing for a basic unity of Marx's thought, one should not attribute these problems to a mere lack of understanding of Marx or to a deficient interpretation; on the contrary, they may indicate real difficulties in the development of Marx's thought. The interpretation must point to those real difficulties, not cover them up. Additionally, the effort of interpretation must not be mistaken for a proof of the superiority of Marx's arguments, something which can be assessed only in the critical confrontation of them with other theories.

Consciousness and reality

The period in which the concept of ideology first appears is very much concerned with the polarity of subject and object. Marx wants to end every kind of dualism which would sharply separate consciousness from reality, but at the same time wants to maintain the independence of consciousness from external being. Hegel had already criticized the Kantian dualism between consciousness and being. Marx is aware that idealism emphasizes the activity of the subject in opposition to modern materialism. He makes this idealist idea the basis of his criticism of Feuerbach, who still sees material reality 'in the form of the object or of contemplation, but not as sensuous human activity, practice, not subjectively'.[5]

Yet Marx is also aware that Hegel had taken subjective activity too far, that it had become the speculative construction of material reality, with the consequent loss of all objectivity external to the subject. The unity between consciousness and reality occurred within thought. Being had been identified with thought. Feuerbach had first recognized the difference between the subject and thought and had affirmed the external character of the object with respect to the subject. So Marx used Feuerbach's ideas to criticize Hegel.

The problem which Marx faces in building a new theory of consciousness is twofold: how to reconcile materialism with the fact that reality should not be conceived as a given object which does not include the subject's activity; and how to reconcile idealism with the fact that being cannot be reduced to thought. While materialism makes consciousness a reflection of external reality, idealism makes reality the product of consciousness. Materialism splits up in two separate worlds what Marx thinks to be a unity whereas idealism dissolves one world into the other. Marx propounds a basic unity between consciousness and reality which nevertheless retain a distinction.

Marx is explicitly trying to integrate contributions from idealism and materialism and in order to sharpen his critique tends to oppose each of them in terms of the other;[6] this poses difficult problems of interpretation as it often results in one-sided formulations. Images like 'phantoms', 'inversions on the retina' and '*camera obscura*' may suggest that consciousness somehow arbitrarily distorts a reality which would otherwise be seen clearly in its true dimension. At the same time images like 'reflexes' and 'sublimates' suggest that, on the contrary, consciousness is a mere reflection of external reality. This is a source of confusion which not only shows the lack of integration of some of Marx's statements, but also contributes to obscure Marx's own solution.

Yet one should remember that the context of these expressions is one of criticism of idealism. Marx wants to assert, above all, that consciousness is not independent of material conditions. Because he is struggling against the idealist conception of consciousness, he emphasizes that

consciousness can never be anything else than conscious existence, and the existence of men is their actual life-process.
. . . men, developing their material production and their material intercourse alter, along with this their real existence, their thinking and the products of their thinking. Life is not determined by consciousness but consciousness by life.[7]

This is one of the most crucial materialist assumptions behind Marx's approach to consciousness. Consciousness is not autonomous from men's forms of existence; its contents do not arise arbitrarily. What men think is necessarily referred to and conditioned by the historical reality of society. 'Consciousness is, therefore, from the very beginning a social product, and remains so as long as men exist at all.'[8] Consciousness, like language, originates in basic human necessities, in the need for cooperation with other men to survive. This is why at the beginning there is only consciousness of the immediate environment, social and natural, and it is very limited. With the advance in the division of labour, consciousness may go beyond the immediate sensuous environment and may begin to believe that it is 'pure', autonomous and emancipated from the world. Yet this very belief, this illusion, is conditioned by the stage reached by social relations. Marx insists upon this idea time and again:

the mode of production of material life conditions the social, political and intellectual life process in general. It is not the consciousness of men that determines their being, but, on the contrary, their social being that determines their consciousness.[9]

In short, Marx is putting forward the priority of being *over* consciousness, as against idealism which had dissolved being *into* consciousness.

These statements about consciousness being determined by life, when taken in isolation from Marx's critique of the old materialism, can be taken to suggest that consciousness merely reflects external reality. Hence in ideology it would be reality which deceives a passive consciousness. If consciousness cannot be anything else than conscious existence, then consciousness may appear a mere reflection of existence. Material reality appears as a separate world which conditions consciousness from without. No wonder that certain interpretations therefore maintain that every element in consciousness has its equivalent or particular cause in material existence; so consciousness is a secondary sort of phenomenon, not worth studying in itself, because, ultimately, it can be reduced to its material base.

That Marx conceives of this relation in quite a different way is perfectly clear from his criticism of Feuerbach and the old materialism.[10] Feuerbach's conception of the sensuous world, Marx says, is confined to mere contemplation of it:

He does not see how the sensuous world around him is, not a thing given direct from all eternity, remaining ever the same, but the product of industry and of the state of society; and, indeed, in the sense that it is a historical product, the result of the activity of a whole succession of generations. . . .[11]

Marx's statement that consciousness cannot be anything else than conscious existence must be understood in the context of his critique of the old materialism for its belief that men were just the passive products of circumstances and education.

However important these counterbalances may be in order to understand Marx's thoughts at this stage, there are also some limitations which go beyond the problem of one-sided formulations and which are inherent in the general way Marx approaches the problem. In effect, at this time Marx was working out his general theoretical framework, which he later summarized in the famous *Preface* of 1859. So his formulations are bound to emphasize, above all, the change of perspective with respect to idealism and the Feuerbachian critique of religion. As yet there is no total awareness about the problems which science faces in order to understand reality. It appears that to accomplish this it is sufficient to shift the focus of attention from religious and moral to material life.

This shift is, of course, indispensable. But in order to fully understand the relationship between consciousness and reality, the concrete analysis of material life is required, that is, the study of the specific material conditions of the capitalist mode of production. However, as this analysis remains to be carried out – *Capital* is the full realization of this project – there is still little awareness of the difficulties which material life opposes to that task and of the existence of deceptive forms which must be penetrated beyond their appearance. At this stage a somehow over-simplified idea of science is said to be able to replace speculation by just representing and describing material life.

Be this as it may, the sense of Marx's critique of Feuerbach is this: what seems to be the objective reality is by no means a pure datum; on the contrary it is to be understood as the historical product of man's practice. In turn, men's practice is not merely subjective. Reality includes man's activity and for this reason practice has also an objective character. Hence, the subject-object relationship becomes neither a relation of mere contemplation of an external objective reality nor a relation of ideal creation of reality, but a relation mediated by practice. It is by means of the concept of practice that Marx tries to solve the problem of the relation between consciousness and reality.

According to Marx 'all social life is essentially practical' and 'all the mysteries which lead theory to mysticism find their rational solution in human practice and in the comprehension of this practice'.[12] How does he show that practice is at the basis of social life and how does he understand it? When Marx expounds the premises of materialist method in *The German Ideology*, he maintains that his premises are 'the real individuals, their activity and the material conditions under which they live, both those which they find already existing and those produced by their activity'.[13] Practice is therefore a certain kind of activity. Yet not all forms of activity are practice. In the first thesis on Feuerbach, Marx recognizes that idealism has developed the active side, in contradistinction to materialism; but it has done so abstractly – it does not know real, sensuous activity. Thus Marx distinguishes the activity of consciousness as such from practical activity.

First of all men have to produce their material existence. So their first activity is in relation to nature, the production of their means of subsistence. As Marx puts it, 'the first historical act is the production of the means to satisfy human needs, the production of material life itself'.[14] Hence, practice first appears as labour, as human transformation of the world aimed at reproducing material life.

This shows a second feature of practice. It is intentional activity, it has a goal. 'Men can be distinguished from animals by consciousness,' Marx affirms. 'They begin to distinguish themselves from animals as soon as they begin to produce their means of subsistence.'[15] This presupposes a purposive action. Practice is not activity opposed to consciousness but is conscious activity; otherwise it would be only a blind activity, pure animal instinctive activity. As Marx later clarifies it in *Capital*,

what distinguishes the worst architect from the best of bees is this, that the architect raises his structure in imagination before he erects it in reality. At the end of every labour-process, we get a result that already existed in the imagination of the labourer at its commencement.[16]

A third aspect Marx emphasizes is that practice is not only the transformation of nature but also the transformation of men themselves. Practice should be understood not merely as the production of the physical existence of men, but also as an activity expressing their life.[17] In this sense Marx surpasses Aristotle's distinction between *praxis* and *poiesis*.[18] What men are coincides with their practice. Therefore, practical activity cannot be opposed to other aspects of man. Practice is man's specific way of being. It is not an external determination, a sort of appendage to theory or even the application of theory. Practice determines man in its totality. It is the activity which produces not only material means but also men and their social life.

The production of life, Marx says, 'appears as a double relationship'.[19] Productive practice implies a certain mode of cooperation, presupposes the intercourse of individuals with one another and, consequently, a certain division of labour. Practice is therefore the intentional activity which produces material and social life. Both aspects cannot be separated; the production of material life can only be social; it is framed within a mode of cooperation, within certain social relations. Yet practice cannot be entirely identified with labour.[20] In fact, Marx distinguishes two kinds of practice.

Firstly, he considers labour or, more generally, a reproductive practice. This is the most basic expression of practice, the process by which men create their material existence. Yet this kind of practice has some peculiar features. 'As soon as the distribution of labour comes into being, each man has a particular, exclusive sphere of activity, which is forced upon him and from which he cannot escape'.[21] Men's practice, by producing social life and the division of labour, fixes the forms of cooperation so that practice appears as forced upon men, as a power over individuals.

The importance Marx gives to this fact is clear from his own words:

This fixation of social activity, this consolidation of what we ourselves produce into an objective power above us, growing out of our control, thwarting our expectations, bringing to naught our calculations, is one of the chief factors in historical development up till now.[22]

This is the basis upon which Marx builds up one of his main principles for the analysis of society:

men make their own history, but they do not make it just as they please; they do not make it under circumstances chosen by themselves, but under circumstances directly encountered, given and transmitted from the past.[23]

The important thing to remark here is that these 'given circumstances' are the consolidation of what men themselves produce by means of their practice.

By being framed within social relations which are the result of its own activity, labour can only reproduce these social relations time and again. Labour is a condition of freedom in that by means of labour man satisfies his needs and can liberate himself from the constraints of nature; yet, as labour takes place under specific social conditions, it is not in itself liberating. By itself labour does not react against, but on the contrary can only be carried out under, the sway of social relations of production which impose themselves as an external determination. That is why it reproduces the relations of domination.

Here arises for Marx the need for a second kind of practice, revolutionary practice, which aims at transforming social relations so that labour may become framed in social relations which are no longer relations of domination. Marx recognizes that in history up to his time it is an empirical fact that individuals have become enslaved under a power alien to them, which they themselves have practically produced. But he adds:

it is just as empirically established that, by the overthrow of the existing state of society by the communist revolution . . . this power, which so baffles the German theoreticians, will be dissolved. . . .
. . . *all-round* dependence, this natural form of the world-historical cooperation of individuals, will be transformed . . . into the control and conscious mastery of these powers. . . .[24]

This practice of transformation of social relations of production also coincides with the change of men themselves. As Marx puts it, 'the coincidence of the changing of circumstances and of human activity or self-changing can be conceived and rationally understood only as revolutionary practice'.[25]

Yet revolutionary practice does not arise arbitrarily out of men's free will. Marx criticizes Stirner precisely because 'he imagines that people up to now have always formed a concept of man, and then won freedom for themselves to the extent that was necessary to realize this concept. . . .'[26] Marx thinks that people have won freedom to the extent that productive forces have so permitted. That is why, until the revolutionary expansion of productive forces in capitalism, all past revolutions were necessarily restricted. The practice of the revolutionary class had to exclude the majority, as there was not enough to satisfy all needs. Hence the narrow-minded-ness of the conquering class and the impossibility of a communal conscious mastery over the structures produced by practice.

In order to abolish the dependence upon this objective power, that is, in order that a revolutionary practice could effectively produce a system in which men control social relations, two practical premises must be given. On the one hand existing power

> must necessarily have rendered the great mass of humanity 'propertyless', and produced at the same time, the contradiction of an existing world of wealth and culture, both of which conditions presuppose a great increase in productive power . . . and, on the other hand, this development of productive forces . . . is an absolutely necessary practical premise. . . .[27]

Given these conditions, revolutionary practice may, for the first time, become conscious of them and attempt to change the external power so that it could be controlled by the whole community.

Hence, *reproductive practice* is activity as determined and forced upon men by circumstances; *revolutionary practice* is activity which, conscious of the determination of circumstances, is aimed at transforming them. Reproductive practice is carried out within given social relations and has as many objects as the complexity of the division of labour demands; revolutionary practice makes these social relations the very object of its activity. Reproductive practice does not by itself question the social framework within which it operates, whereas revolutionary practice seeks to change that framework, whose conditioning is acknowledged. In this sense, the object of revolutionary practice is the social totality and not partial aspects of it.

Revolutionary practice does not oppose reproductive practice as totally free activity opposes necessary activity. Yet the former cannot be reduced to a mere result of the latter. Revolutionary practice can arise only when certain practical premises are given, but it is not the automatic product of these conditions. Revolutionary practice is neither arbitrary nor absolutely prefigured. In this sense, it mediates between necessity and freedom.[28] The domination of material conditions over individuals sets them the cooperative task of replacing such domination by the domination of individuals over conditions. But it is up to man to accomplish the task. This is why Marx contends that communism is not 'a state of affairs which is to be established' but the real movement which abolishes the present state of things.[29]

The emergence of ideology

Men's practice produces social conditions which become independent of men's will; this fact determines the constitution of social reality as a contradictory reality. According to Marx 'the division of labour inside a nation leads at first to the separation of industrial and commercial from agricultural labour, and hence the separation of *town* and *country* and to the conflict of their interests'.[30] As the division of labour develops, new separations and divisions appear: between commercial and industrial labour; between material and mental labour; among the individuals cooperating inside every branch of production; and so on.

The various phases of development of this division of labour appear as so many different forms of ownership and consequently as a division of the conditions of labour, as a division between capital and labour, as the opposition between private interest and communal interest: in sum, as the separation of the individuals in social classes. The conditions under which men carry out their practice are the conditions of the rule of a definite class which holds contradictory relations with other classes:

> Thus society has hitherto always developed within the framework of a contradiction – in antiquity the contradiction between free men and slaves, in the Middle Ages that between nobility and serfs, in modern times that between the bourgeoisie and the proletariat.[31]

Contradictions in reality do not emerge from the mere fact that human practice crystallizes itself into objective social relations and structures, into an objective power. This is a necessary result of practice. The problem is man's lack of control of this power: man is controlled by those structures instead of being the conscious master of them. The division of labour is a result of man's reproductive practice, but not a consciously intended result. This fact, in its turn, is conditioned by the development of productive forces. The necessary consequence of the limitations of productive forces has been a development which can satisfy the needs of a few (dominant class) at the expense of the majority (dominated classes). So the division of labour can only manifest itself as a division of contradictory classes, as the exclusion of the majority from any development.[32]

The basis upon which Marx approaches the concept of ideology is this contradictory character of social reality, which is brought about by the restricted productive forces and the division of labour.

Reviewing in 1859 the results of the investigation of past years, Marx provided two important clues. First, he affirms that consciousness must be explained from the contradictions of material life; second, he states that

mankind always sets itself only such tasks as it can solve; since looking at the matter more closely, it will always be found that the task itself arises only when the material conditions for its solution already exist or are at least in the process of formation.[33]

From this one may deduce that men cannot solve in consciousness those contradictions which they are unable to solve in practice.

As contradictions emerge and reach consciousness before men can solve them in practice, they are given distorted solutions in the mind. In this sense Marx affirms that 'the phantoms formed in the human brain are also, necessarily, sublimates of their material life-process . . . .'[34] As men in their reproductive practice are unable to solve these contradictions, they project them in ideological forms of consciousness. Ideology is, therefore, a solution in the mind to contradictions which cannot be solved in practice; it is the necessary projection in consciousness of man's practical inabilities.[35]

By attempting to solve in consciousness contradictions which are not overcome in practice, ideology necessarily negates and conceals them. As Poulantzas puts it 'ideology has the precise function of hiding the real contradictions and of *reconstituting* on an imaginary level a relatively coherent discourse which serves as the horizon of agents' experience . . . .'[36] Marx repeatedly describes this negation of real contradictions as an inversion of reality, but he does not mean an arbitrary inversion produced by consciousness. 'If the conscious expression of the real relations of these individuals is illusory, if in their imagination they turn reality upside-down, then this in its turn is the result of their limited material mode of activity . . . .'[37] Ideology, therefore, appears as a sublimation in consciousness of the limitations of human practice which leads to the negation of social contradictions.

For Marx, therefore, ideology does not arise as a pure invention of consciousness which distorts reality, nor as the result of an objectively opaque reality which deceives a passive consciousness. Ideology arises from a 'limited material mode of activity' which produces both contradictory relations and, as a consequence, distorted representations about them; thus it unites in one phenomenon consciousness and reality. Marx is much less interested in finding out whether ideology is produced by this or that particular class or whether it is externally imposed by reality on these classes, than in showing the origin of ideology in a kind of practice, a restricted practice which is the basis of both the contradictory reality and ideology.

Ideology cannot, then, be 'dissolved by mental criticism . . . but only by the practical overthrow of the actual social relations which gave rise to this idealistic humbug . . . .'[38] Revolutionary practice is the only way to overcome ideology at its roots by solving the real contradictions which give rise to it. Marx insists that 'the real, practical dissolution of these phrases, the removal of these notions from the consciousness of men, will . . . be effected by altered circumstances, not by theoretical deductions'.[39] Not that mental critique should be eliminated. Marx is constructing precisely a theoretical critique of ideology. But this necessary critique does not suffice by itself.

With this concept Marx criticizes the German ideologists who want to liberate men by criticizing and thereby dissolving ideas. They believe the chains of men are illusions of consciousness and not material relations. By combating phrases they hide the real chains, the real contradictions which arise in practical life. As Marx says:

> It has not occurred to any one of these philosophers to inquire into the connection of German philosophy with German reality, the relation of their criticism to their own material surroundings.[40]

As the conditions under which productive practice is carried out are always the conditions of the rule of a definite class, the ideological hiding of contradictions necessarily serves the interests of that class. Ideology is not only a result of the division of labour and of the objectivation of practice into contradictory classes; it is also a condition for the functioning and reproduction of the system of class domination. It plays this role precisely by hiding the true relations between classes, by explaining away the relations of domination and subordination. Thus, social relations appear harmonious and individuals carry out their reproductive practices without disruption.

In this sense ideology legitimates the class structure and, in general, the whole social structure, thus it becomes indispensable for their reproduction. For this reason it necessarily serves the interests of the dominant class. For Marx each new class, in order to carry through its aim, is compelled to represent its interest as the common interest of all the members of society, that is, expressed in ideal form: it has to give its ideas the form of universality, and represent them as the only rational, universally valid ones.[41]

Initially the class making a revolution truly represents the common interests of all the non-ruling classes. But soon it develops its own particular class interest and contradictions appear with other classes. By concealing these contradictions, ideology allows the dominant class to continue to appear 'not as a class but as the representative of the whole of society'.[42]

In capitalist society class differences are negated, and a world of freedom and equality re-constructed in consciousness; in pre-capitalist societies, class differences are rather justified in hierarchical conceptions of the world. In both, ideology negates contradictions and legitimates the structure of domination. In sum, ideology for Marx, as a distorted consciousness, has a particular negative connotation whose two specific and connected features are, firstly, that it conceals social contradictions and, secondly, that it does it in the interests of the dominant class. Hence, ideology is a restricted kind of distortion which does not exhaust the range of possible errors of consciousness. The relationship between ideological and non-ideological consciousness cannot be conceived simply as the relationship between falsehood and truth. Non-ideological consciousness can still be erroneous for reasons other than the concealment of contradictions in the interest of the dominant class.

As contradictions are historical, so is ideology. An ideological distortion is not an immanent attribute of consciousness nor is it confined to the given situation in which it emerged. Non-ideological consciousness may become ideological.[43] Ideology has to be judged by its reference to actual social practice, to the concrete evolution of contradictions. At the beginning of a mode of production, for instance, the conditions under which individuals produce are not external to them in so far as the contradictions typical of this mode are temporarily absent. Marx affirms that it is when contradictions enter on the scene that men can realize the one-sidedness of the conditions under which they produce.[44] This is also the moment when ideology appears as the concealment of those contradictions.

According to Marx, before contradictions appear, the consciousness of the new ruling class corresponds to the forms of intercourse; in this sense it is not ideological. Contradictions and ideology operate from the very beginning of the mode of production, but those contradictions and ideology affect the former dominant class, defeated but still struggling for survival. They are not the contradictions typical of the new mode of production. The new ideological forms come about when these specific contradictions appear. As Marx puts it,

the more the normal form of intercourse of society, and with it the conditions of the ruling class, develop their contradiction to the advanced productive forces, and the greater the consequent split within the ruling class itself as well as the split between it and the class ruled by it, the more untrue, of course, becomes the consciousness which originally corresponded to this form of intercourse. . . .[45]

It is important to stress that ideology for Marx not only arises as a historical phenomenon; its very character also changes as contradictions evolve. The sharper these contradictions become, the more ideology 'descends to the level of mere idealizing phrases, conscious illusion, deliberate hypocrisy'.[46] Marx cannot be particularly concerned with ascertaining whether ideology is a deliberate attempt to deceive by a particular subject or whether it is a necessary deception induced by reality – his conception emphasizes the unity of consciousness and reality through practice. However, the union between subject and object, between consciousness and reality is also historical and evolves through different configurations.

A. Schmidt has pointed out that this historical character of the subject–object relation makes it possible to detect the dominance of the objective moment at certain periods, and of the subjective moment at certain other periods, just as the proportions between labour and the materials of nature vary in the products of labour.[47] It appears that, for Marx, the more the contradictions develop, the more ideological distortions become a 'deliberate hypocrisy' of the subject, for the very acuteness of contradictions would destroy the apparent harmony of structures and institutions. This is why Marx affirms that 'the more their falsity is exposed by life, and the less meaning they have for consciousness itself, the more firmly they are asserted, the more hypocritical, moral and holy becomes the language of this normal society'.[48] Yet one, has to emphasize that Marx sees always a participation of both subject and object in the production of ideology. The proportion of each aspect may vary, but ideology is never pure invention disconnected from reality or a mere objective deception imposed by reality on the subject.

Ideology and superstructure

Marx examines the concept of ideology in this stage in conjunction with a connected but different problem, the determination of all forms of consciousness by material reality. This is the source of many confusions, some of which affect Marx himself. In effect, occasionally one has the impression that the term 'ideological' is used to make general reference to all forms of consciousness, theories and intellectual representations corresponding to a certain economic base. From here various interpreters derive the term 'ideological superstructure'. But in the majority of cases ideology refers to a particular, distorted kind of consciousness which conceals contradictions.

These two meanings should not be confused, and it seems to me that there are grounds in Marx's writings for distinguishing them and giving them different names. Apart from one place,[49] Marx never uses the expression 'ideological superstructure'. In the 1859 *Preface*, he refers to the 'legal and political superstructure' and to the 'forms of social consciousness' which correspond to the base.[50] When he uses the term superstructure to identify these forms of social consciousness, he does not add the word 'ideological', but describes it as a 'superstructure of distinct and peculiarly formed sentiments, illusions, modes of thought and views of life' or as an '*idealistic superstructure*'.[51] Although the term 'idealistic' entails a negative connotation, the quotation from *The eighteenth Brumaire of Louis Bonaparte* does not seem exclusively to refer to distorted thoughts. However, a notion that clearly expresses the difference between ideology and a more general superstructure of ideas is not found in Marx. I propose the expression '*ideational superstructure*' to signify this distinction.

When Marx refers to consciousness as a structural level, one may say he is including all forms of consciousness. Not all of them have an ideological character in the sense of being a distortion which conceals contradictions. All of them are socially determined, but only some of them are ideological. Therefore *what may be considered necessary for all society as a structural level is the ideational superstructure – not ideology, which is a particular kind of consciousness dependent upon contradictions*. Consciousness necessarily survives the eventual end of social contradictions. Ideology, on the contrary, only arises in antagonistic kinds of society. Of course, ideology is indispensable to the reproduction of a contradictory social formation, indispensable to the reproduction of a contradictory social formation, but its necessity is restricted to that kind of society.

In the ideational superstructure of society, according to Marx, the ruling ideas are the ideas of the ruling class.[52] But this does not make all of them ideological. The class origin of ideas is not a sufficient condition to make them ideological. At this stage of Marx's development, his idea is not yet fully clear. On many occasions he seems to treat as ideological all forms of consciousness coming from the ruling class. However, a distinction is anticipated in his historical treatment of ideology and contradictions: Marx recognizes that originally some forms of consciousness of the ruling class correspond to the form of intercourse and, therefore, are not ideological. This is something which Marx fully clarified when he undertook the critique of political economy.

Here one can only point to the fact that a distinction between ideational superstructure and ideology implies that the class character of certain ideas does not suffice to characterize them as ideology and, moreover, that not all errors or distortions are necessarily ideological. In *Theories of Surplus Value*, it seems to me, is found a more definite statement in this sense. Marx is criticizing Storch because he does not conceive material production historically: Storch 'deprives himself of the basis on which alone can be understood *partly the ideological component parts of the ruling class, partly the free spiritual production of this particular social formation*'.[53] Here a distinction is clearly drawn between ideological and non-ideological ideas in the ideational superstructure, which, as one knows, is dominated by the ideas of the ruling class. On the other hand, the fact that ideology should not be confused with a more general superstructure of ideas does not preclude its being structured. It only restricts its existence to a sector within a vaster structure.

None the less, this distinction between ideational superstructure and ideology does not solve the problems stemming from the attribution of superstructural character to all forms of consciousness. The characteristics of the juridico-political superstructure differ from the characteristics of the ideational superstructure. As it is described by Marx, the political superstructure emerges out of the need for regulating the class conflict.[54] Class domination requires a juridical structure, institutions and repressive apparatuses which regulate life and protect property and trade. The state is thus the embodiment of the power of the dominant class which supervises the division of labour. As Marx puts it, 'the state is nothing more than the form of organization which the bourgeois necessarily adopt . . . is the form in which the individuals of a ruling class assert their common interests . . . .'[55]

|For Marx, the political superstructure presents a remarkable unity; only one state arises directly out of the base and, in turn, makes that base work in the interest of the ruling class.[56] If one considers the whole of social consciousness as a superstructure, the unity disappears. It is not like the political superstructure, in which only one state apparatus and one juridical organization exist which are functional for the reproduction of the system. In the ideational superstructure one may find conflicting theories and ideas, some of them not in the least functional to the system. True, the ruling ideas are the ideas of the ruling class so that, in the main, the forms of social consciousness correspond to the system of domination. Yet the importance of disruptive ideas cannot be underestimated.

If one wished to make the political superstructure equivalent to the ideational superstructure, one would have to accept the possibility of various juridical systems or states, as long as one of them was dominant. This is clearly absurd in Marx's perspective. The normal solution, to postulate the 'ideological superstructure', makes more sense in this particular context, for ideology as such is entirely functional to the system, like the state and the legal apparatus. But then one faces another problem, the question as to whether there may be a non-ideological consciousness. If the answer is affirmative – and it seems clear to me that Marx envisaged his own thought as being non-ideological – then what can one make of it? Is it outside the superstructure or is it a part of it?

This problem seems to be insoluble under the assumption of an ideological superstructure. Either this superstructure would leave sectors of consciousness aside, and we would not know where to locate them, or it would encompass totally opposite forms of consciousness, all of them, alas, ideological. The critical meaning Marx intends for the concept of ideology would be lost. It seems to me preferable to distinguish ideology from ideational superstructure, accepting that the latter includes all forms of consciousness, ideological and non-ideological, and is not a superstructure in the same sense as the political superstructure. But, of course, this is not elaborated by Marx himself and still presents some unsolved problems.

From the general mechanism of ideology to the specific analysis of capitalism

Marx's application of the concept of ideology in the period I have depicted emphasizes the distortions in theoretical consciousness. Marx is mainly concerned with the inversions of German philosophy, which 'descends from heaven to earth' and explains practice from the formation of ideas instead of explaining ideas from practice. The hiding of contradictions is mainly carried out by attributing independent existence to ideas, as if they could rule over material life. So the problems of mankind are attributed to wrong ideas instead of focusing on the real and practical contradictions.

True, Marx differentiates the 'illusions' of common people from ideological theories when he distinguishes the active members of the class from the thinkers of the class.[57] Yet he is mostly concerned with the thinkers. Besides, although the 'illusions' of spontaneous consciousness correspond in general with the development of contradictions in society, the more detailed correspondence between the ideological forms and the concrete forms of economic reality is not analysed. There is only a general reference to the fact that individuals are subjected to the sway of things, but there is no analysis concerning how things are in practice invested with personal characteristics and the subjects appear as things. This is not due to any mistaken approach. It is due to two related factors. First, the degree of generality which Marx's preliminary investigations impose upon his thought: he is producing the basic general premises of his approach to society. Second, the elaboration of these premises is accomplished in the context of a critique and unmasking of philosophy and other theoretical forms which presume to solve human conflicts by mere criticism.

Feuerbach and other Hegelian critics had tried to discover by analysis the earthly core of religion, thus resolving it into the human essence. Marx on the contrary proposes to develop from the actual material relations of life the corresponding forms of religious consciousness. In short, he starts at the opposite end. That is why he insists that ideologists turn reality upside-down. Yet Marx, at this stage, only outlines a general theory based on material relations; he does not analyse very deeply these relations in the capitalist mode of production. That programme is to be carried out later on.

The essential elements of the concept of ideology are laid down in this period of Marx's intellectual development and in the context of the problematic subject–object which Marx tries to solve with the concept of practice. But, again, the study of material practice is carried out only from a general point of view. Marx wants to stress that historical practice is the point of departure as against philosophy. He arrives at the general conclusion that reproductive practice leads to the domination of material conditions over individuals and that revolutionary practice is necessary to change those circumstances. A new period in Marx's intellectual development starts when he initiates a concrete study of the specific material conditions which need to be overcome in the capitalist mode of production.

With the *Grundrisse*, this new stage of Marx's intellectual development begins. As M. Nicolaus has shown, the *Grundrisse* seems a turning-point in many respects.[58] Not the least, Marx's search for an appropriate methodology and for the proper beginning of political economy, which had remained unsettled in the 1857 *Introduction*, can be seen to arrive at new conclusions while he is writing the *Grundrisse*. A re-reading of Hegel's *Logic*, to which Marx concedes importance,[59] seems to have been decisive. Nicolaus notes, for instance, that in the very last page of the *Grundrisse* Marx finds the proper beginning in the analysis of the commodity, contrary to his ambiguous discussion in the 1857 *Introduction*. This is later confirmed both in the 1859 *Preface*,[60] where he explicitly disavows the *Introduction*, and in *Capital*, which begins with the analysis of commodities.

The culminating point of the new developments initiated in the *Grundrisse* is *Capital*. Yet this new phase is not a radical change of perspective; on the contrary, it is the continuation of the programme outlined in *The German Ideology*. There Marx recognized a reproductive practice and the constitution of an objective power over and against the individuals; in *Capital* he completes the analysis of this practice in detail and spells out the forms which this objective power assumes. In *The German Ideology* Marx arrived at the necessity of a revolutionary practice; *Capital* constitutes the study of the conditions for it to arise.

In a letter to Engels, Marx expounds the inner connections between the three volumes of *Capital* and ends his analysis thus:

> At last we have arrived at the phenomena which serve as the *starting point* for the vulgar economist: rent originating from the land, profit (interest) from capital, wages from labour. But from our point of view the thing now looks differently. The apparent movement is explained.

. . . since these three [wages, rent, profit (interest)] constitute the respective source of income of the three classes of landowners, capitalists and wage labourers, we have, in conclusion, the *class struggle* into which the movement and the analysis of the whole business resolves itself. . . .[61]

So it is by no means casual that Marx begins *Capital* with the analysis of commodities and that the manuscript is interrupted when he is about to analyse classes. From practice as objectified in commodities Marx arrives at revolutionary practice in which 'the whole business resolves itself'. K. Kosik has argued that *Capital* can be understood as the Odyssey of concrete historical practice which passes through different stages and forms in which it is objectified and disguised, to end its pilgrimage, not in the mere knowledge of its forms, but in revolutionary activity.[62] Thus, commodity is the concrete, historical form of practice which in successive transformations becomes money, capital and surplus-value, to end in the class struggle. In this sense Marx's concern with practice has not disappeared.

The study of economy is in fact the study of objectified forms of practice. As Kosik puts it 'the economy is the objective world of men and their social products, it is not the objectified world of the social movement of things'.[63] Capitalism is characterized by the domination of the object over the subject, of capital over labour, of conditions of production over the producer, of dead labour over living labour. But this is, for Marx, the result of men's reproductive practice. Marx analyses it not only to know how the system works and reproduces itself, but also to show the conditions of its supersession. Both Marx's analysis and the real movement of the system resolve themselves in the class struggle.

Essence and appearance

The analysis in detail of the various forms of reproductive practice in the capitalist mode of production is shown, in *Capital*, under a new light. The objectified forms of practice present themselves disguised in fantastic appearances which conceal their true character. 'A commodity appears, at first sight, a very trivial thing, and easily understood', yet 'its analysis shows that it is, in reality a very queer thing . . . .'[64] The value-relation which constitutes a thing as a commodity appears on the surface as a relation between things, whereas its real essence is a definite social relation between men. Labour and its product assume, therefore, a mysterious character.

This is something specific to the capitalist mode of production. During feudalism, social relations between men were objectified in classes and personal dependency, yet these relations, in their various forms of labour, appeared as their own personal relationships and not in the guise of social relations between things. The immediate social form of labour was the particular and natural form of labour, not its abstract form, which is typical of the production of commodities.[65] In both cases there is compulsory labour, yet in capitalism this is not seen on the surface.

'Surplus-value itself does not appear as the product of the appropriation of labour-time, but as an excess of the selling price of commodities over their cost-price . . . .'[66] Thus, under the form of profit, the surplus-value extracted from the workers becomes unrecognizable. The difference in magnitude between profit and surplus-value conceals the origin and nature of profit 'not only from the capitalist, who has a special interest in deceiving himself on this score, but also from the labourer'.[67] Marx is not only concerned now with theoretical forms of consciousness, which he tackles in his critique of political economy, but also with the consciousness of the common man.

The inability of political economy to distinguish between profit and surplus-value and the

confusion of the theorists best illustrates the utter incapacity of the practical capitalist, blinded by competition as he is, and incapable of penetrating its phenomena, to recognize the inner essence and inner structure of this process behind its outer appearance.[68]

So not only the economists, but labourers and capitalists are deceived by the form profit which hides surplus-value. This is specific to and typical of the capitalist mode of production. Surplus-value existed before the capitalist system emerged, but then it was evident on the surface, in so far as surplus-labour was accurately marked off from the necessary labour. The surplus-labour which a medieval peasant did on behalf of his master was distinctly separated from the necessary labour he did for his own maintenance.[69]

This division between necessary labour and surplus-labour is also obscured by another form, the wage-form. '. . . wages are not what they *appear* to be, namely, the *value*, or *price, of labour power*.'[70] The very expression 'value of labour' is, for Marx, as absurd as the expression 'value of the earth'. Yet it arises from the relations of production themselves. It is a category for 'the phenomenal forms

of essential relations'.[71] The expression suggests that all labour
has been paid for, and in this sense, it conceals the distinction
between necessary labour and surplus-labour.

In this manner Marx analyses the various forms which practice
and its products assume in the capitalist mode of production. The
objectified forms of practice present themselves as external appearances of essential internal relations, as phenomenal forms of the
essence. Appearances are not mere illusions nor is the essence more
real than the appearance. Both essence and appearance are real.[72]
In other words, reality itself is the unity of essence and appearance.
The latter conceals, but at the same time manifests the former.
As Marx puts it

the final pattern of economic relations as seen on the surface, *in their real
existence* and consequently in the conceptions by which the bearers and
agents of these relations seek to understand them, is very much different
from, and indeed quite the reverse of, their inner but concealed essential
pattern and the conception corresponding to it.[73]

Phenomenal forms are, therefore, as real as the essence and yet
invert the concealed essence. This inversion occurs because, at the
level of the essence, social relations are in turn inverted. In effect,
according to Marx, objectified labour assumes a colossal independence and confronts labour as an alien power. Yet, the emphasis
should be placed not merely on the fact of objectivation, but also
on the fact that this objective power belongs not to the worker but
to capital. The process of objectivation of practice, therefore,
appears from the standpoint of labour as a process of dispossession
or from the standpoint of capital as appropriation of alien labour.
Objectified practice appears as the antithesis of live practice. Marx
refers to this as a 'twisting and inversion' which is not a 'supposed
one existing merely in the imagination of the workers and the
capitalists.'[74] A real inversion at the level of the essence is responsible
for the inversion produced at the level of the appearances.

This is why to Marx, the way in which surplus-value is transformed
into the form of profit is

a further development of the inversion of subject and object that takes
place already in the process of production . . ., even in the simple relations
of production this inverted relationship necessarily produces certain
correspondingly inverted conceptions, a transposed consciousness which
is further developed by the metamorphoses and modifications of the actual
circulation process.[75]

Except for a few passages, Marx does not use the term ideology any more. Yet the concept is still involved in the analysis of essence and appearances in the capitalist mode of production. Ideology remains a projection in the mind of men's practical inabilities, but this practical limitation appears now as responsible for the production of the phenomenal forms. Reproductive practice not only produces objectified inverted relationships, but also, and for that very reason, it produces and projects into consciousness inverted appearances. Phenomenal forms are spontaneously reproduced in consciousness in so far as they are produced by the reproductive practice.

Therefore, ideological consciousness can now be said to be a consciousness which remains fixed in the external appearances that conceal inverted social relations (the essence). Hence, ideology does not invent anything, nor is it a negation of reality as such, in so far as phenomenal forms are real. Yet the ideological representation is not an immanent attribute of reality which deceives a passive consciousness, but the projection into consciousness of petrified appearances produced by men's practice. Ideology negates the inverted character of social relations; it takes an aspect of reality, the appearances, and gives them an autonomy and independence which they do not actually have. In this sense ideology fetishizes the world of appearances, separates it from its real connections.

This is why Marx says of the wage-form:

this phenomenal form, which makes the actual relation invisible, and, indeed, shows the direct opposite of that relation, forms the basis of all the juridical notions of both labourer and capitalist, of all the mystifications of the capitalistic mode of production, of all its illusions as to liberty, of all the apologetic shifts of the vulgar economists.[76]

The appearance, the value of labour or wage, is separated from the hidden actual relation which is the value of labour-power. The former appears spontaneously in consciousness as the real thing.

In *The German Ideology* Marx also characterized the concealment of contradictions as an inversion. Yet he mostly focused on those inversions of the German philosophy which tried to explain social relations from ideas. Now Marx turns to the greater range of ideological distortions and inversions which are common in the spontaneous consciousness of the bearers and agents of the economic relations. He no longer privileges the analysis of theoretical forms of ideology but explains the ideology of common workers and capitalists. He is now interested in showing that 'the distorted form in which the real inversion is expressed is naturally reproduced in the views of the agents of this mode of production'.[77]

Of course, he continues to consider theoretical forms of ideology like vulgar economy, but this is thought to 'express in theoretical terms the notions of the practical men who are engrossed in capitalist production, dominated by it and interested in it'.[78] Another innovation is that now Marx not only detects in general an inverted and contradictory reality which is simply concealed, but also analyses in detail this inverted reality in the capitalist mode of production, thus showing the mediation of phenomenal forms between ideology and the contradictory reality.

This is why Marx can now rephrase his critique of the German ideology in terms of appearances:

relations can be expressed only in ideas, and thus philosophers have determined the reign of ideas to be the peculiarity of the new age. . . . This error was all the more easily committed, from the ideological standpoint, as this reign exercised by the relations . . . appears within the consciousness of individuals as the reign of ideas.[79]

The phenomenal forms of social relations do not produce by themselves a univocal form of deception or mystification. On the contrary, the practical standpoint of the subject is important. Where the philosopher sees the reign of ideas, the economist may see the reign of things.

N. Geras has drawn a valuable distinction between the mystification which consists of reducing the social objectivity of phenomenal forms to a natural objectivity and the mystification which reduces social objectivity to social subjectivity.[80] To Marx the material forms assumed by the social qualities of labour can be conceived as mere symbols. Thus some writers have been led to hold that 'the value of gold and silver is imaginary' or that the phenomenal forms are 'arbitrary fictions'. 'Unable to account for the origin of the puzzling forms assumed by social relations between man and man, people sought to denude them of their strange appearance by ascribing to them a conventional origin.'[81] On the other hand, the value of a commodity like gold or silver can also be thought of as a property of the thing itself.

This is important: first of all, it shows that the various forms of ideological distortions in capitalist society are connected in the practical reproduction of social relations and their appearances, and yet remain different in the particular way in which mystification operates; secondly, it shows that ideology is neither a mere subjective creation of the subject's imagination, nor a mere imposition of reality upon the subject's passive consciousness. In effect, for Marx, phenomenal forms are not subjective fictions. If the relationships between men in labour appear as a social attribute of commodities, this is not a mere creation of consciousness. Thus he argues against Hodgskin, who 'regards this as a pure subjective illusion which conceals the deceit and the interests of the exploiting classes. He does not see that their way of looking at things arises out of the actual relationship itself . . . .'[82]

Yet this very fact, that the mystification stemming from phenomenal forms cannot be reduced to only one form of distortion, excludes the opposite version which sees ideology as the product of external 'given circumstances' which deceive a receptive mind. Phenomenal forms are spontaneously reproduced in consciousness, not as an unavoidable, automatic result, but as a consequence of men's own engagement in the reproductive practice which produces them. If ideology was a mere attribute of a certain deformed reality contemplated by the human mind from without, how could a non-ideological consciousness be possible? But Marx conceives the problem in terms of a practice which is limited and which could be liberated by a different, revolutionary practice.

So revolutionary practice is, for Marx, the only way to overcome ideology. Revolutionary practice changes the conditions within which reproductive practice must necessarily produce misleading appearances. This does not diminish the importance of ideological critique. Revolutionary practice is a conscious, a theoretically informed, practice. Even more, the theoretical critique in itself has an important bearing on the undermining of ideology. 'Once the interconnection is grasped, all theoretical belief in the permanent necessity of existing conditions collapses before their collapse in practice.'[83] Yet the ideological distortion, by which the social character of labour appears to men as an objective character of the products themselves, does not disappear when it is discovered that value is an expression of the human labour spent in the production of those products.[84] In order for this mystification to disappear, the conditions of labour should change. As Marx puts it, 'the whole mystery of commodities, all the magic and necromancy that surrounds the products of labour as long as they take the form of commodities, vanishes therefore, so soon as we come to other forms of production'.[85]

The essential features of ideology continue to be those which Marx previously clarified, in *The German Ideology*, although they are expressed in a different manner. In effect, ideology is reaffirmed as a consciousness which conceals contradictions in the interest of the dominant class. The inverted character of ideological consciousness corresponds to the real inversion of social relations, and this inversion is closely connected with their being contradictory or antithetical. The ideological notion which stems from the inversion contained in the fetishism of capital, for instance, conceives capital as able to self-expand and produce interests. This notion comes near to the popular notion and is also propounded by vulgar economists,

partly because the inner connections are least apparent here and capital emerges in a form in which it appears to be an independent source of value, partly because its *contradictory* character is totally concealed and effaced in this form and no contradiction to labour is evident.[86]

A further example is provided by the ideological notions which arise from the fetishism of commodity. In commodities the social relations between men assume the form of relations between things and thereby conceal the contradiction that concrete labour has to pass for abstract human labour, the antithesis between the personification of things and the reification of persons.[87] The ideological notions which stem from the wage-form, in turn, conceal the contradiction between the labourer's full day of work and the capitalist's appropriation of unpaid surplus-value.

All these contradictions are forms of the basic class contradiction.[88] Every economic operation in society corresponds 'to a definite mode of production which itself corresponds to class antagonism. There is no individual exchange without the antagonism of classes.'[89] So, by concealing contradictions, ideology serves the interests of the ruling class, which can display the present order of things as natural and in the interest of all sections of society. Ideology serves the interests of the dominant class not because it has been produced by the ideologists of the class – which may or may not be the case – but because the concealment of contradictions objectively works in favour of the dominant class's interests.

Precisely because of the contradictory character of real relations, Marx conceives of the essence as historical and not as something definitively given:

the capitalist process is not just a production process pure and simple. The contradictory, socially determined feature of its elements evolves, becomes reality only in the process itself, and this feature is the predominant characteristic of the process. . . .[90]

This is why the real relations are not static. For Marx the essence is not definitely fixed once and for all; it is not something which could be grasped simply by drawing away a curtain of appearances and unveiling an eternal truth.

Marx distinguishes two essential moments in the evolution of capitalist social relations. Initially, contradictions do not appear on the surface; that is, they are latent or potential. As the process develops, contradictions become real or apparent and may precipitate a crisis.[91] It is above all in crises that the contradictions and antagonisms of capitalist production reveal themselves, in a striking fashion. 'The crises are always but momentary and forcible solutions of the existing contradictions. They are violent eruptions which for a time restore the disturbed equilibrium.'[92] For instance, a crisis of over-production shows the contradiction between the production of surplus-value and its realization. The crisis is temporarily solved by a fall in production. But the basic contradiction survives between the tendency to expand production and the tendency to increase the value of capital.

The historical character of social relations is the basis upon which Marx propounds to understand the products of consciousness. He contends that 'in order to examine the connection between spiritual production and material production it is above all necessary to grasp the latter itself not as a general category but in *definite historical form*'.[93] As the essential feature of ideology is the concealment of contradictions, the historical evolution of real relations according to the two broad phases above mentioned becomes crucial. While contradictions are latent or potential, there is no basis for ideology. In effect, the reproductive practice typical of the capitalist mode of production is not settled at the beginning. Capital results from the process of dissolution of the preceding social formation and not from its own reproduction.[94] Thus the phenomenal forms are not yet fully developed and men do not project them in ideological forms of consciousness.

When contradictions come to the surface, ideology arises. For this to occur capital should be reproduced upon the basis of wage-labour and the extraction of surplus-value. Then phenomenal forms arise and conceal the very nature of surplus-value. During the first phase the bourgeoisie is not in direct opposition to the proletariat but, rather, antagonistic to the nobility. So the 'spiritual' production of the bourgeoisie at this moment is not ideological; on the contrary, it is critical of feudal ideology. Ideology exists as the attempt to legitimate a mode of production in dissolution. The classics like Adam Smith and Ricardo, Marx says,

represent a bourgeoisie which, while still struggling with the relics of feudal society, works only to purge economic relations of feudal taints, to increase the productive forces and to give a new upsurge to industry and commerce. The proletariat that takes part in this struggle and is absorbed in this feverish labour experiences only passing, accidental sufferings, and itself regards them as such.[95]

Marx firmly believes that Ricardo is right for his time when he regards the capitalist mode of production as the most advantageous for production in general. The fact that Ricardo's thought is in the interest of the bourgeoisie does not make it ideological; not all class-orientated thought is ideological as far as Marx is concerned. It must conceal contradictions in order to become ideological.[96] This happens during the second phase in which the bourgeoisie is in direct opposition to the proletariat, in so far as the capitalist reproductive practice has asserted itself, thus creating the appearances which men project into ideological forms of consciousness.

This is why the consideration of material production as a historical process is so crucial for Marx. The understanding of the ideational superstructure depends on it; furthermore, it is for Marx the only basis upon which a distinction can be drawn between the 'ideological component' of the ruling class and the 'free spiritual production' of the social formation.[97] Some problems which arise from the apparent treatment of ideology as both a distorted consciousness and the general superstructure of ideas can now be given a solution. Marx is clearly reserving the term ideology to indicate a distorted form of consciousness and, at the same time, is recognizing that the 'spiritual' production of bourgeois society cannot be reduced in its entirety to the ideological level. Also there may be other errors and conceptual shortcomings in the 'free spiritual production' of society. Free here means 'free from ideology', but not necessarily free from other sources of distortion or limitations. Marx's critique of political economy is not always a critique of ideology; sometimes it is a critique of the narrow methodological standpoint and of other limitations which are necessary, given the development of science, but which in their historical context are not ideological.

Some difficult questions

The presentation of Marx's thought on ideology within the context of his intellectual development has allowed the consideration of it both in its fundamental unity and in the differences of emphasis as it evolves. Yet this does not exclude the existence of real problems and unsolved questions which generate conflicting interpretations. The source of the difficulty is to be found in Marx's own treatment of the concept. I have already pointed to the possibility of confusion derived from the lack of a clear distinction between ideology conceived as a specific phenomenon and the general social determination of all forms of consciousness. The mistaken and misleading notion of 'ideological superstructure' emerges from that confusion. In more general terms Marx deals with the concept of ideology within the context of a double perspective. On the one hand he emphasizes the relationship between consciousness and practice; on the other he stresses the relationship between base and superstructure.[98] The logic and consequences of each perspective are not exactly the same. While the former relates consciousness to a practice which produces primarily but not exclusively the economic relations of society, the latter conveys the image of consciousness being related to a separate economic structure.

It can be argued that these two perspectives are in fact not so different since, for Marx practice mediates between consciousness and social being. But the problem is whether social being can be identified with economic conditions. Several authors have rightly disputed this identification. Jakubowski, for instance, claims that the contrasting pair 'base and superstructure' is different from the pair 'being and consciousness'. Social being is certainly founded upon the economy, but cannot be restricted to it. The fact that social being determines consciousness does not imply that social being simply means economic relations. Likewise, the superstructure cannot be identified with consciousness since it also contains 'highly material' political elements.[99] Kosik has also noted that social being does not coincide with given conditions or with the economic factor.[100]

The base–superstructure relationship is not equivalent to the practice–consciousness relationship. The discrepancy is the source of two connected orders of difficulties. Firstly, although these two polarities are not exactly alike, it seems that neither can be sustained in isolation from the other. In effect, if one takes the former without considering the latter, consciousness may appear to be determined by external economic structures. By itself, this determination may seem unmediated and direct; that is, consciousness may appear as a pure reflection of the base. If on the contrary one takes the practice–consciousness relationship without considering the base–super-structure relationship, reality appears not as a mere object but as a practically produced world and, therefore, consciousness of it is necessarily mediated by practice. Yet this practice, by itself, may appear as undetermined, as the product of man's free will. So the reduction of one polarity to the other may lead to either a theory of reflection or an idealist theory of indetermination.

Second, ideology assumes different connotations according to the polarity which serves as a context. Under the base–superstructure relationship, ideology appears as a secondary ideal structure which is directly determined by the economic structure. Under the practice–consciousness polarity, ideology appears as the free and conscious product of a subject, as a false consciousness which protects some class interests. While for the former ideology is necessary, for the latter it appears illusory. The emphasis upon the necessity of ideology under the first polarity produces a tendency to consider it, at least partially, as a positive fact of social life, as performing a necessary function for society. On the contrary, ideology, considered as a false consciousness or illusion, is always contingent and negative.

As neither conception seems to do justice to Marx's thought when taken in isolation, a certain form of integration appears necessary. Marx's indictment of common sense serves us as a methodological warning that we should strive to see both their unity and distinction:

It is characteristic of the entire crudeness of 'common sense', which takes its rise from 'the full life' and does not cripple its natural features by philosophical or other studies, that where it succeeds in seeing a distinction it fails to see a unity, and where it sees a unity it fails to see a distinction. If 'common sense' establishes distinct determinations, they immediately petrify surreptitiously, and it is considered the most reprehensible sophistry to rub together these conceptual blocks in such a way that they catch fire.[101]

One can try to see in the base–superstructure image a twofold meaning. It attempts to show that consciousness cannot be analysed on its own, that it has a foundation in material reality. It also attempts to show the primacy of economic relations in the social being, without meaning to reduce the latter to the former. In its turn, the theory-practice polarity emphasizes the foundation in practice of all knowledge so that the dependence upon material reality is not understood as a dependence upon a given, objective world, separated from the subject. Yet this practice would be itself determined by the objectivations and crystallizations of past practice.

Although this interpretation is possible, Marx himself did not explicitly propose it; on the contrary, he shifted from one polarity to the other without much analysis. The use of the base–super-structure polarity in isolation from the theory–practice polarity is problematic and has contributed to the emergence of confusions and conflicting interpretations. Various authors have shown the ambiguity of the distinction between base and superstructure. Williams, for instance, sees that the distinction may acquire, instead of a metaphorical and relational meaning, a conceptual and descriptive meaning which would purport to indicate the existence of separate observable areas of social life.[102] Of course, reality itself refuses to be compartmentalized. Jakubowski has shown that certain economic relations often make their appearance directly in legal form, which is why he thinks that base and superstructure are separable only for methodological purposes.[103] In the same sense, Rossanda warns against a conception which introduces a dichotomy between two different spheres and conceives of their reciprocal relationship in a mechanistic manner. This conception leads to two kinds of errors; the superstructure is considered subordinate to the base or, conversely, as autonomous from it. As neither autonomy nor subordination solve the problem she proposes to understand the terms of this relationship as a specific co-presence.[104]

The hypostasis of two different spheres of society is implicit in Aron's criticism, that it is difficult to know which elements of social reality belong to which sphere.[105] In general, the base refers to the economy and forces of production. But science, according to Marx is a force of production,[106] and yet it is also knowledge and therefore must belong to the superstructure. The ambiguity is not only spatial. As the superstructure is founded upon the base the idea can also arise that the base is temporally prior to the superstructure. A combination of the temporal and spatial way of understanding the relationship is at the root of conceptions which see the superstructure as a contingent and secondary sort of phenomenon. If the super-structure is caused by the base, then in order to understand con-sciousness it is necessary to reduce it to its material conditions. Further, to exempt certain areas of knowledge from this secondary and contingent character, the only choice is to exclude them from the superstructure. This is the view which Timpanaro takes. He is concerned with the existence of objective truths which science has attained in pre-socialist societies, sometimes through politically conservative scientists. So, from his point of view, science cannot be simply considered as a superstructure. Instead, he restricts the concept of superstructure so that it does not include the totality of cultural activity. By transferring without modification the notion of superstructure to the domain of scientific knowledge one risks, he argues, 'making the latter as relative and subjective a phenomenon as religion or law'.[107]

As one can see, Timpanaro has identified the notion of super-structure with a negative concept of ideology so that all true knowledge is outside its sphere. The problem is, nevertheless, that Marx did not exclude any form of knowledge from the 'forms of social consciousness' or 'ideational superstructure'.

These are just a few of the problems which may arise from Marx's treatment of the concept of ideology. I have already pointed to some possible solutions which may avert the most serious pitfalls. But one must acknowledge that they are based on yet another effort of interpretation and that, therefore, one will not find them as such in Marx's writings.

3   From Engels to Durkheim: the continuing debate on ideology

Orientations of the debate

The magnitude of Marx's contribution to the concept of ideology makes him a necessary point of reference for nearly all new developments and controversies about the concept. However, his was not the only perspective in which the phenomenon of ideology was analysed. Broadly speaking, it is possible to distinguish the debate within Marxism itself from the new contributions which emerge outside its boundaries. In both areas, the evolution is far from unilineal. Within the Marxist field, various currents of interpretation adopt different points of view in order to understand ideology. These currents follow, more or less, the alternative orientations which stem from Marx's own treatment, both in the sense of emphasizing specific elements which Marx integrated with others and in the sense of stressing the writings of a particular period of his life.

Two main orientations have become known, one for its positivist leanings and the other for its 'historicist' approach. In the first orientation one can locate the tradition arising from Engels's interpretation, which originates a debate in which Lenin, Plekhanov and Labriola participate. In the second orientation one can locate the early Lukács and Gramsci. Imperfect and relative as this classification may be, it shows the two broad trends. The debate within the Engelsian tradition underlines the base–superstructure perspective and seeks a correct understanding of the determination of knowledge by the economic base; the 'historicist' approach emphasizes the theory–practice perspective and seeks to elucidate the role of class practice as crucial to understanding ideology.

Parallel to the Marxist debate, important developments occur in the social sciences which contribute different insights on the concept of ideology. The nineteenth century's intellectual atmosphere had emphasized man as an eminently rational creature and had put great hopes in reason as the only means to understand and solve any social problem. The twentieth century witnesses the beginning of a certain scepticism with respect to the role of reason, and many authors focus upon the importance of non-rational elements in both man and society. In broad terms two main orientations can be distinguished.

There is a trend very much concerned with the subjective and psychological phenomena which are suppressed by reason; its main representatives are Freud and Pareto. Both insist on the fact that most human actions in society respond to basic impulses and instincts and that the human mind tries to conceal this by giving a rational account of irrational behaviour. Hence, a kind of psychological concept of ideology emerges from their conceptions, although the term ideology is not used.

A second orientation, represented by Émile Durkheim, follows the contrary, Baconian tradition; it starts by a critique of the subjective elements which interfere with rational knowledge, thus developing a notion of ideology, in opposition to science, which shows a positivist slant. Rationalism is here very much alive. Subsequently Durkheim focuses upon the importance of religious phenomena, which he studies not only from a speculative point of view but also from a functional perspective. This shows a change of attitude with respect to the eighteenth and nineteenth centuries. Ideology becomes a collective representation instead of an innate pre-notion or purely distorted knowledge. Despite important differences between Freud and Pareto's psychological approach and Durkheim's concept of ideology, both are concerned with subjective processes, which seem unconnected with specific social contradictions. In this sense both approaches represent an alternative to the Marxist tradition.

The Engelsian tradition: the problem of the economic factor and the change in the meaning of ideology

One of the problems derived from the base–superstructure polarity is that social reality may appear divided into independent sectors, some of which generate others and thereby constitute themselves as primary explanatory causes. From here emerged the theory of the economic factor. Society is conceived as an aggregation of factors; some are causes, others effects. The 'economic factor' is the most important cause, whereas the superstructure is a mere effect constituted by derivative factors.[1] Engels was the first to react against the oversimplification of the economic factor and the rigid conception of cause and effect. In a letter to Bloch he argues that

according to the materialist conception of history, the *ultimately* determining factor in history is the production and reproduction of real life.
Neither Marx nor I have ever asserted more than this. Hence if somebody
twists this into saying that the economic factor is the *only* determining one,
he transforms that proposition into a meaningless, abstract, absurd
phrase.[2]

Engels accepts that production is the decisive factor, in the last
instance, but stresses time and again that the superstructures are not
merely derivative. On the contrary, 'although the material mode of
existence is the *primum agens* this does not prevent the ideological
spheres from reacting upon it and influencing it in their turn, but
this is a secondary effect'.[3] Engels also warns against conceiving
the economic factor as the cause, the sole active agent, whereas
everything else is considered the effect.[4] On the contrary, he argues
that interaction takes place upon the basis of economic necessity.
The ideological spheres have no independent historical development,
but they do have an effect on history.[5]

Engels applies these principles to Marxism itself. On the one hand
modern socialism appears as determined by the class antagonism
existing in society between capitalists and workers; on the other
hand, in its theoretical form, is the extension of the principles laid
down by French philosophers of the eighteenth century. 'Like every
new theory, modern socialism had, at first, to connect itself with the
intellectual stock-in-trade ready to its hand, however deeply its roots
lay in material economic facts.'[6] Other Engelsian formulae are less
clear and apparently propound a kind of reflection theory. In trying
to account for Marx's and his own separation from Hegel, Engels
keeps referring to concepts as 'images' or 'reflections' of real things
and to 'the dialectics of concepts' as a 'conscious reflex of the
dialectical motion of the real world'.[7]

Lukács is particularly critical of Engels's conception of dialectic
and of his use of the concept of reflection. True, Engels recognizes
that the world is not to be comprehended as a complex of ready-made
things but as a complex of processes. But if there are no things,
Lukács asks, what then is 'reflected' in thought?[8] Korsch in turn
refers to Engels's idea of interaction and contends that 'no scientist
can be contented with the answer given by Engels . . .'. In his view,
Engels's phrases 'are but useless attempts to adhere to the "dialectical" unity of substance, causality and interaction in the Hegelian

philosophical "idea" ".[9] For Korsch neither 'dialectical causality' nor scientific causality supplemented by 'interaction' can account for the relations existing between the base and the superstructure. By analogy with Marx's treatment of production, distribution, exchange and consumption, Korsch propounds to understand the base and the superstructure as moments of a totality or differences within the unity.[10]

Following this line of criticism, Stedman Jones has argued that Engels's solution, by emphasizing interaction as based upon necessity, involuntarily takes as a model Hegel's solution for the relationship of Nature to the Notion. Hegel contends that on the surface of nature, contingency must be recognized: but underneath, there is necessity concealed.[11] Hence, consciousness, even being allowed to react on the surface, is ultimately determined by an objective and necessary substructure with laws over and above men's practice.

One may dispute the 'given' character of the base or its 'necessary' character as against the 'contingent' character of consciousness. Both base and superstructure are products of human practice. To this extent their reality does not differ. As Kosik has argued, the primacy of the economic does not derive from its being a different or more concrete reality, but from the central meaning which practice, as labour, has in the production of human reality.[12]

Despite his criticism of the theories of the economic factor for their unilaterality, Engels himself does not get rid of the conception of society as composed of different factors which carry different weights. This is why he has to resort to 'interaction' based upon necessity and the distinction between primary and secondary effects. In this sense, Korsch's scepticism about Engels's solution is justified. Yet his own ultimate solution does not do justice to Marx's thought either. He thinks Marx often uses his terms figuratively, as when he speaks of a 'correspondence' between the base and the superstructure. Korsch suggests that one should not adhere too strictly to these words. He is against smoothing over apparent contradictions in Marx by scholastic interpretations. According to him Marx presents the history of society at one time as a history of the class struggle, at another time as the product of economic forces. Thus, he claims there are 'two independent forms of Marxian thought, equally original and not derived one from the other'.[13] This seems to me just as debatable as Engels's compromise. Although a problem may exist, does one have to split up Marx's thought into two independent worlds in order to solve it?

Labriola and Plekhanov attempt to overcome the problem by opposing to the economic factor the theory of the economic structure.[14] Contrary to the theory of factors, they think that society should be conceived as constituted as a whole by the economic structure; that is, by the social relations that men enter into when they produce and by the means of production. The economic structure is the unity of all spheres of social life. A historico-social factor, on the contrary, is an abstraction, justified by the desire to understand the inner connections of social phenomena, but which does not stand the light of criticism for it dismembers the activity of social man.[15]

Labriola argues that factors have never been seen acting independently. All facts in history recall the conditions of the economic structure, yet all facts are also 'preceded', accompanied and followed by determined forms of consciousness.[16] Of course, the economic structure determines all the rest, but it is not

a simple mechanism whence emerge, as immediate, automatic and mechanical effects, institutions, laws, customs, thoughts, sentiments, ideologies. From this substructure to all the rest the process of derivation and of mediation is very complicated, often subtle, tortuous and not always legible.[17]

Labriola distinguishes between the situation of the legal–politica order and that of ideas. The economic structure determines directly the legal–political order, and only in 'second place' and 'indirectly' the order of ideas. In the products of thought, particularly in their artistic and religious forms, the mediation between the base and the product is not easy to sort out. A long experience in social psychology is required to 'reduce' these secondary products to the social conditions they idealize.[18] Likewise, Plekhanov contends that

the law, the state system and the morality of any given people are determined directly and immediately by its characteristic economic relations. These economic relations also determine – but indirectly and mediately – all the creations of the mind and imagination. . . .[19]

Despite the just criticisms of the theory of factors, it does not seem to me that the theory of the economic structure clarifies everything. It is more or less clear that the economic structure is determinant not in the sense of producing automatic, mechanical effects, but it is much less clear what positive meaning is then attached to that determination. One cannot but notice the lack of the concept of practice as the mediating instance between consciousness and being. Labriola and Plekhanov are still entangled in the problem of how to sort out the complicated 'mediations' between the economy and consciousness. True, the theory of the economic structure is meant to surpass a narrow conception of the economy as a factor among others.[20] Yet in searching for a mediation in social psychology rather than in practice, a conception of 'factor' is somehow re-introduced by the back door. The economy appears as a given fact, completely external to the individual. Psychology is supposed to be able to sort out the way in which this base impresses itself upon the mind. In other words, this is a more subtle attempt at 'reducing' consciousness to its social conditions.[21]

Engels's critique of the reductionism to the economic base was continued in the same direction by Labriola and Plekhanov in their critique of the economic factor, then reversed in the opposite direction by Lenin's early approach to the subject. In a text written in 1894, Lenin over-emphasizes the importance of economic necessity as against the subject's consciousness and will.[22] In his view Marx's decisive contribution to science is proving the scientific necessity of socialism by an objective analysis of capitalism and history. The conception of history is no longer based upon the will of governments and authorities but upon a rigorous study of the evolution of social formations. This evolution, which ineluctably leads to socialism, appears as a historico-natural process. Marx arrived at this basic idea 'by singling out the economic sphere from the various spheres of social life, by singling out *production relations* from all social relations as being basic, primary determining all other relations'.[23]

By a process of reduction, Lenin develops a rather restricted notion of economic structure and makes it the main explanatory cause. 'Only the reduction of social relations to production relations and of the latter to the level of the productive forces provided a firm basis for the conception that the development of formations of society is a process of natural history.'[24] Lenin claims that Marx's analysis in *Capital* never explains things by resorting to factors other than the relations of production. And yet, the point is that by explaining the structure only by the relations of production, Marx always studies the corresponding superstructures.[25] Hence Lenin sees no need for an analysis of the superstructure in itself. This could be reduced to essential economic relations and, in this way, satisfactorily understood. Consciousness is therefore reduced to its economic conditions.

In this view, social movement is ruled by laws which are above human practice and independent of consciousness and will. Men cannot change these objective laws. On the contrary, these laws determine human purposes and consciousness, and social movement is treated as a natural process in which human intention does not play any role. Therefore, socialism will come about not so much as a result of a human conscious decision but as the result of historical necessity. According to Lenin, socialism is inevitable 'by virtue of the very laws of capitalist development'. Marx stopped his scientific study of capitalist society after showing that its development 'has such and such a tendency, that it must inevitably perish and turn into another, a higher organization'.[26] It is not that practice does not play any role; it is only that it is a determined practice, conditioned by the economic structures. Therefore, practice and consciousness are conceived as instruments of the structural determinism. To this extent their explanation must be found not in themselves but in the economic structures.

Yet Lenin's explanation of Marx's own theory does not really take into account this set of principles. Marx's contribution is exalted as a scientific break-through which substitutes a scientifically objective analysis for a subjective approach which recognized the oppression of the masses and wanted a new society based upon a superior ethic. Marx, according to Lenin, demonstrated the necessity of both exploitation and its overcoming. Yet this scientific breakthrough appears itself undetermined, as the work of a scientific genius. In Engels modern socialism appeared not only as the extension of the debate of French philosophers, not only as a scientific achievement, but also as the expression of the class antagonism existing in society; in Lenin this aspect is totally disregarded. Hence, although consciousness in general appears as a secondary sort of phenomenon, derived from and determined by economic relations, science seems to gain an especial status and there is no mention of its own determination.

This is even more noticeable in *What Is to Be Done?*, written in 1902. There is found the thesis of the importation of science into the labour movement. Following Kautsky, Lenin contends that socialism and class struggle arise from different premises, neither deriving from the other. Science is produced outside the class struggle as the inevitable outcome of philosophical and economic theories developed by intellectuals.[27] So, the indetermination of science is now confirmed in positive terms. Yet beyond this fact, the role of consciousness in general also changes. No longer is it merely the reflection of economic structures. The spontaenous consciousness of the working class is said to reflect bourgeois ideology.

Lenin justifies this by explaining that bourgeois ideology is older than socialist ideology, so it is more developed and possesses more means of dissemination.[28] Hence, he implicitly acknowledges the mediation of a superstructural factor in the determination of working-class consciousness. Just as bourgeois ideology mediates in a negative sense, science comes from without to mediate in a positive sense. It is science that may liberate the spontaneous consciousness of the proletariat. One cannot but notice, though, that the mediation is attributed to consciousness as carried by the party, and not to practice.

For Lenin science does not arise in connection with class struggle nor does it have as its object class practice, but the relations of production. And yet this science appears as determinant of revolutionary practice. Hence practice continues to be an instrument of an external determination. In *What the Friends of the People Are*, practice is the instrument of economic necessity. Now in *What Is to Be Done?*, practice appears as the instrument of consciousness, either as bourgeois ideology or as science. No doubt the superstructure has gained a more active role but at the cost of being, both disconnected from class practice in its origin, and externally constitutive of class practice in its function. Nothing could be farther away from Marx's thought.

True, some of these theses are subsequently reviewed when Lenin goes through Hegel's logic. There he recognizes that 'practice is higher than theoretical knowledge, and that 'man's consciousness not only reflects the objective world, but creates it'.[29] Knowledge continues to be a reflection of nature but not 'a simple, not an immediate, not a complete reflection'. Man comes closer to the truth step by step.[30] Yet this is a simple theoretical recognition of what he had already implicitly found in *What Is to Be Done?*: that the working class's spontaneous consciousness did not fully express a true cognition of its objective situation. Besides, in spite of his partial consideration of practice within the theory of knowledge, the order of the concepts continues to give primacy to abstract thought. As Lenin puts it, 'from living perception to abstract thought, *and from this to practice*, – such is the dialectical path of the cognition of *truth*, of the cognition of objective reality'.[31]

Engels's late treatment of the concept of ideology within the polarity base–superstructure did not, however, innovate in the basic negative meaning which he and Marx had given to the concept in *The German Ideology*. Even if ideology appears as a reflection of economic relations in consciousness, Engels simultaneously asserts that these relations appear inverted. As he puts it, 'this inversion, which, so long as it remains unrecognized, forms what we call *ideological outlook*, influences in its turn the economic basis . . .'.[32] Yet the preference given to the treatment of ideology within this relationship inaugurates a tradition which was soon to lose sight of the inverted character of ideology. This occurs because obviously the relationship between base and superstructure does not exclusively refer to distorted forms of consciousness but to all forms of consciousness. All the products of thought are determined by the base, irrespective of their validity.

Hence, by itself, the relationship between base and superstructure does not distinguish inverted from non-inverted forms of consciousness. The more ideology is understood within this polarity the more it tends to be substituted for all forms of social consciousness. This theoretical development converges with the political practice of social democracy at the end of the nineteenth century.[33] In the political struggle against the bourgeoisie, the critique of its ideology was made from the point of view of the proletariat, and from this the idea arose that such a critique was made from a different 'ideological' point of view. Just as there were bourgeois ideologists, so there were proletarian ideologists who represented the interests of the proletariat.

Lenin synthesizes this double movement and begins to use the concept of ideology in the sense of a set of cognitions and theories which express the interests of a class. There is a bourgeois ideology as much as a proletarian ideology.[34] In general, there are class ideologies. This being so, ideology must be stripped of any inherent characteristic which makes it a necessary inversion. The concept may now encompass distorted as much as true forms of consciousness and, therefore, does not by itself entail a negative meaning. The falsity of bourgeois ideology is due not to its ideological character but rather to its bourgeois origin. Lenin's conceptualization not only expressed a particular theoretical development which overstressed the polarity base–superstructure, but also expressed a political practice which seemed to give credibility to the theory–practice polarity.

This is why such a conception is taken up by authors like Lukács and Gramsci despite their opposition to positivist interpretations of Marx and his concept of ideology. Ideology as superstructure is compatible with ideology as a class *Weltanschauung*. Thus a move from ideology to class 'ideologies' is firmly established which loses the originally negative sense of the concept. The cognitive validity of ideology is set aside as a different problem to be solved independently from the fact that all class knowledge is ideological. For Marx ideology had to be judged in relation to contradictions in society, irrespective of its social origin. Ideology was always distorted knowledge and always worked in the interests of the dominant class. But not all intellectual production of this class was thought of as ideology. When ideology becomes a *Weltanschauung*, its validity tends to vary according to the imputation of a class background. True, neither Lenin nor Lukács nor Gramsci would have supported a criterion of validity exclusively based upon the attribution of class origin. Yet the risk is present as a tendency when the problem of the cognitive evaluation of ideology is separated from the essential definition of ideology.

The most significant consequence of this evolution from a restricted negative concept in Marx to a general positive concept from Lenin onwards, is the loss or dissolution of the concept itself. Detached from its critical connotation, ideology loses what for Marx was its essential feature and becomes a concept which covers the whole range of social and political thought, whatever its origin, function or validity. Thus the value which the concept had in Marx's work as a tool of analysis and critique has almost disappeared. For those who try to maintain, at least partially, the original critical meaning of the concept, another consequence is that, in equating some ideologies with science and others with pre-scientific or non-scientific knowledge, the assessment of what is ideological and what is non-ideological soon becomes a problem of truth and error. The reference to social contradictions in society is lost and ideology is confused with all sorts of errors or simply with pre-scientific consciousness. Thus, even maintaining some negative and critical connotation, ideology loses its specificity.

The 'historicist' conception of ideology: Lukács and Gramsci

Lukács (1885–1971) is usually taken as the most typical exponent of a historicist conception of ideology.[35] Indeed the influence of

German historicism as developed in Heidelberg, particularly by Dilthey, had a profound influence upon Lukács's early writings.[36]

Yet Lukács later modified his view-points in several respects. A case in point is Lukács's attitude towards Engels and the theory of reflection. As I have already mentioned, in the 1920s Lukács was strongly critical of Engels's concept of dialectics and of the theory of reflection. In his view, in the theory of reflection

we find the theoretical embodiment of the duality of thought and existence, consciousness and reality, that is so intractable to the reified consciousness.[37]

In 1945, on the contrary, Lukács affirms that

It is a fundamental thesis of dialectical materialism that any apperception of the external world is nothing but the reflection of a reality existing independently of the consciousness, in thoughts, conceptions, perceptions, etc., of men.[38]

Instead of rejecting the theory of reflection, the later Lukács propounds, following Lenin, a dialectical understanding of it which would rule out all mechanism. He quotes, approvingly, letters of Engels which deal with the base–superstructure relationship and adheres to his solutions without reservations. The change is so radical that one wonders whether in this respect he can still be accused of historicism. Indeed even Lukács's early writings are more balanced than one is led to believe by certain 'structuralist' authors. Lukács's critique of the dualism of the reflection theory seems very appropriate from a Marxist point of view: he rejects both the theory of reflection and the other idealist extreme whereby things appear as reflections of concepts. His solution is Marx's solution in the *Theses on Feuerbach*, namely to link consciousness and reality through practice.

One cannot say that for Lukács practice is totally indetermined, or the result of man's absolute freedom. As he puts it, 'this praxis has its objective and structural preconditions and complement in the view that reality is a "complex of processes" '.[39] In order to define class consciousness he reaffirms, as an essential principle of scientific Marxism, the independence of the real motor forces of history from man's consciousness. The unity of consciousness and existence is not an identity resulting from a reflection or correspondence between each other, but the result of both being aspects of the same historical process. The consciousness of the proletariat is 'by no means the invention of the proletariat, nor was it "created" out of void'.[40] At the same time, emancipation 'does not take place mechanically parallel to and simultaneously with economic developments. It both anticipates these and is anticipated by them.'[41]

Yet Lukács also accentuates the role of consciousness as the ascribed world-view of the class to a point in which it may appear as a substitute for the concrete practice of the class. The thought of the proletariat has a practical character; it is a theory of practice which 'transforms itself into a practical theory that overturns the real world.'[42] It seems as if thought could change the world. If Marxism is revolutionary it is because 'it understands' the process or 'demonstrates' the line of future development. Thus ideology appears not only as a consequence of the economic structure of society but also as the precondition of it. Marxism as the ideology of the proletariat puts it 'into a very particular frame of mind,' for *'the strength of every society is in the last resort a spiritual strength. And from this we can only be liberated by knowledge.'*[43] Yet the proletarian consciousness does not depend upon the historical practice of the class; rather it is conceived as an imputed rationality which flows from the class being. The concrete history of the class produces an empirical or psychological consciousness which is reputed to be false, and thus cannot be liberating.

That is why the ideological obstacle to the proletarian consciousness, legality, although 'it does not always entail a conscious betrayal or even a conscious compromise', can be described as a 'natural and instinctive attitude towards the state'. 'The disease itself is the inability to see the state as nothing more than a power factor.'[44] There is no mention of this 'disease' being anchored in the forms of objectified practice. On the contrary, practice is recognized as limited and conditioned because of the limitations of consciousness. Therefore consciousness tends to gain an autonomy more in accordance with Dilthey's concept of historical consciousness than with Marx's concept of consciousness. In the same way as Dilthey's 'current of life' manifested itself in partial objectivations, which were not total expressions of it, Lukács's class consciousness expresses itself in partial psychological forms which do not exhaust the real class consciousness.

Lukács's early writings coincide with some of Gramsci's most important developments in the distinction between the sphere of ideology and the sphere of coercion. Although force is the last argument in society, through ideology men submit freely to the social system without a permanent need for the use of force. Society could not survive 'if it were compelled to use force every time it is challenged'.[45] That is why a change of society can be brought about only when the ideological belief of both the ruled and the rulers has been smashed. Here, some elements of Gramsci's concept of hegemony are implicitly expressed by Lukács.[46] For a class to make a revolution, the possession of the consciousness able to organize society is essential. Yet unlike Gramsci, Lukács expressly emphasizes that 'this does not preclude the use of force'.

The attention Lukács pays to the reified forms of the economic is not necessarily a symptom of his recognition of ideologies as mere reflection of reality. He has accepted the theory of reflection and maintains that the inversions of the categories of the human being constitute the necessary fetishization of capitalist society; yet he insists that 'in men's consciousness, the world appears completely different from what is in reality, disfigured in its structure, separated from its authentic relations'.[47] He does not realize that for Marx the ideological inversion corresponds to a real inversion of the social relations, not only to the inversion of their appearances. One can find in Lukács an overemphasis of the role which the subject plays through its consciousness in the origin of ideology.

Gramsci (1891–1937) also follows the trend away from a purely negative concept of ideology. For him ideology is a superstructural expression of a contradictory reality, an expression of the 'kingdom of necessity' which embraces every class in society. Marxism, also an expression of historical contradictions, is bound to disappear, together with other expressions of the reign of necessity, in the reign of freedom. Structures and superstructures form a 'historical bloc', so the latter are 'the reflection of the ensemble of the social relations of production'.[48] Gramsci insists that the superstructures are an objective reality, where men gain consciousness of their positions and goals. Therefore Marxism is a superstructure like every other class ideology.

However, Gramsci is aware of the danger of confusion in the use of the concept of ideology in relation to the superstructure. He recognizes

that there is a potential element of error in assessing the value of ideologies, due to the fact (by no means casual) that the name ideology is given both to the necessary superstructure of a particular structure and to the arbitrary elucubration of particular individuals.[49]

So he confronts two interpretations: ideology as necessary super-structure and ideology as 'pure appearance', 'useless', 'stupid'. He thinks the second sense has become widespread and has denatured the theoretical analysis of the concept. He maintains, on the contrary, that 'the thesis which asserts that men become conscious of funda-mental conflicts on the level of ideology is not psychological or moralistic in character, but structural and epistemological . . .'.[50]

Although this approach cannot be accused of historicism, it may still induce confusion in so far as it does not distinguish between two different notions – the distorted character of ideology and the arbitrary character of ideology. One can agree that ideology is not an arbitrary phenomenon without insisting that it is not distorted: ideology may be both necessary and distorted. So when Gramsci affirms that 'the bad sense' of the word has denatured the concept, one can agree only as long as he is referring to the arbitrary character of ideology. In the case of the distorted character of ideology, the opposite is true: the 'good sense' of the word has become widespread after Lenin, as Gramsci's own concept shows it, and it is this positive concept, applied to Marxism and other proletarian expressions, that has denatured the original meaning of ideology.

Be that as it may, Gramsci distinguishes two kinds of ideologies: historically organic ideologies (those 'which are necessary to a given structure') and arbitrary or 'willed' ideologies.[51] Gramsci favours the former concept, giving rise to the conception of ideology as a class *Weltanschauung*. As he puts it, 'one might say "ideology" here, but on condition that the word is used in its highest sense of a conception of the world'.[52] In this conception the problem is how a world-view may preserve the unity of the social bloc. Ideologies serve as a 'cement' which unifies it; but not all of them are equally successful.[53]

Despite the fact that all ideologies belong to the reign of necessity, Gramsci makes a distinction between Marxism and the others. On the one hand 'all hitherto existing philosophies . . . have been mani-festations of the intimate contradictions by which society is lacerated'; on the other hand they have not been 'the conscious expression of these contradictions'.[54] The superiority of Marxism, on the contrary, is based upon its being the most conscious expression of those contradictions. It does not only grasp contradictions but also 'posits itself as an element of the contradiction'.[55] While other philosophies are in themselves contradictory in so far as they seek to conciliate opposite interests, Marxism does not seek to solve peacefully the contradictions; on the contrary, it is the theory of those contradictions.

In contrast with Lenin, who thought the primacy of Marxism was based on its scientific character, detached from class contradictions, Gramsci bases the superiority of Marxism on its being the 'most conscious' expression of contradictions. For Lenin, Marxist science came from without, carried by the party, in order to overcome a spontaneously deficient consciousness. To Gramsci, the philosophy of praxis, as well as the party or Modern Prince, represents a collective will. Lenin holds the traditional conception of the educator which Marx had criticized in the *Theses on Feuerbach*; Gramsci holds that the Modern Prince is an educator who needs to be educated. It is the proletariat itself which produces its organic intellectuals.

While Lenin's scientific ideology had to struggle against spontaneous consciousness, Gramsci's philosophy of praxis expresses a historical spontaneous direction. Education does not suppress but purifies; it is a 'catharsis',

the passage from the purely economic (or egoistic passional) to the ethico-political moment that is the superior elaboration of the structure into super-structure in the minds of men. This also means the passage from 'objective to subjective' and from 'necessity to freedom'.[56]

Yet Gramsci's identification of 'subjectivity', 'super-structure' and 'freedom', as against 'objectivity', 'structure' and 'necessity', also differs from Marx's standpoint. As Hoare and Nowell Smith have pointed out, Marx affirms that the realm of freedom 'can blossom forth only with this realm of necessity as its basis'.[57] Gramsci seems to locate freedom in a superstructural, subjective sphere which surpasses all necessity. A similar displacement occurs with the concept of civil society: in Marx it is located in the economic base, whereas in Gramsci it assumes a mere superstructural character.[58]

Gramsci's most important contribution, though, is his treatment of the relationship between ideology and the state. Gramsci characterizes western societies for the predominance in them of civil society as against the predominance of the State in eastern societies. From here he deduces the central importance of class hegemony, that is, the ability of a class to assume a moral and intellectual leadership over the other classes without resorting to coercion. If applied to bourgeois domination, this emphasis may imply that, in order to overthrow bourgeois power, an ideological hegemony must first be achieved by the working class.

Perry Anderson has shown how illusory is this sharp separation between the ideological hegemony of the bourgeoisie and State power; on the contrary, the very existence of the bourgeois State is in itself 'the principal ideological lynchpin of Western Capitalism'.[59] Anderson describes the basic relation between the State and civil society in the west as an asymmetry, coercion located in the State, consent located in both civil society and the State. This characteristic would have eluded Gramsci's attempts to solve the problem. More damaging is Anderson's clear demonstration of Gramsci's persistent slippage of concepts. Terms like State, hegemony and civil society receive several different connotations which contribute to three different versions of their relationship.[60]

Despite its inconsistencies, some of them naturally induced by the conditions under which it was produced, Gramsci's thought has the originality of pointing towards the peculiarities of the cultural situation in the west and to the consequences deriving from bourgeois rule by consent and ideological hegemony. Yet in separating ideology from political society, Gramsci abandons the possibility of understanding one of the most important bases of ideological domination in bourgeois society. Moreover, his concept of ideology as a class world-view, like Lukács's, tends to overrate the role played by consciousness in both the production of ideology and the overcoming of capitalist society.

Like Lukács's tenet that the true strength of society is spiritual and that, therefore, knowledge is required to overcome it, Gramsci emphasizes ideological hegemony in contrast to political coercion. Lukács had expressly contemplated violence in addition to the need for knowledge; in Gramsci this is far less clear. In some other respects though, Gramsci goes beyond Lukács. While Lukács asserts only negatively that class consciousness is not a creation out of a void, Gramsci positively affirms that every ideology is an expression of the contradictions of the reign of necessity.

Freud and Pareto: the re-emergence of a psychological concept of ideology

Although some of the intellectual developments before Marx could be said to have implicitly produced a psychological concept of ideology, Sigmund Freud (1856–1939) made undoubtedly the first powerful and systematic study of the human psyche which contributes specific insights into some psychological mechanisms which closely resemble ideological phenomena. In effect, elements of a concept of ideology emerge in the mechanism of transposition or projection. Freud studies it in connection with such pathological states of mind as paranoia. Yet he affirms that the mechanism is 'very commonly employed in normal life'.[61] It consists of an internal impulse which is concealed and distorted by its transposition into an objective sphere. As Freud puts it, 'an internal perception is suppressed, and, instead, its content, after undergoing a certain kind of distortion, enters consciousness in the form of an external perception'.[62] One can notice the inversion of the mechanism with regard to Marx's concept of ideology. In Marx an external contradiction receives a distorted solution in the mind; in Freud an internal contradiction receives a distorted solution by being transposed into the external sphere.

Similarly, the mechanism of rationalization, which Freud studies in connection with diseases such as obsessional neuroses, suggests a kind of ideological phenomenon. The neurotic patient naturally misunderstands some occurrences of his disease 'and puts forward a set of secondary motives to account for them – rationalizes them, in short'.[63] Just as the neurotic makes up reasons for justifying his conduct, man's mind seeks arguments to conceal his inner desires and appetites. Inasmuch as society does not tolerate man's instinctive impulses, he needs to justify them by giving them the appearance of rationality. In fact people's conscious interpretations of their memories, phantasies and nocturnal dreams may all be rationalizations of an unconscious motive. Again, the mechanism of ideology appears inverted in so far as the contradiction being dealt with is a psychological conflict between inner impulses which prompts the attempt to find a logical though distorted explanation.

Although these two psychological phenomena operate with a mechanism similar to that of ideology – even if inverted – they still remain a process mainly at the individual level. This obviously marks a difference with the traditional concept of ideology which, whatever its origin, had normally been thought of as having social consequences. But of course, it is possible to understand individual psychological mechanisms as having a collective impact which could be crucial for the production of ideology. Thus, after Freud, Wilhem Reich tries to explain the emergence of fascist ideologies in terms of psychological processes. Although he seeks an integration with Marxism, Reich emphasizes the sexual repression behind fascism. Hence he can affirm that 'race ideology is a pure biopathic expression of the character structure of the orgastically impotent man'.[64] Fascism is not a national characteristic or the patrimony of a class; it is 'the sum total of all the *irrational* reactions of the average human character'.[65] In this 'average human character' is a repressed intermediate layer of cruel and sadistic impulses, a kind of Freudian unconscious; in a situation of crisis it emerges unrestrained, falling upon a scapegoat while simultaneously rationalizing the discharge of these impulses in theories of the superior race and the conspiracy against it.

What is interesting from the point of view of the conception of ideology is that Reich believes the determinations of the material structure of society are not sufficient to understand ideology. The character structure of the masses has to be taken into account. Ideology not only reflects the economic process of society but also imprints it in the psychic structure of individuals: ideology has not only reproduced itself in man but, what is more significant, 'has become an active force, a material power in man'.[66] Ideology has become the character structure of men, and the basic traits of that character are formed in early childhood. This would be why ideology is more conservative and lags behind changes in the rest of society. Therefore, ideology reflects a material process corresponding to the childhood of people; to this extent ideology becomes identified with a psychic structure of masses which is somehow fixed. This is why the age-long sexual repression plays the main role in shaping ideology and supersedes the determination of specific social contradictions.[67]

However, one does not need to resort to other authors to see the social projection of some Freudian psychological mechanisms. Freud himself sees it, above all in his analysis of two other phenomena. First, among the mechanisms of defence he mentions identification with the aggressor as a process which plays an important role in the formation of the super-ego and the control of impulses. By this mechanism man defends himself against an object which provokes anguish by partially assimilating it or by internalizing some of its features. The child, for instance, when overwhelmed by the fear produced by an aggressor, may tend to imitate the personality of the aggressor in an attempt to overcome his unbearable anguish. This mechanism of identification is seen by Freud as one of the factors which can explain the attachment of the oppressed people to the cultural ideal of the oppressors.

In any given society, the cultural ideal is capable of producing a narcissistic satisfaction not only in the favoured classes but also in the suppressed,

since the right to despise those that are outside it compensate them for the wrongs they suffer in their own group. True, one is a miserable plebeian, tormented by obligations and military service, but withal one is a Roman citizen, one has one's share in the task of ruling other nations and dictating their laws. This identification of the suppressed with the class that governs and exploits them, is, however, only a part of a larger whole. Thus the former can be attached effectively to the latter, in spite of their animosity they can find their ideals in their masters.[68]

So, according to Freud's explanation, the ideological domination of the ruling class is guaranteed by the psychological process of identification with the aggressor. Although the dominated classes cannot enjoy the benefits of the cultural ideal of society, their narcissistic satisfaction is nevertheless induced by the mechanism of identification.

The analysis of religion shows other important connections between psychological mechanisms and social institutions which have a bearing upon the concept of ideology. To Freud, religious ideas are 'the most important part of the psychical inventory of a culture'.[69] Religion is an illusion which fulfils 'the oldest, strongest and most insistent wishes of mankind'.[70] This illusion is not necessarily a delusion, in the sense of an error which conflicts with reality. The main factor in the motivation of religion is wish-fulfilment, and this cannot be proved or refuted. In the same way as Feuerbach thought that religion corresponded with the infantile stage of mankind, so Freud contends that the mechanisms of religion are based upon man's state of helplessness with respect to nature, as a little child is helpless and dependent upon his parents. The child's relation to his father is ambivalent in that he perceives him as a danger but also as one from whom protection should come. The same ambivalence is deeply imprinted on religion. Men know that they need protection against the uncertainties of life and thus create gods with the traits of the father-figure. At the beginning

Man makes the forces of nature not simply in the image of men with whom he can associate as his equals – that would not do justice to the overpowering impression they make on him – but he gives them the characteristics of the father, makes them into gods, thereby following not only an infantile, but also, as I have tried to show, a phylogenetic prototype.[71]

As man's state of helplessness remains even after science has deprived nature of its personified character – when the child grows up, he finds he is destined to remain a child for ever[72] – the father-longing and the gods also remain. They have now to reconcile men with their own death and with the deprivations encountered in their social life. So, Freud sees religion as an illusion which crystallizes in God those human wishes that derive from man's helplessness. Again, a kind of ideological mechanism is operating. Although Freud does not want to pass judgement on the reality value of religion, he acknowledges that the emergence of scientific spirit has affected religion. 'The more the fruits of knowledge become accessible to men, the more widespread is the decline of religious belief.'[73] Just as the child spontaneously overcomes most of the necessary neuroses which the process of growing up brings about, so mankind will also overcome the neuroses of its development. Thus religion appears as

the universal obsessional neurosis of humanity. It, like the child's, originated in the Oedipus complex, the relation to the father. According to this conception one might prophesy that the abandoning of religion must take place with the fateful inexorability of a process of growth, and that we are just now in the middle of this phase of development.[74]

Freud is aware of the criticism that he is also indulging in an illusion, namely, the end of religion and its replacement by other ideas. For these new ideas, whatever they are, must be transmitted through education and therefore are bound to assume all the psychological characteristics of religion. For it is a natural defect of culture 'that it imposes on the child, governed by his instincts and intellectually weak, the making of decisions to which only the matured intelligence of the grown-up can do justice'.[75] Freud accepts that he cannot be certain about this; yet he finds that his illusion is preferable and more likely than the religious illusion. In this he shares in the hopes of the Enlightenment about a more rational society, free from ideological distortions. As he puts it,

we believe that it is possible for scientific work to discover something about the reality of the world through which we can regulate our life. If this belief is an illusion, then we are in the same position as you, but science has shown us by numerous and significant successes that it is no illusion.[76]

Hence, Freud's psychological conception of ideology ends up recognizing in science the only force capable of overcoming ideology. This feature, curiously enough, he shares with the positivist conception of ideology. Ideology has lost its determination in the specific contradictions of society and is now rooted in the psychical structure of individuals. This is why Freud is critical of the Marxist conception. He argues:

the communists believe that they have found the path to deliverance from our evils. According to them, man is wholly good and is well-disposed to his neighbour; but the institution of private property has corrupted his nature.[77]

As the hostility between classes is supposed to be created by the possession or dispossession of private property, the assumption is made that if private property were abolished, hostility would disappear. Freud does not want to argue against the economic wisdom of abolishing private property, but he sees in the hopes that accompany it an untenable illusion. The abolition of private property may check *one* of the sources of aggression, but this is not the only one because 'aggressiveness was not created by property'.[78]

For Marx ideology can be overcome only by altering in practice the material conditions of society; for Freud ideology has deeper roots in human nature and no change in the organization of society can guarantee its overcoming. Science, with its progressive advance, will bring about the defeat of ideology. But, of course, Freud does not realize that his rationalistic hope in science leaves aside the problem of the social determination of that very science. Science appears an absolute force; no consideration is given to the fact that its achievements, which incidentally Marx also recognizes, can be obtained within the framework of contradictory social relations. Therefore, as long as these contradictions remain, whatever the scientific progress, ideology will remain too. It is precisely because ideology is rooted in social contradictions that science can unmask it but not overcome it. Besides, it is difficult to see how an ideology rooted in the psychical structure of the individual minds can ever be overcome by reason. Culture and education must necessarily impose a form of authority over the individual, and this very fact continues to provoke his mechanisms of defence and thus the production of ideology. Ultimately, all psychological conception of ideology ends up trapped by the eternal and universal existence of ideology.

This problem also befalls V. Pareto (1848–1923) but, if anything, it becomes even more accentuated. Basic to Pareto's sociology is the assumption that non-rational actions and beliefs constitute by far the most important part of society and that reason plays a very small role in shaping social institutions. Induction, Pareto says, 'makes us recognize how great a part in social phenomena is played by non-logical behaviour'.[79] In comparing the believers' faith with experimental truth he maintains that 'we must take care to avoid the error – which a certain materialist metaphysics makes – of attributing to logic and experience a greater power and dignity than that allowable to dogmas accepted by sentiment'.[80] The notion of ideology emerges because, simultaneously with the great extension of non-logical behaviour in society, men have a kind of innate tendency to cover that behaviour with a veneer of logic. 'Human beings have so strong a tendency to attach logical developments to non-logical actions that everything and anything can serve as a pretext for them to indulge in this favourite occupation.'[81]

The distinction between *residues* and *derivations* basically corresponds with the idea of irrational actions being logically accounted for. The residues are manifestations of sentiments which correspond to certain human instincts; derivations are the intellectual elements which try to justify the residues.[82] For Freud the mechanism of rationalization gave an appearance of rationality to inner impulses and desires; for Pareto derivations justify residues as if they were the results of rational considerations. Derivations are born from man's hunger for thinking. But this hunger is satisfied in different ways, not only by experimental theories but also by pseudo-experimental reasonings. Derivations make man conceal before himself the irrational origin of many of his actions. Hence Pareto sets himself the task of 'removing these "logical" masks to reveal the things which are hidden beneath them'.[83] In other words, Pareto wants his theory to become a critique of ideology.

However, what appears in common people to be a spontaneous tendency to delude themselves has further reasons in the case of writers and theoreticians. Pareto wonders why authors minimize non-logical behaviour and replace it by logical behaviour. Beyond a natural inclination he finds another powerful motive: 'If we suppose that certain actions are logical, it then becomes much more easy to embody these in a theory than if they were non-logical.'[84] Furthermore, most intellectuals want to preach what ought to be instead of what is; besides, many of them consider non-logical actions as irrelevant if not reprehensible – things, like superstitions, which ought to be unmasked by reason. But in preaching that man ought to act by reason alone intellectuals close their eyes to reality. This is why Pareto attacks the easy critics who hold the church responsible for the creation of prejudices. In fact magic and superstition exist everywhere and their interpretations 'are the servants not the masters, of the thing itself'.[85] Hence

it is not by the logical devices of the church, of governments or of any other institutions of authority that belief in such non-logical behaviour comes to be imposed. It is the other way about: it was the non-logical behaviour which imposed on these institutions the necessity of finding logical devices to explain them.[86]

Like Freud, Pareto asserts that he is not concerned with the intrinsic truth of religion and advances a methodological proposition which is also crucial to Durkheim: 'Religions, beliefs and the like will only be considered externally inasmuch as they are social facts, and entirely apart from their intrinsic merits.[87] Freud has the hope that religion will finally be replaced in its task of motivating civilized behaviour by other secular motives; both Pareto and Durkheim have a more cautious approach. Pareto, like Durkheim, refuses to equate the experimental truth of a theory with its social utility:[88] many propositions of religion are puerile, but there is no logical right to draw the conclusion that religion is puerile or harmful to society.[89] While Freud conceived the possibility of men's emancipation from internal and external constraints, Pareto thinks it is useless to try to do away with them. The art of government, Pareto argues in Machiavellian style, 'lies in finding ways to take advantage of sentiments, not in wasting one's energies in futile efforts to destroy them'.[90] The elites and their statesmen very rarely resort to logical arguments to convince the people. On the contrary they prefer derivations, the influence of interests and sentiments. Even science itself has become a faith; to this extent government can resort to science, as a derivation, in order to modify people's opinions. This is not difficult 'for the common man is satisfied with a remote, a very remote, semblance of a logico-experimental element in derivations'.[91]

Therefore, Pareto holds a rather sceptical vision. His theory of derivations denounces as ideological almost every aspect of man's activity and spiritual production. True, logico-experimental science is conceived of as the opposite to ideology. Yet, unlike Freud, Pareto has no hope that science will be able to get rid of derivations. Even more, science itself has become a derivation. 'The worship of "reason", "truth", "progress" and other similar entities,' Pareto argues, 'is to be classed as non-logical behaviour, as are all cults.'[92]

Hence, ultimately, ideology is not only universalized and made inevitable but it becomes, also, a necessary instrument of government by the elites in order to promote their social measures. The achievement of practical ends requires the existence of ideological motives. Marx had recognized the distance between what men actually do and the ideas they make of their actions. But this phenomenon was the result of specific historical conditions and contradictions which could eventually be overcome. By making ideology a psychological phenomenon rooted in human nature, Pareto absolutizes it and takes to its extreme a position which Freud had tried without total success, to avoid.

Durkheim's conception of ideology

Although Durkheim (1858–1917) does not provide a systematic analysis of the concept of ideology, at least he uses the term and proposes a certain understanding of it. This can be found in *The Rules of Sociological Method* (*The Rules*, henceforth) and is complemented by subsequent writings, the most important of which is *The Elementary Forms of Religious Life* (*The Forms*, henceforth). The context in which Durkheim first deals with ideology is the attempt in *The Rules* to lay the foundations of sociology as a science of social facts. Starting from the methodological tenet that social facts should be considered as things, Durkheim sees that men form some ideas or pre-concepts on things, which naturally tend to substitute themselves for the real things. These ideas or preconceptions may become the subject of science and speculation instead of the things themselves. A science concerned with these ideas can only produce what Durkheim calls an 'ideological analysis', that is to say, it becomes a science which 'proceeds from ideas to things, not from things to ideas'.[93]

At the beginning, all sciences come across these preconceptions. Even physics and chemistry, when they first appeared, found there already existed some crude notions concerning physico-chemical phenomena, because thought is prior to science and man cannot live without forming ideas. At the very moment that a new phenomenon becomes the subject of science, these preconceptions, like Baconian idols, try to substitute themselves for the real things so that 'instead of observing, describing, and comparing things, we are content to focus our consciousness upon, to analyse, and to combine our ideas. Instead of a science concerned with realities, we produce no more than an ideological analysis.'[94] Durkheim finds it obvious that this method cannot give objective results; the ideas are like a veil drawn between the scientist and the things, concealing them from him. They are particularly active in sociology, because social things are a product of human activity and hence tend to appear as the application or embodiment of certain ideas.

To this ideological analysis Durkheim opposes sociology as a science of facts. But in order to constitute sociology as a true science, these preconceptions must be eradicated. Pareto was convinced that sociology up to his time had almost always been presented dogmatically and warned us not to be deceived by Comte's attaching the label 'positive' to his philosophy;[95] so Durkheim believes that sociology up to his own time has merely dealt with preconceptions and not with things. Thus he also criticizes Comte, who was not consistent with the positivist programme, who abandoned his affirmation that social phenomena are natural facts, and who made the object of his sociology a pre-notion (the idea of constant progress of mankind throughout history) which turns out to be absolutely unverifiable through objective observation. In proceeding thus, Durkheim argues, 'not only does one remain in the sphere of ideology but one assigns to Sociology a concept which is not even truly sociological'.[96] The same mistake is made by Spencer, who rejects the idea of progress only to replace it by another pre-notion, the idea of cooperation.

Therefore, Durkheim defines ideology in contrast with science. Following the Baconian tradition he depicts it as those preconceptions or idols which constitute an obstacle to the scientific understanding of reality. These ideas are 'illusions that distort the real aspect of things' and produce an 'imaginary world'.[97] The scientist 'must emancipate himself from the fallacious ideas that dominate the mind of the layman'.[98] However, ideology is not a mere distortion which has no function; these ideas harmonize men's actions with their environment. Men need to regulate their behaviour by means of certain notions which allow them to adjust to reality. Pre-notions have precisely this adaptive role although they are theoretically false.[99]

The analogy with Bacon's idols has nevertheless certain problematic consequences for Durkheim's conception of ideology. Not the least is that in trying to secure a science of social facts Durkheim arrives at the paradoxical result that the social origin of ideology itself is disregarded. In effect, preconceptions seem to be inherent in human nature. Men, Durkheim argues, cannot live without forming some ideas about their environment, and the presence of these ideas cannot be doubted because one can perceive them within oneself. They are the product of repeated experiences and acquire the authority of the habit derived from repetition. 'We feel their resistance when we try to shake them off.'[100] Hence, ideology does not appear as a totally indeterminate and casual phenomenon. Men spontaneously produce and fix by habit these ideas in order to adjust themselves to reality. But this determination is not social. Just as most of the Baconian idols were conceived as innate obstacles of the human mind, so Durkheim's ideology appears as a phenomenon inherent in the nature of man's intellect. Ideological analysis, Durkheim says, 'conforms so closely to the *natural bent* of the human mind that it is to be found in the beginning of the physical sciences'.[101] Even when sociological science has been founded and its fundamental methodological rule established, '*the mind is so naturally inclined* to underrate and disregard this particular truth that a relapse into the old errors will inevitably follow unless sociologists are willing to submit themselves to a rigorous discipline'.[102] There is no link between ideology and social reality. Ideology is simply an illusion derived from an innate predisposition of the human mind and fixed by habit. Although a crucial phenomenon for the emergence of a science of social facts, ideology is not itself considered as a social fact.

Durkheim's subsequent analysis of religion introduces a context from which new elements for a conception of ideology could be derived. However, the relationship between these new elements and the former conception is ambiguous. Durkheim does not explicitly abandon his early concept of ideology, some traces of which can be found in *The Forms*, but his analysis of religion is carried out upon different bases. Does Durkheim keep his original concept, in which case religion cannot be considered as ideology? Or does Durkheim implicitly drop the first approach to ideology, in which case ideology becomes a collective representation and religion is included within it?[103]

Durkheim's early treatment of ideology as a spontaneous illusion which distorts the aspect of things cannot include religious representations as 'collective representations which express collective realities'.[104] On this view, religion cannot be a tissue of illusions. While Feuerbach understood religion as a projection of the human essence into a transcendental sphere, Durkheim understands religion as an expression of society, 'a system of ideas with which the individuals represent to themselves the society of which they are members, and the obscure but intimate relations which they have with it'.[105] Feuerbach found religion an illusion projected by man which splits the subject into a good alien being (god) and a bad being (man). For Durkheim, 'the collective ideal which religion expresses is far from being due to a vague innate power of the individual, but it is rather at the school of collective life that the individual has learned to idealize.'[106] Religious practice is not alienating but, on the contrary, 'strengthens the bonds attaching the individual to the society of which he is a member'.[107] Hence, all societies need religion: 'There can be no society which does not feel the need of upholding and reaffirming at regular intervals the collective sentiments and the collective ideas which make its unity and its personality'.[108]

While Durkheim's early concept of ideology is born in opposition to science, religion does not differ from science in its nature or basic attitude. Both science and religion express reality and try to connect things together, to classify them and to systematize them. Even more, for Durkheim the essential ideas of scientific logic and the fundamental categories of thought are of religious origin. But 'if religion has given birth to all that is essential in society, it is because the idea of society is the soul of religion'.[109] Hence, there can be no antinomy between science and religion because both come from the same source, the collective consciousness. True, the collective origin of religious ideas does not mean that they are at once adequate for their object. Religion ignores the spirit of criticism and how to escape from subjective prejudices. Science brings in a new methodology which enables it to overcome these deficiencies.

But these perfectionings of method are not enough to differentiate it from religion. In this regard, both pursue the same end; scientific thought is only a more perfect form of religious thought. Thus it seems natural that the second should progressively retire before the first, as this becomes better fitted to perform the task.[110]

Yet only the speculative function of religion is taken up by science; the reaffirmation of collective sentiments continues as the eternal function of religion.

So there exists a clear contrast between Durkheim's analysis of religion and his early concept of ideology. Is this due to a change in the concept of ideology or to the fact that he is analysing a different phenomenon? In principle the latter position is attractive because it avoids the assertion of a radical change of perspective which is not acknowledged by the author himself. Had he abandoned his former theory, it is likely that he would have given some indication of it, especially if he intended to replace it with a new theory. But there is no explicit attempt to substitute his analysis of religion for the concept of ideology. On the contrary, certain elements in *The Forms* may suggest that even in analysing religion the former concept of ideology is implicitly maintained.

In effect, the substance of ideology was those ideas or pre-notions which substituted for things, that is to say, for those social facts which ought to be considered as things. Religion is a social fact and therefore should be studied as a thing. But there are pre-notions about religion, ideological ideas which substitute themselves for the real thing. Durkheim seems to recognize two sources of them. Firstly he affirms that

from the fact that a 'religious experience', if we choose to call it this, does exist and that it has a certain foundation . . . it does not follow that the reality which is its foundation conforms objectively to the idea which believers have of it.[111]

Secondly, not only believers but also philosophers have misunderstood religion in so far as 'unfortunately, the method which they generally employ is purely dialectic: they confine themselves to analysing the idea which they make for themselves of religion'.[112] So, Durkheim implicitly evokes his old conception of ideology, according to which religion itself is not ideological but the idea which some people have of religion is ideological. Although the term ideology is no longer used, the phenomenon described follows the conception elaborated in *The Rules*. Religion would be a social fact but instead of analysing it as a thing, philosophers would be content to analyse the idea or pre-notion which they have made for themselves of religion. The difference of terminology would be merely formal: what in *The Rules* was called 'ideological analysis' is called 'dialectic method' in *The Forms*.

However, there are also strong arguments in favour of the position which sees a change in the concept of ideology. When Durkheim analyses the process of idealization in religion he is alluding to the same mechanism of ideology, but, simultaneously, he is giving to it a different foundation. In effect, Durkheim believes that although reality clearly appears in the midst of mythologies and theologies, it nevertheless does it in an idealized form. This idealizing, typical of religion is defined as the faculty 'of substituting for the real world another different one, to which they [men] transport themselves by thought'.[113] It is obvious that this definition evokes the mechanism of ideology as illustrated in *The Rules*, namely, the substitution of an 'imaginary world' for the real world. Yet to the question of whence this idealization comes, Durkheim gives now a strikingly different answer. In *The Rules* the source of ideology was explained in terms of a 'natural bent' of the human mind; in *The Forms* it is affirmed that

some reply that men have a natural faculty for idealizing. . . . But that is merely changing the terms of the problem; it is not resolving it or even advancing it. The systematic idealization is an essential characteristic of religions. Explaining them by an *innate power of idealization* is simply replacing one word by another which is equivalent of the first; it is as if they said that men have made religions because they have a religious nature.[114]

Implicitly, this is a very forceful critique of the former conception of ideology.

In *The Rules* ideology was not itself considered a social fact; that is, it was an obstacle to science but not an object to science. Now Durkheim states that 'the formation of the ideal world is therefore not an irreducible fact which escapes science; it depends upon conditions which observation can touch; it is a natural product of social life'.[115] In *The Rules* men spontaneously formed their ideas in order to adapt themselves to their environment, whereas now idealization is not due 'to a vague innate power of the individual' but, on the contrary, the individual has learned to idealize 'at the school of collective life'.[116] According to this argument the concept of ideology has changed. The very mechanism of ideology as described in *The Rules* can be found in religion, but now it has a social foundation. Durkheim would have finally arrived at conceiving the social determination of ideology.

How should this social determination be understood? First of all, Durkheim wants to separate himself from · any crude theory of reflection which he identifies, somehow mistakenly, I think, with Marxism. He insists that his theory is not ·'a simple restatement of historical materialism' and that 'in showing that religion is something essentially social, we do not mean to say that it confines itself to translating into another language the material forms of society and its immediate vital necessities'.[117] Social determination cannot mean that consciousness is a mere epiphenomenon of its material base, nor does it entail any debasing or diminution of its value.[118] Second, in positive terms, Durkheim understands social determination as meaning that concepts are collective representations, that is, 'they correspond to the way in which this very special being, society, consider the things of its own proper experience'.[119] A collective consciousness, 'the highest form of psychic life', is the source of all logical thought and of the basic categories with which the human mind works. The collective representation presents 'guarantees of objectivity by the fact that it is collective: for it is not without sufficient reason that it has been able to generalize and maintain itself with persistence'.[120]

However, this general conception of social determination still does not discriminate between ideology and other forms of knowledge. For although Durkheim does not accept a qualitative difference between religion and science there must surely exist a social foundation for their distinction. To this Durkheim replies that although collective representations cannot be wholly inadequate for its subject, neither are they adequate at once:

> If society is something universal in relation to the individual, it is none-theless an individuality itself, which has its own personal physiognomy and its idiosyncracies; it is a particular subject and consequently particularizes whatever it thinks of. Therefore collective representations also contain subjective elements, and these must be progressively rooted out, if we are to approach reality more closely.[121]

In other words, the specific determination of ideology springs from the particular character of collective representations which, in its turn, derives from the personal physiognomy of the social individuality.

In *The Rules* ideology was explained in terms of a natural bent inherent in the minds of individuals; in *The Forms* ideology seems to be explained in terms of a natural bent inherent in the mind of society considered as a subject. The social determination of ideology is resolved into an idiosyncracy, the innate subjectivity of the collective individual which particularizes whatever it thinks of. But this transposition almost entirely blurs the distinction between the two conceptions of ideology which we have been evaluating. Even if one accepts the existence of a social subject, the difference between the innate bent of individuals and the innate bent of the collective individual seems secondary. Ideology has effectively become the *a priori* condition of all individuality, even if this happens to be a social individuality. To this extent, it makes little difference whether Durkheim abandoned his first conception or not. If anything, it seems to me that the inclusiveness of the collective consciousness, postulated so forcefully in *The Forms*, must make one accept the existence of a change in the concept of ideology. No element of consciousness can be outside the collective consciousness, not even ideology.

It could be argued that the difference between the two conceptions is not as small as I make it: for instance, the relationship between ideology and science are deeply affected and radically vary according to the position one judges correct. While in *The Rules* there was a strong opposition between ideology and science, in *The Forms* Durkheim rejects the idea of an antinomy between them because they come from the same source. However, this difference is more apparent than real. What has changed is that Durkheim has now identified the same origin for ideology and science in the collective experience of society. But by no means has he underrated their distinction. On the contrary, religion is supposed to retire progressively before science, and science tends to substitute for religion in all its cognitive and intellectual functions. Durkheim sees a real evolution: 'the concept which was first held as true because it was collective tends to be no longer collective except on condition of being held as true'.[122] Besides, he is strongly critical of those who have used the 'dialectic method' to understand religion, and he does not accept the idea of religion which the believer has. What has really happened is that in *The Forms* Durkheim has discovered a double function of ideology. In *The Rules* he had already recognized that ideology has a necessary intellectual function. Now he adds to the speculative function the social function of expressing collective sentiments. This is why science cannot, now, refuse, to grant to ideology its right to exist. However, science must take over its intellectual function and must refuse its right to dogmatize or claim a special competence. In *The Rules* he had considered only this function, and so had stressed the opposition to science. Now he emphasizes the other function, and the antinomy between ideology and science seems to disappear. But in reality it is maintained in the same terms in all that concerns their intellectual function.

Durkheim criticizes the conception that explains man's faculty for idealizing in a sort of innate power. It is, he says, as if one said that men have made religions because they have a religious nature. Yet he ends up implying something not essentially different, namely, that men have made religions because society has a religious nature. The recourse to the subjectivity of a hypostatized individual only masks the fact that ideology is conceived as a spontaneously given *a priori*. For social determination to have any real meaning it has to be specific; otherwise it is an empty form which cannot be adequately distinguished from its repeated individual manifestations. This fact shows an important difference between Durkheim's conception of determination and Marx's. While Durkheim traces ideology back to the subjectivity of the general form of society, Marx specifies historical practices, contradictions and material conditions which, within society, determine it. For Marx it was crucial to grasp material production not as a general category but in definite historical form in order to examine its connection with spiritual production. Durkheim, on the contrary, tends to conceive of representations as social in the sense that there is a collective subject that 'thinks' them.

Durkheim accuses Marx of reducing consciousness to a mere epiphenomenon of its morphological basis. But he can be accused in turn of reducing consciousness to the result of a hypostatized collective experience. By describing the social as prior to men's practice, Durkheim somehow substantializes it as a kind of second nature. The logical consequence is that social facts like, ideology, become normative with respect to men's practice, whatever their value and whatever men do about it. Religion will never dispense with its form of speculation, and this is why truly human thought is described as 'the ideal limit towards which we are constantly approaching, but which in all probability we shall never succeed in reaching':[123] to get rid of ideology is, ultimately, the impossible task for the collective individual to dispose of its subjectivity. Durkheim's conception of ideology suffers the same problem that befalls Freud's. Both are rationalists and expect science to get rid of ideology, yet the very logic of their conceptions makes the task impossible. Hence, in a strange way and despite Durkheim's disregard for psychology, his conception of ideology ends up very near a psychological conception. While Freud looks for the substratum of ideology in the individual psyche, Durkheim looks for it in the collective consciousness. But in both cases ideology, separated from historical social contradictions, has become attached to a general form, be it the Oedipus complex or the collective idiosyncracy. Both substrata appear as given, ahistorical facts which substitute for specific determinations.

4 The historicist tradition: Mannheim's sociology of knowledge and Goldmann's genetic structuralism

Introduction

Following Lukács's influential analyses in the sociology of literature and culture, Mannheim and Goldmann continue the neo-Kantian tradition which German historicism had inaugurated. Both underline the basic distinction between natural sciences and social sciences, and the peculiarity of the methodology applicable to social sciences. When analysing social life, it is argued, a particular kind of understanding is required since the object of knowledge partially involves the subject. Yet both put the case for a certain kind of integration between causal explanation and interpretation of cultural phenomena. Mannheim as much as Goldmann is strongly influenced by Lukács's interpretation of Marxism and seeks to support the analysis of cultural phenomena upon the identification of a class world-view or *Weltanschauung*. However, while Mannheim consciously separates himself from Marx and wants to supersede his theory of ideology by the more general sociology of knowledge, Goldmann finds Marx one of the genuine founders of his genetic structuralism.

In the general pattern for analysing cultural phenomena, the concept of ideology is understood in connection with the notion of a class world-view, that is, the general system of ideas, aspirations and feelings which is common to the class and which unites its members. This determines the preference for a positive concept of ideology over the traditional 'false consciousness' approach. Yet while Goldmann still keeps an epistemological distinction between the outlooks of various classes, Mannheim relativizes all standpoints, including Marxism. In spite of this difference, the treatment of ideology as a class *Weltanschauung* has similar consequences in that ideology loses all specificity as a concept. In the world-view of the class all intellectual and cultural products find their ultimate support, and thus become indistinguishable from ideology itself.

Consciousness and reality: between relationism and relativism

Like Lukács, with whom he collaborated in his youth, Mannheim (1893–1947) was strongly influenced by both Marxism and German historicism, especially through Dilthey. Unlike Lukács he never became a real Marxist, although in his maturity he also moved away from the most idealist tenets of *Geistesgeschichte*. The neo-Kantian 'interpretative' tradition seems to have had a much greater and more long-lasting impact upon Mannheim's conceptions than upon Lukács's. Even when he fully develops his sociology of knowledge, drawing extensively from Marx's theory of ideology, Mannheim maintains that 'the sociology of knowledge is closely related to, but increasingly distinguishable from the theory of ideology which has also emerged and developed in our time'.[1] Mannheim wants to surpass an allegedly narrow Marxist point of view in order to outline a general theory of the social determination of knowledge and a sociological methodology of analysis. His early writings though, do not elaborate on the social determination of knowledge and, on the contrary, rely heavily upon a *verstehende* approach.

In effect, in his essay 'On the interpretation of Weltanschauung' Mannheim insists that cultural products require the interpretation of meanings which cannot be carried out by the methods of the natural sciences. *Weltanschauung* as the global outlook of an epoch assumes a central role in this task since interpretation involves the location of cultural products within a totality of which they constitute meaningful parts. As he puts it 'the crucial question is how the totality we call the spirit, "Weltanschauung", of an epoch can be distilled from the various "objectifications" of that epoch – and how we can give a theoretical account of it'.[2] Mannheim acknowledges the several methodological difficulties inherent in this question. *Weltanschauung* is a totality located beyond each partial objectivation, yet culture is permanently in process of historical evolution. Additionally, as Dilthey had suggested, there are irrational aspects of *Weltanschauung* which are not easily reducd to a scientific analysis. Yet Mannheim insists that it is possible to transpose contents grasped in atheoretical experience into scientific terms.[3] One has to reject the methods of the natural sciences in order to analyse cultural products, but these are susceptible to a scientific analysis specific to the particular characteristics of the object.

The task of inserting a cultural objectivation in its *Weltanschauung* could be accomplished at three different levels of meaning. The objective meaning, the obvious identification of an action; the expressive meaning, the subjective intention of the subject, and the documentary meaning, the total meaning that comes out of the analysis of all the implications of an action. The latter is the most comprehensive and coincides with the total outlook or *Weltanschauung* of an epoch. This is why it has to be conceived of as eminently historical and changeable. As Mannheim puts it

unlike the two other types of interpretation, documentary interpretation has the peculiarity that it has to be performed anew in each period, and that any single interpretation is profoundly influenced by the location within the historical stream from which the interpreter attempts to reconstruct the spirit of a past epoch.[4]

As Mannheim elaborates his version of a sociology of knowledge, he moves away from this first approach and begins to lay a greater emphasis upon the social determination of cultural objects.[5] He still keeps many concepts drawn from the historicist tradition but now incorporated into a conception which privileges genetic sociological explanations. A feature of this new approach is the existential determination of thought which involves, first, that certain types of knowledge do not emerge out of immanent or purely logical laws but are decisively determined by extra-theoretical or existential factors and, second, that these existential factors are not only important to the genesis of knowledge but also to its content, scope and validity.[6] Following Marx, Mannheim contends that 'social relations and processes comprising the prevailing pattern of social life are determinants of the mental life corresponding to that particular social structure',[7] and that 'there are modes of thought which cannot be adequately understood as long as their social origins are obscured'.[8]

Like Hegel and Marx, Mannheim criticizes classical epistemology for considering the cognitive process as a theoretical contemplation. He puts forward the idea of practice as the basis of a new conception in certain spheres of knowledge: 'It is the impulse to act which first makes the objects of the world accessible to the acting subject . . .'.[9] He also rejects an individualistic or psychogenetic approach to meaning. The sociological point of view must seek the genesis of meaning in the context of group life. 'Knowledge is from the very beginning a co-operative process of group life, in which everyone unfolds his knowledge within the framework of a common fate, a common activity, and the overcoming of common difficulties'.[10]

Nevertheless two important features of historicist origin are kept and integrated into these premises by Mannheim. First of all, he restricts his approach to a particular kind of knowledge which he calls 'existentially-determined' and which is concerned with historical, political and, in general, cultural matters. This is a kind of thought whose results are 'partly determined by the nature of the thinking subject' and which are a 'function of a particular viewpoint or perspective'.[11] Mannheim insists that cultural objects cannot be treated by the methods of the natural sciences; in this sense the traditional historicist distinction between *Geisteswissenschaften* and *Naturwissenschaften* is upheld. What is more, Mannheim not only separates these two spheres by virtue of the different methodological approaches to them but also seems to exclude natural sciences from the direct determination of social factors. As he puts it, 'in mathematics and natural science, progress seems to be determined to a large extent by immanent factors, one question leading up to another with a purely logical necessity'.[12]

This contention about the immanent development of natural sciences seems excessive and arbitrary. There is little justification for depriving such an important sphere of consciousness of social determinations. There may be an undeniable difference between the social determination of historical sciences and the social determination of natural sciences, in so far as the effects upon scientific contents are concerned. Yet Mannheim absolutizes the distinction so as to divide human consciousness into two separate worlds. This dualism leads to epistemological idealism in the field of natural sciences and encourages relativism in the field of social science.

Secondly, the determination of social and cultural sciences by social factors is mediated by 'the total system of a world outlook' or *Weltanschauung*.[13] Mannheim seeks to avoid a direct association between classes and knowledge, between interests and consciousness, so as to surpass vulgar Marxism which directly links the spiritual products of mind with the economic interests of a class.[14]

We cannot relate an intellectual standpoint directly to a social class; what we can do is find out the correlation between the 'style of thought' underlying a given standpoint, and the 'intellectual motivation' of a certain social group.[15]

So the style of thought should be related to a system of attitudes, which in turn could be related to an economic system in a kind of 'circuitous route'. The extra-theoretical factors which affect 'existentially-determined' thought are not merely economic interests but rather a class or group outlook which infiltrates each individual manifestation.

From here Mannheim goes on to a different version of the interpretative levels of an intellectual phenomenon. Now he distinguishes the ideological from the sociological interpretation.[16] The ideological is an interpretation from within a particular thought which remains trapped in the immanence of that thought. The sociological is an interpretation from without which seeks to refer knowledge to the wider social context, whence come the clues with which to grasp its meaning. When one tries to interpret thought from within, its content appears as 'idea', when one tries an extrinsic approach its content appears as 'ideology', that is, it 'is taken as the function of an "existence" posited outside of it'. This functionalizing means 'the uncovering of all existentially conditioned relationships that alone make possible the emergence and the impact of an intellectual phenomenon'.[17]

Examples of extrinsic interpretations are provided by Mannheim in two essays in which the phenomena of 'competition' and 'generation' assume a decisive role in the shaping of mental structures.[18] Thus for instance, generations as sociologically significant phenomena tend to influence consciousness in a manner similar to the way a given class situation affects its members' thought. As Mannheim puts it,

the fact of belonging to the same class, and that of belonging to the same generation or age group, have this in common, that both endow the individuals sharing in them with a common location in the social and historical process, and thereby limit them to a specific range of potential experience, predisposing them to a certain characteristic mode of thought and experience....[19]

This general statement in the case of generations is in the case of competition historically concretized. In effect, Mannheim describes four historical periods within which competition among social groups in their struggle for power assumes different forms, thus determining different interpretations of the world. The mode of thought based on consensus or spontaneous co-operation between groups (traditional and folk wisdom, proverbs, myths, etc.) is found in its pure form in socially homogeneous strata or societies. The mode of thinking based on a monopoly position (theology and the medieval–ecclesiastical world-view, Chinese *literati*) exists in societies where a social group controls power to the exclusion of other groups. The atomistic competition between several theories, in its turn, derives from historical competition between the social groups liberated from ecclesiastical tutelage and in search for political power. The mode of thought, based upon concentration round one interpretation of various formerly competing groups, follows the atomistic period, thus determining fewer but more dominant world-views (for instance the unification of European conservative thought).[20]

There is a certain lack of precision in the picture that Mannheim draws of social groups responsible for styles of thought, particularly in the period of 'atomistic competition'. The competing groups mentioned are as varied as the church, the court nobility, the big bourgeoisie, the official church and lower ranks of the church, the absolute state, high finance, and so on. Obviously there may be confusion and overlap between institutions, classes and smaller groups, since no distinction of hierarchy is made among them and their conflicting theories. The struggle between realists and nomina-lists, the opposition between the church and the absolute state, and the conflict between the bourgeoisie and the nobility appear at the same level without any indication as to which one is more relevant and without considering the possibility that one of them could be the fundament of the others.

The functional meaning bestowed by sociological interpretation upon intellectual phenomena is also called 'relationism' by Mannheim. The procedure of the sociology of knowledge is said to be 'relational' because it seeks to relate thought to a certain mode of interpreting the world which in turn depends upon a certain social structure. How is this relationism, which bestows a functional meaning, related to the intrinsic meaning of intellectual phenomena? That is, are these two meanings connected at all?

Mannheim puts forward two alternative solutions. The first emphasizes the importance of functional meaning:

It insists that extrinsic interpretation, while relativizing 'immanent meaning' by functionalizing it, at the same time bestows a new sense on it, precisely by incorporating it into a higher context of meaning.[21]

Here, the intrinsic truth of an intellectual phenomenon is somehow affected by the functional interpretation.

The second solution emphasizes the importance of immanent meaning and neglects the 'existential element' of historical thought.

Historical thought is assimilated to purely theoretical thought and therefore has to be judged by immanent criteria. A strong separation between functional meaning and intrinsic meaning is propounded which makes both levels incommensurable. This solution has within it two further alternatives. One position maintains that the investigation of intellectual phenomena should be kept within the limits of intrinsic meaning. Functional knowledge is possible but irrelevant and meaningless. The other position considers 'only functional meaning as valid and rejects any discussion on an immanent basis as "merely ideological" – as Marx did'.[22]

Mannheim presents these three possibilities without explicitly committing himself to any, but it is quite plain that he favours the first solution. Hence he faces the questions of how functional meaning affects the truth of an intellectual phenomenon and whether or not this relationism leads to relativism. Mannheim recognizes that, in conceiving of thought as related to the author's social position, a process of 'self-relativization' of thought has occurred. But he insists that it is possible to distinguish self-relativization' from epistemological relativism:

One may very well assert that thought is 'relative to being', 'dependent on being', 'non-autonomous', 'part of a whole reaching beyond it', without professing any 'relativism' concerning the truth value of its findings. At this point it is, so to speak, still open whether the 'existential relativization' of thought is to be combined with epistemological relativism or not.[23]

Mannheim's answer to this open-ended question varies. In 'The problem of a sociology of knowledge' he stresses the independence of each aspect. Referring to the 'unmasking turn of mind' which characterized modern thought in its struggle against the theocratic tradition, Mannheim asserts that this turn of mind 'does not seek to refute, negate or call in doubt certain ideas, but rather to *disintegrate* them . . .'.[24] He traces a distinction between 'denying the truth of an idea and 'determining the function it exercises'. He can therefore affirm that

when I do not even raise the question (or at least when I do not make this question the burden of my argument) whether what the idea asserts is true, but consider it merely in terms of the extra-theoretical function it serves, then, and only then, do I achieve an 'unmasking' which in fact represents no theoretical refutation but the destruction of the practical effectiveness of these ideas.[25]

Likewise, in 'The ideological and sociological interpretation of intellectual phenomena' Mannheim refuses to be drawn into the epistemological question of whether or not truth is impaired by functional interpretation. In *Ideology and Utopia*, nevertheless, Mannheim goes further, maintaining that the social genesis of an idea does have a distinct bearing upon its validity: 'the analyses characteristic of the sociology of knowledge are, in this sense, by no means irrelevant for the determination of the truth of a statement'.[26] This is what he calls, 'particularization', the verification of the fact that sociological interpretation does not merely establish the relationship of the cultural object with the social world but simultaneously particularizes its scope, and the extent of its validity.[27] The alternative, which makes functional meaning incommensurable with immanent meaning, comes up with two equally deficient accounts of truth: either what can be established about the author's social position tells us nothing concerning the truth-value of his statements; or, conversely, the validity of knowledge is entirely denied by showing its structural relationship to a given social situation. Mannheim propounds a middle-of-the-road solution separate from both these extremes. Relationism neither denies validity upon the basis of mere functional meaning nor rejects extrinsic interpretations as meaningless for the problem of truth. By means of 'particularization', relationism 'restricts' the claim to truth, limits the absolute scope of validity.

Yet Mannheim holds that relationism does not necessarily lead to relativism, only 'that certain qualitative truths cannot even be grasped or formulated, except in the framework of an existential correlation between subject and object'.[28] We may speak, he says, of an infiltration of the social position of the researcher into the outcome of his study. This does not mean 'that there are no criteria of rightness and wrongness in a discussion', merely 'that it lies in the nature of certain assertions that they cannot be formulated absolutely, but only in terms of the perspective of a given situation'.[29] Mannheim accepts that truth is affected by particularization; at the same time he acknowledges that relationism does not fully reveal truth and is no substitute for a direct discussion between divergent points of view. Mannheim cannot conceal the pains he takes to separate himself from relativism. Yet he does not dispel the danger.

True, he opposes a relativism conceived of as a positivist theory of knowledge which maintains the absolute validity of the mathematical model of thought and rejects historical knowledge as 'relative' and 'unreliable'.[30] But the problem remains as to how the validity of social thought is affected by relationism. Ultimately

Mannheim seems sceptical of the possibility of reaching the truth. Every point of view appears limited and narrow and the emphasis is laid upon the search for an ever more inclusive and synthetic point of view, which is never definitively achieved by any single standpoint. Of course, according to Mannheim, the point is to determine which social standpoint offers the best chance for reaching an 'optimum of truth'.[31] But this does not solve the basic problem, as Mannheim realizes. Still, he prefers the dangers of relativism to the pitfalls of epistemological absolutism.

Various concepts of ideology; from ideology to the sociology of knowledge

An important stage in the process of 'self-relativization' of knowledge, as we saw, was the modern 'unmasking turn of mind', a way of deprecating ideas which, according to Mannheim, was vital in the struggle against the medieval monopolistic theocratic thought. This was the origin of the concept of ideology. Marx contributed a great deal to the concept's development but its meaning has evolved ever since. Mannheim sets himself the task of analysing the different conceptions which underlie the term. This enterprise is undertaken not only from an analytical point of view – which leads to a static scheme – but also from a historical perspective. According to the latter, Mannheim sees ideology developing from a particular conception to a total conception, and from the special formulation of the latter to its general formulation, that is, the sociology of knowledge.

The particular conception of ideology consists of a certain scepticism with which one judges the adversary's ideas. These are regarded as more or less conscious deceptions which disguise the pursuance of partial interests. This conception operates at a psychological level and designates a phenomenon which oscillates between a mere lie and a conceptual error, this lie or error being only a part of the opponent's consciousness. Bacon's pre-conceptions and Machiavelli's scepticism about the real interests behind public statements are quoted as forerunners of the modern concept of ideology.[32]

The total conception of ideology refers, on the contrary, to a phenomenon concerned 'with the characteristics and composition of the total structure of the mind', of an age or social group.[33] The total conception operates at a sociological level, in contrast with the psychological approach of the particular conception. It calls into question the opponent's total *Weltanschauung*; it challenges the whole outlook of a social group, not merely the partial ideas of individuals. That is why the total conception entails a radical criticism. Historically this was first accomplished by the critique of the rising bourgeoisie which disintegrated the feudal world-view. The philosophy of consciousness represented by Kant, the historical perspective contributed by Hegel, and Marx's substitution of the proletariat for the *Volksgeist* are mentioned as the principal stages in the arising of a total conception of ideology.[34]

However important, Marx's conception is considered to represent only a special formulation of the total conception of ideology. Special because, according to Mannheim, it is interested in analysing the opponent's ideas but not its own. Just as Napoleon had used the term ideology to discredit the ideas of his critics, the proletariat uses ideology as a weapon against the ruling class. But the notion of ideology, Mannheim contends,

cannot, in the long run remain the exclusive privilege of one class . . . it is no longer possible for one point of view and interpretation to assail all others as ideological without itself being placed in the position of having to meet that challenge.[35]

This is why a new stage arises after Marx, whereby the total conception ceases to be a 'special formulation' and becomes a 'general formulation' interested in the analysis of all points of view, including its own.

With this general formulation of the total conception, the transition from the theory of ideology to the sociology of knowledge is accomplished. Now, it is said, socialism has no longer the 'exclusive privilege' of tracing bourgeois ideas to ideological foundations. Classes and groups of the most diverse standpoints can now use this weapon to try and discredit the ideas of all the rest.[36] This signals an important change in the concept of ideology, which is now based upon the fact that all social knowledge is determined by the social structure. According to this new general total conception, the consciousness of all parties through history has been of an ideological character, since social determination affected all of them. Mannheim contends that when the theory of ideology becomes the sociology of knowledge, a qualitative change occurs: what was a party weapon becomes a scientific method of research. This new method has, as its main purpose, the task of finding the factors in the social situation which determine, and consequently relativize, the thought of each social group.

The general total conception of ideology could be approached by two alternative methods of inquiry called by Mannheim 'the non-evaluative general total conception' and 'the evaluative general total conception'. The non-evaluative is characterized by freedom from value-judgements: it merely seeks to relate the social structure to the intellectual point of view without advancing any further judgement as to the validity of the ideas to be analysed. The evaluative combines the non-evaluative approach with an epistemologically oriented approach, so the problem of truth acquires relevance. We have seen that Mannheim evolves from a position which maintains a strong separation between the depreciation of ideas and the assessment of their truth to a position which recognizes the inevitability of the former leading to the latter. In *Ideology and Utopia* Mannheim accepts that historically speaking a transition towards an evaluative approach is needed 'by the fact that history as history is unintelligible unless certain of its aspects are emphasized in contrast to others'; this entails selection and accentuation of certain factors and, thus, value-judgements.[37] One may wonder whether a true non-evaluative approach has ever been possible.

None the less, the evaluative approach does not accept absolute or supra-temporal values. Norms and values are socially and historically determined; therefore they permit the judgement of ideas only with reference to a given situation. The evaluative conception has to separate the genuine from the ideologically distorted in norms and modes of thought.

Mannheim describes three classes of ideological distortion. First, he considers an ethical attitude invalid 'if it is oriented with reference to norms, with which action in a given historical setting, even with the best of intentions cannot comply'.[38] The ideological character of a theory is proved when its categories prevent man from adapting himself to the historical period. The example Mannheim proposes is the norm that forbids lending with interest. This norm can work only in a traditional society; in a period of rising capitalism it becomes incapable of practical acceptance.

A second kind of ideological distortion has recourse to absolutes and ideals in order to cover up the real relations:

This is the case when we create 'myths', worship 'greatness in itself', avow allegiance to 'ideals', while in our actual conduct we are following other interests which we try to mask by simulating an unconscious righteousness. . . .[39]

A third kind of ideological distortion arises when a form of knowledge is no longer adequate for comprehending the actual world, as when a landowner who administers his estate in a capitalistic way insists on viewing his relations to the labourers in patriarchal categories.[40]

Mannheim ends his analysis of the general evaluative formulation of the total conception of ideology with this description of three different types of ideological distortions; yet the general total conception was said to be the theory of ideology as developing into the sociology of knowledge. So at the most sophisticated level of its development, the concept of ideology is nevertheless dissolved. Mannheim supersedes the theory of ideology by a more general sociology of knowledge. The theory of ideology is therefore restricted 'to unmask the more or less conscious deceptions and disguises of human interest groups, particularly those of political parties';[41] the sociology of knowledge would occupy itself with relating each line of thought to its social setting. The theory of ideology is concerned with lies or consciously created illusions, whereas the sociology of knowledge would analyse the necessary one-sidedness stemming from the social determination of knowledge. In contrast to the sociology of knowledge, therefore, the term ideology acquires a moral and denunciatory connotation. Mannheim proposes to avoid it as far as possible, replacing it by the less controversial term 'perspective' of a thinker.[42]

Mannheim applies the principles I have briefly described in various concrete analyses. The essays on competition and generations are good examples, and the essay on 'Conservative thought' is the most relevant. From it one can derive a methodology of research which can be outlined in a few stages. First of all, Mannheim proposes the determination of the style of thought. The description of any theory or thought should be referred to a general *Weltanschauung* or style of thought, a general system of thinking within which several theories could arise. This reference or 'imputation' consists of reconstructing a kind of ideal type of a world-view, identifying the main features of an integral and comprehensive outlook:

We want to look at the thinkers of a given period as representatives of different styles of thought. We want to describe their different ways of looking at things as if they were reflecting the changing outlook of their groups....[43]

There are two classes of imputation.[44] The first deals with general problems of interpretation. It looks for a 'basic intention' or 'perspective', a basic way of approaching the world, an inner core or drive which determines the character of the style of thought.[45] The second constitutes the style of thought as a hypothesis with which to examine various authors and their articulated theoretical statements. This, which can be considered the second stage in the methodology, is a more precise imputation which seeks 'to produce the concrete picture of the course and direction of development which has actually taken place'.[46] The history of the style of thought is here revealed in its actual manifestations and the main theoretical principles which arose in the struggle against other styles of thought are elucidated.

These first two stages take a given thought as a unit or final product in itself. A third stage is necessary which can be called genetic process or sociological imputation. By this Mannheim understands the tracing back of the currents of thought to the social forces, classes or groups which determine them, that is, the analysis of how a theory or intellectual trend reflects the interests, aspirations and characteristics of the social group which is behind it and through which it finds expression.[47] Two factors are taken into account: the composition of the classes or groups in which the theory originates and the direction of the historical development of the structural situation.[48]

Thus Mannheim is able to relate romantic and feudalistic conservatism to the German social structure after the French Revolution. Germany was at that time rather backward in its capitalist economic development. Accordingly, it lacked a strong bourgeoisie which could follow the example of the French Revolution. Instead of the bourgeoisie, the state bureaucracy took up the challenge and, supported by the absolute state, carried out the reforms required for capitalist expansion. The nobility opposed these transformations, so the struggle, which in France occurred between the monarchy and the people, was transposed in Germany into a struggle between the nobility and the monarchy. In France the nobility and the king were allies, in Germany they were disunited. As Mannheim puts it 'the situation found its ideological expression in a feudalistic reaction. The feudalistic conservatism of the nobility assumed a romantic colouring'[49] which opposed the modern world.

Ideology and utopia; the historical totality and the end of utopia

When analysing the kinds of ideological distortion above mentioned, Mannheim arrives at a further distinction of importance, the distinction between ideological thought and utopian thought. The term 'ideological' is reserved for a special sort of distortion which 'fails to take account of the new realities applying to a situation' and which 'attempts to conceal them by thinking of them in categories which are inappropriate'. According to Mannheim, this mentality has not yet 'grown up to the present'.[50] The utopian distortion, on the other hand, transcends the present and is orientated towards the future; it originates in a mentality which is 'beyond the present'.

However, not every state of mind which transcends the present is utopian: 'Only those orientations transcending reality will be referred to by us as utopian which, when they pass over into conduct, tend to shatter, either partially or wholly, the order of things prevailing at the time'.[51] So, an additional prerequisite for the utopian mentality is a tendency to destroy in practice the *status quo*. According to Mannheim, it is not always easy to distinguish ideologies from utopias: both are beyond present reality and, therefore, a value-judgement is required as to what reality is. One can safely expect the representatives of a given order to think of reality as the present structures, which support their interests; consequently, they label as utopian all transformatory points of views. Conversely, those who want a change think of reality as those facts of social life which point towards a new order that will represent their interests; they consequently label as ideological the conservative point of view. Mannheim therefore distinguishes absolute utopias from relative utopias. The former are those which 'in principle can never be realized', while the latter are those which seem to be unrealizable 'only from the point of view of a given social order which is already in existence'.[52]

Another difficulty is that often one may find a fusion of utopian and ideological features in the world-view of a class. Mannheim gives the example of the ascendant bourgeoisie whose idea of freedom was a real utopia which wanted to shatter the medieval order, an aim which, finally, became partially realized. Yet that very utopia can be seen now to contain ideological elements: the postulated freedom concealed a new sort of unfreedom.[53] Mannheim ultimately arrives at the conclusion that the distinction between ideology and utopia can only be fairly assessed by looking into the past and using the criterion of realization: 'ideas which later turned out to have been only distorted representations of a past or potential social order were ideological, while those which were adequately realized in the succeeding social order were relative utopias'.[54]

This solution by confining ideological analysis to the past, makes difficult the elucidation of ideologies and utopias in the present. At least Mannheim provides no criteria for this case. Take Mannheim's example of the interest on loans. The attitude of the church in its opposition to interest is thought ideological. Yet this was not clear when the conflict was actually happening, just as bourgeois freedom was not at that time a realizable utopia for everybody. Had Mannheim lived during the controversy between rising capitalism and declining feudalism he would not have been able to tell whether the church opposition to interest, and the bourgeois principle of freedom, were ideologies or utopias, making impossible the analysis of the present social reality.

According to Mannheim, both ideology and utopia distort reality in so far as their ideas do not fit into reality. Both kinds of thought are not adequate or 'situationally congruous': ideology because it conceals reality, utopia because it exceeds its limits; one mentality because it is antiquated with respect to the present, the other because it is in advance of it. The avoidance of these distortions constitutes for Mannheim a 'quest for reality': 'thought should contain neither less nor more than the reality in whose medium it operates'.[55] By introducing the adequacy of thought to reality as the criterion of its utopian or ideological character, Mannheim implicity elevates the given state of a society to the category of principle which decides between truth and distortion. The dangers of the conception are obvious, not least the petrification of society as a kind of second nature. The problem, as we said before, is that the various groups whose outlooks contradict one another experience the same reality in different ways. This fact, which causes the same object to appear differently, is nevertheless, in Mannheim's view, not a barrier to the knowledge of reality. On the contrary, this knowledge is enriched and becomes more comprehensive when it assimilates divergent perspectives.

Mannheim is not sceptical about the possibility of grasping reality as a totality. The limitations and partiality of every point of view do not impede comprehension of the whole. On the contrary, only by accepting these limitations does the whole become accessible.

Of course, the concept of totality acquires a new meaning in Mannheim's thought. It is no longer the 'immediate and eternally valid vision of reality attributable only to a divine eye', not a 'self-contained and stable view', but a view which entails both 'the assimilation and transcendence of the limitations of particular points of view'.[56] The dominant feature of the era which follows the period of 'atomistic competition' is the tendency towards the concentration of world-views around a few poles. Hence, a synthesis in the realm of ideas is achieved through the polarization of thoughts in broad doctrinal currents. This is the new sense which totality acquires nowadays.

Mannheim believes that syntheses 'owe their existence to the same social process that brings about polarization; groups take over the modes of thought and intellectual achievements of their adversaries under the simple law of "competition on the basis of achievement" '.[57] Contrary to beliefs that competition can only polarize and that intellectual divergences cannot be mediated, Mannheim affirms that syntheses do arise in the very process of polarization: 'in the socially differentiated thought process, even the opponent is ultimately forced to adopt those categories and forms of thought which are most appropriate for orientation in a given type of world order'.[58]

When analysing the prospects of scientific politics, Mannheim again asks if different styles of thought can be fused with one another and undergo synthesis. And once more he answers positively:

the course of historical development shows that such a synthesis is possible. Every concrete analysis of thinking which proceeds sociologically and seeks to reveal the historical succession of thought-styles indicates that styles of thought undergo uninterrupted fusion and interpenetration.[59]

Yet syntheses are never absolute. The process of fusion is permanently advancing and reformulating itself. No partial point of view can achieve a definitive and permanent synthesis. The understanding of the whole rests upon the acceptance of the limited scope of each point of view and, therefore, consists in the broadest possible extension of the horizon of vision by assimilating and transcending every standpoint, a continuous process which cannot be transformed into a supra-temporal vision.

Who are the bearers and agents of the process of synthesis? At this point Mannheim introduces the role of the 'unattached intelligentsia' or 'free-floating intellectuals', for which he is well known. Precisely because intellectuals can adapt themselves to any point of view and can choose their affiliation without being immediately bound by a class outlook, they may perform a unique role in achieving synthesis. Due to the partial character of each class outlook, a true synthesis is not likely to be achieved by any particular class, not even those classes which occupy a middle position. A relatively classless group which is not too firmly anchored in the social structure may, nevertheless, accomplish the task. As Mannheim puts it,

we owe the possibility of mutual interpenetration and understanding of existing currents of thought to the presence of such a relatively unattached middle stratum which is open to the constant influx of individuals from the most diverse social classes and groups with all possible points of view. Only under such conditions can the incessantly fresh and broadening synthesis, to which we have referred, arise.[60]

Mannheim warns his readers against misinterpreting his view. He does not claim that the class links of the individual disappear. But their importance is clearly weakened. At least, they play a role secondary to education, the new link which binds intellectuals. Mannheim contends that one of the characteristics of modern life unlike other periods, is that intellectual life is not the patrimony of an exclusive social class such as the priesthood but of an unattached social stratum recruited from an 'increasingly inclusive area of social life'.[61] This stratum cannot be understood by a 'class-oriented' sociology because, although situated between classes, it is not a middle class. It is affected by class interests, but these interests represent a variety of classes and in their interaction they subject the individual to all sorts of intellectual tendencies which are thus tied one with another.

It seems to me clear that Mannheim's general approach to the social determination of knowledge is incompatible with his theory of the free-floating intellectuals. The fact that all existentially determined thought is relativized to a social situation is inconsistent with the lack of attachment of its authors. Mannheim seems to accept the difficulty of self-detachment when he affirms:

nothing is more self-evident than that precisely the forms in which we ourselves think are those whose limited nature is most difficult for us to perceive, and that only further historical and social development gives us the perspective from which we realize their particularity.[62]

Yet he does not relate this particularity to a specific social background of the intellectuals. One wonders how this could possibly be without contradicting the very process of relationism.[63]

According to Mannheim, the only two kinds of utopian mentality which insist nowadays on an absolute perspective of totality are Marxism and the conservative–historical tradition. Yet he claims a contemporary trend which leads to a relative departure from the utopia. 'The total perspective tends to disappear in proportion to the disappearance of the utopia.'[64] An epoch has arrived in which the problem of totality is entirely disregarded. History is no longer a process leading to an ultimate, more rational end. On the contrary, history becomes more and more like undifferentiated space, where there is no room for a conception of a definite progress.

Socialist thought, which hitherto had unmasked all its adversaries' 'utopias' as ideologies, never raised the problem of determinateness about its own position. It never applied this method to itself and never checked its own desire to be absolute. It is nevertheless inevitable that here too the utopian element disappears with an increase in the feeling of determinateness. Thus we approach a situation in which the utopian element through its many divergent forms has completely (in politics, at least) annihilated itself.[65]

This annihilation is the outcome of a new relativist and sceptical outlook produced by a widespread awareness of the partiality of the various points of view. The partiality in its turn results from the increasing realization of the social determinateness of all ideas and perspectives. A detached, impersonal point of view is to Mannheim a false ideal; totality and objectivity are now understood in a different way, as a process always striving to enlarge the human perspective by assimilating new points of view. This trend, of course, contradicts the absolute perspectives of utopias and finally destroys them. It leads towards a 'realism', a 'matter-of-factness' which eliminates the 'reality-transcending' element from consciousness.[66] Although Mannheim sees the obvious risks which such a mentality brings upon mankind – such as the decay of the human will to shape history, the loss of ideals and the reification of man – he does not envisage any possible way of escape. At this point it is difficult to assess whether Mannheim is just asserting a fact he does not like or whether he is unconsciously arriving at the logical conclusion of his own theoretical premises.

The loss of ideology

Mannheim's treatment of the concept of ideology follows a con‑ tradictory pattern, oscillating between two versions which are never properly reconciled. In the first version he seems to universalize the concept to the point that it becomes the same as the social determination of historical knowledge. In this sense he affirms that the thought of all parties throughout history has been of an ideological character and that no particular point of view can claim an especial vantage point from which to judge the others without being itself subjected to the same judgement. In this context ideology is used not as a negative value-judgement, but designates a *Weltanschauung* associated with a given social situation.[67] In the second version, he seems to restrict the concept of ideology to the conscious deception of groups of interests so that the more general fact of the social determination of knowledge appears as the preoccupation of the sociology of knowledge and no longer of the theory of ideology. True, it can be argued that Mannheim is only trying to depict the historical evolution of the concept of ideology which, by becoming general and total, loses its exclusive character and may be used by all sectors and classes as a critical tool. This universalization apparently leads to the sociology of knowledge and to the replacement of the concept of ideology by a more scientific concept like the 'perspective' of a thinker.

None the less, in both versions the concept of ideology is fraught with problems. In the first version every point of view has an ideological character. It is therefore very difficult to envisage what is really specific to the concept of ideology. When the concept is universalized in such a way that it may cover all parties in all epochs, it ends up with very little meaning and loses its critical capability. In the second version ideology is confined to the conscious lies and illusions of political parties and groups. It is not that ideology could not exist as a conscious deception; we know that it takes this form on many occasions. The problem arises when one reduces the ideological phenomenon to this one case, leaving aside the vaster field of distorted knowledge produced as a result of social contradictions but not as conscious lie. Ideology is psychologized. It assumes a moral connotation which unduly links it more with political decisions than with objective contradictions. Hence ideology risks losing its anchorage in social reality to become a kind of free decision attributable to the will of social groups.

Mannheim's continual use of the term ideology with both these meanings introduces a great deal of confusion. All his criticism of Marxism seems to be based upon the first universal conception. While recognizing that the fact that all social knowledge is determined by a particular social position is not necessarily a source of error, he nevertheless criticizes Marxism for not bringing its own theory into the category of ideology and gaining consciousness of its own partiality. According to Mannheim, Marx did not reach the general total conception of ideology because he perceived the relations between human thought and social reality only in the case of the opponent. He adds that, this was probably due

to a subconscious reluctance to think out the implications of a concretely formulated insight to a point where the theoretical formulations latent in it would be clear enough to have a disquieting effect on one's own position. Thus we see how the narrowed focus which a given position imposes and the driving impulses which govern its insights tend to obstruct the general and theoretical formulation of these views and to restrict the capacity for abstraction.[68]

This criticism is evidently based upon a slippage of the concept of ideology. Marx did not perceive the social determination of knowledge only in the case of his opponents. He accepted the social determination of his own thought. The fact is that he did not understand ideology as the universal determination of knowledge, so that in spite of recognizing his own 'determinateness' and connections with the working-class movement, he had no reason at all to call his own theory an ideology.[69] For Marx ideology was a distorted knowledge which concealed contradictions in the interest of the dominant class. Hence he could not possibly conceive of his own theory as an ideology. Ideology was not an abstract problem of error against truth, but neither was it the general assertion of the social determination of knowledge.

This is precisely the source of Mannheim's shortcomings: the problem of the separation between immanent meaning and functional meaning. As we saw, for Mannheim an intellectual phenomenon appears as an idea in so far as it is considered 'from within'; it assumes the character of ideology when considered 'from without'. This contrast between idea and ideology leads to an epistemological dualism which separates the ideological from the intrinsic meaning of thought. All happens as if knowledge could be ideological in spite of, and for reasons different from, its immanent value. Hence the ideological phenomenon is confined to the functional meaning. We have seen that Mannheim hesitates as to how this functional meaning affects the truth of knowledge. It seems unable to refute or cancel its validity. In this sense Mannheim refers to a 'depreciation' or 'destruction' of ideas without necessarily passing judgement upon their validity. Yet he finally agrees that relationism is followed by 'particularization'; that is, the functional meaning somehow restricts the claim to validity of social thought.[70]

Curiously enough, Mannheim criticizes Marx because he believes Marx considers only functional meaning as valid and rejects any consideration of an immanent meaning. We can see now that the reverse is true: Mannheim makes the mistake of which he accuses Marx. For Marx never conceives of the existence of two separate spheres, one of which (the functional) is capable of altering the other (the immanent). Marx considers a single process of production of knowledge which carries inherently both its social determination and the question of truth, that is, of whether or not it is adequate to reality. Truth does not differ from the class practice within which knowledge is brought about, but neither is it made entirely dependent upon that practice. The social background is not considered to be 'extrinsic' with respect to an 'intrinsic' value, but it does not depreciate automatically each standpoint either. Hence Marx criticizes the inversions of social theories and simultaneously maintains the validity of his own, whereas Mannheim leaves rather untouched the core of theories to stress everywhere their partiality.[71] Sociology of knowledge is consequently unable to criticize the content of any thought and confines itself to insisting upon the social setting of each one.

In this sense, Adorno points out, the sociology of knowledge has failed. It has failed before philosophy:

for the truth content of philosophy it substitutes its social function and its conditioning by interests, while refraining from a critique of that content itself, remaining indifferent toward it. It fails equally before the concept of ideology, which it will stir into its broad beggarly broth; for the concept of ideology makes sense only in relation to the truth or untruth of what it refers to.[72]

One can perfectly agree that ideology does not exhaust itself in the problem of error and truth as put forward in its most abstract formulation. Ideology, as I have already argued, is not simply an error. Yet to pretend that the problem of truth is not necessarily involved in or could be separated from the concept of ideology (as Mannheim continually suggests) is another extreme which distorts the concept of ideology.

Ultimately, Mannheim does not avoid epistemological relativism. The distinctions he often repeats, between the evaluative approach and the non-evaluative approach, between relationism and particularization, do not solve the problem. When the non-evaluative approach is put forward, the relativization of truth is implicitly present, for all the differences Mannheim notes between impairing the truth of an idea and destroying it in practice. In the end it is very difficult to conceive of the critical liquidation of ideas without affecting their truth. On the other hand, when the evaluative approach is presented, relationism appears the fundament of the relativization of truth. Nowhere is the possibility considered that the necessary determination of knowledge does not necessarily lead to a distortion, or to a diminished claim to validity. There is no need for a return to an epistemological absolutism; Marx rejected it and yet did not fall into relativism. For Marx maintained the possibility of an objective truth, even though he conceived of it as a historical reality. Mannheim on the contrary, ends up denying the very possibility of a full truth in any 'existentially-determined' thought. As Schaff has pointed out, Mannheim implicitly postulates the ideal of the absolute truth although he explicitly rejects it in practice.[73] One can accept that the relationship between social thought and social structure precludes the existence of eternal truths, yet when Mannheim characterizes every point of view as ideological he implicitly does so just because none of them can reach the absolute truth. The rejection of absolute truth is mistakenly transposed into the denial of all objective truth.

Mannheim supersedes Marx's conception of an objective historical truth by the conjunction of partial truths, none of which can claim any primacy. If any truth exists at all, it can be found in the synthesis of different viewpoints and perspectives which the unattached intelligentsia may achieve. This reconciliation of competing positions does not, however, solve the problem of relativism: such a synthesis is always conceived of as provisional and relative to a position, and nobody can possibly claim the superiority of his own synthesis. Mannheim does not realize that he himself puts forward his theory with an implicit pretension to objective truth, the same as anybody else does. The universal fact of the social determination of knowledge is not sufficient reason for diminishing the claim to validity. Yet even if this was the case, not all kinds of partiality should be considered ideological.[74] The inflation which the concept of ideology suffers in Mannheim's theory can only contribute to the dissolution of the concept itself.

Mannheim's insistence upon the universal social determination of knowledge is confined to the general verification of this fact and rather less interested in the historical forms which that determination takes. Hence, ultimately, ideology becomes a feature rooted in the very structure of human thought in so far as it tackles social subjects.[75] In Marx ideology has a historical character, as it is directly related to the evolution of social contradictions and economic forms. In Mannheim, on the contrary, specific economic forms play no role in determining ideology. To this extent ideology is again psychologized, that is, founded upon the very nature of human thought. Social determination becomes a formal *a priori* condition of thought. Although social reality is not conceived as a hypostatized subject '*à la* Durkheim', it nevertheless becomes a kind of second nature which is always present and given for each point of view. Social determination loses its historical character and becomes a given datum. Hence, with Mannheim the concept of ideology maintains the subjective status which it had before Marx and which it regained with the psychological and Durkheimian conceptions.

Goldmann's genetic structuralism

Goldmann's fundamental hypothesis conceives of all human behaviour as a 'significative structure' to be described and explained by the researcher.[76] According to Goldmann the terms of the methodological problem which faces the human sciences can be expressed as the confrontation between 'comprehension' and 'explanation'. This is an old dispute between explanation by means of laws and causes, which the development of the natural sciences precipitated, and the comprehensive description which non-genetic structuralism propounds. While the former tries to introduce into the human sciences the understanding of social phenomena by means of causes or universal correlations, the latter aims to describe basic, universal and permanent structures.

Goldmann believes that the opposition between comprehensive description and causal explanation can be surpassed by a new perspective, 'genetic structuralism', which considers these aspects as the two sides of the same process seen from two different considerations of the object.[77] Every partial structure is 'explained' by its subsumption under a vaster structure, while at the same time the partial structure is understood in itself by its comprehensive description. If on the one hand all human actions and products are structured, on the other hand these structures are not autonomous and active entities which hold man prisoner. No social phenomenon can be interpreted outside the structures that govern it, but at the same time one must be aware that those structures are themselves 'the result of man's earlier praxis'.[78] Consequently it is necessary to explain the genesis of the structures in so far as they are products, historically created and historically bound to change. If structures were permanent there would be no point in looking for their genesis, but in fact there only exist historical structures resulting from the activity of groups and classes. Structures are therefore always in a process of change, a 'destructuration' of pre-existing structures and a 'structuration' of new structures.

Genetic structuralism is thus based upon the assertion that the significance of social phenomena is given by their being structured and upon the fact that these significative structures are 'the result of a genesis and cannot be understood or explained independently of this genesis'.[79] The genesis of structures must be sought in the wider structure which subsumes it. Every human fact is a process of structuration which tends towards a provisional equilibrium. The equilibrium becomes contradictory and, for that reason, is at the same time a process of destructuration. This dynamism is not merely internal to the structure in question but is closely related to the dynamism of a wider structure which also tends to a provisional equilibrium. The reference to the structure in itself is description or comprehension; the reference to the wider structure which subsumes it is explanation. Thus, Goldmann's examples describe a chain of successively wider structures. For instance, the study of Pascal's *Thoughts* as an internal significative structure is considered a comprehensive description; the insertion of *Thoughts* as a partial structure in the wider structure which is Jansenism, is considered a comprehensive description of Jansenism and an explanatory analysis of Pascal's *Thoughts*. The insertion in turn of Jansenism in the structure of the '*noblesse de robe*' explains Jansenism and comprehends the history of that class. And so forth.[80]

Goldmann finds the origin of this approach in Hegel, Marx and Freud, none of whom actually use the expression 'genetic structuralism'. Hegel and Marx in his view have a common method of tackling historical facts in a reflective way which separates itself from the methodological orientations of natural sciences. Freud analyses deviant psychological phenomena by inserting them in a wider structure and explaining their genesis in early childhood. In general, the three of them would have supported the idea that a partial structure or social phenomenon is in itself significative and could be explained by making reference to a series of wider structures. Yet the 'comprehensive' side of their approaches was overlooked by 'official science'. This aspect was first emphasized by Dilthey quite independently of these authors; only later did Lukács and Piaget give it a positive and rigorous shape within a dialectical conception.[81]

According to this approach, a literary or philosophical work cannot be understood by pure philosophical means, nor by mere empathy. One cannot rely upon the writing itself or upon the author's intentions. The exclusive reference of the meaning of a text to the author's biography encounters very serious difficulties such as the lack of scientific certainty about the psychological imputations and, in general, the arbitrariness of the procedure. Yet this should not bring us back to mere analysis of the text. According to Goldmann there are two main problems here. First is the problem of how to delimit an author's production, how to distinguish the essential texts from those less relevant. Second is the problem that the meaning of a text is far from univocal and varies according to the context.[82] If neither the individual nor the text by themselves represent adequate structures in which to insert the meaning of a work – that is, if they are not appropriate totalities for a scientific study – another structure is needed which could be wide enough and objectively controllable to perform the task. This Goldmann finds in a reference to social classes and their world-views.[83]

In analysing a text, therefore, one has to take into account not only the whole text, that is, its immanent comprehension, but also the explanation of 'the genesis of the structure which enables us to interpret the whole of the text under consideration in a coherent manner'.[84] This structure is the class *Weltanschauung*. According to Goldmann it can be defined as 'the conjunction of aspirations, feelings and ideas which bring together the members of the group (or more frequently of a social class) and oppose them to other groups'.[85] Every philosophical or literary work is an expression of a world-view. This concept enables the researcher to understand why authors as different as Kant, Pascal and Racine have, nevertheless, a similar basic structure of thought which Goldmann labels 'the tragic vision'.[86] The world-view of a class is, ultimately, its class consciousness, which finds various expressions through the works of certain individuals. In so far as these individuals are exceptionally gifted as writers or philosophers they convey with maximum coherence the world-view of the class; that is, they express the 'maximum of possible consciousness' of the class.[87]

Following Lukács, Goldmann distinguishes the real consciousness from the possible consciousness of the class. The real is the consciousness which can be factually found in the class at any given moment on various issues. Its structure and contents vary according to several factors, some accidental, others linked with the very nature of the class. The possible is the consciousness which the class might attain without changing its nature. According to Goldmann the possible consciousness is the fundament of the real consciousness.[88]

Literary and philosophical works therefore are expressions of the maximum of possible consciousness of the class. To this extent they are more the product of the class world-view than individual accomplishments. Literary works can be considered as imaginary transpositions of the class *Weltanschauung;* philosophical works become the conceptual translation of the same. Goldmann insists upon the existence of a trans-individual subject at the basis of the products of consciousness. Between this collective consciousness and the individual consciousness there is no contradiction. If it is true that the collective world-view can exist only in the individual consciousness, on the other hand it is very rarely fully expressed by any single individual. The collective consciousness is not the mere addition of individual consciousnesses, nor is it an entity hanging over individuals or opposing them. In a literary or philosophical work the exceptional individual is identified with the fundamental trends of social life so that he may express with coherence what others hold vaguely or confusedly.

For instance, a comprehensive description of Pascal's *Thoughts* shows his belief in the existence of an abyss between man and God which can only be bridged by a wager. There is an uncertainty about God's existence, prompted by His hidden presence, which makes Him rather inaccessible. Hence, the emphasis is upon the distance, loneliness and uncertainty in the relationships with Him. Racine's tragedies show man refusing the world. His heroes have in common a conflict vision of the world; they live by values which are actually non-realizable, and there is a feeling of paradox and of inauthenticity. God appears in the form of idols, yet is also far away and mute, leaving man alone. Kant's philosophy in its turn resorts to 'practical reasons' to justify the existence of an absent God. God cannot be proved or disproved by scientific reasons. Speculative reason is unable to penetrate the *a priori* of practical reason but neither does it contradict practical reason. What all these authors have in common, according to Goldmann is the tragic world-view.

In the case of Pascal and Racine this world-view is developed by Jansenism and corresponds to the specific mental structures of a determined layer of the small nobility, '*la noblesse de robe*', which is 'torn between its bourgeois origins and ties on the one side, and, on the other, its current alliance with the monarchy, which was just beginning to disassociate itself from the third Estate'.[89] Goldmann establishes a privileged affinity between this threatened class in its new dispossession and the tragic vision of Jansenism. This ideology was produced within a class which was placed in a defensive position and had to respond to aggression by placing itself in a distant seclusion: just as God is recognized but inaccessible, the political power of monarchy is considered to be necessary but far away. While absolutism cannot be contested, simultaneously its extension means the loss of prerogatives and liberties for the class.[90]

Kant's tragic vision is justified by the situation of the eighteenth-century German bourgeoisie 'which aspired to a revolution that it was unable to bring about'.[91] In both cases, the social contradiction of a class, which is being dispossessed and cannot fight the agent of its frustration or is prevented from accomplishing its revolution, is transposed into a tragic vision. The logic of the world-view is somehow similar to the logic of myth in Lévi-Strauss; it refers the terms of a real contradiction to a new conceptual or imaginary opposition which makes the situation more bearable. In the case of Jansenism, the real contradiction between the '*noblesse de robe*' and the absolute monarchy is transposed into the paradox of a hidden God, somehow present but mute. Yet Goldmann's understanding of the nature of contradictions differs from Lévi-Strauss's in that he privileges class struggles and not logic paradoxes of the human species. Besides, for Goldmann the basic explanatory structures are essentially historical and not universal.

The relationship between world-view and ideology is a point on which Goldmann is less clear. On the one hand it appears as if one could identify both terms. When dealing with the problem of truth, Goldmann uses both terms interchangeably. He poses himself the question: 'are all ideologies of equal value, at least, as far as the search for truth is concerned; and is the choice of one over another only a matter of individual preference?'[92] Goldmann's answer seeks to disassociate itself from Mannheim's relativism. Ideologies exist on different planes; some permit a better understanding of reality than others and consequently constitute an important step towards an adequate knowledge of the truth. Contrary to Mannheim's tenet that all socially determined knowledge is of an ideological character and has, therefore, a restricted claim to validity, Goldmann maintains that ideologies have different scientific values. The criteria which allow one to judge start by querying 'which of them permits the understanding of the other as a social and human phenomenon, reveals its infrastructure, and clarifies, by means of an immanent critical principle, its inconsistencies and its limitations'.[93]

Hence, Goldmann concludes that it is possible to choose, 'from among the different world-views, the one which provides the widest possible form and range of comprehension'.[94] In this way he can justify preferring Marx to Saint-Simon: by choosing Marx he understands the basis and limitations of Saint-Simon, not vice versa. Likewise, Goldmann compares Marxism with what he calls 'objective' contemporary sociology and finds that the former understands the latter as useful in concrete investigations but unable to comprehend social life as soon as class struggle makes its appearance. By contrast he contends that 'objective' sociologists are less able to understand Marxism seriously: they are content to create an imaginary and 'easy-to-combat' opponent by distorting Marx's premises. So there are objective bases upon which to judge the validity of world-views and ideologies.

Yet Goldmann also introduces a distinction between ideologies and world-views. Ideologies are partial and distorted, whereas world-views are total. Ideologies are related to social classes in decline which defend their acquired positions and interests, whereas world-views are related to social classes which possess an ideal bearing on the whole of the society.[95] Although this distinction is put forward as a mere hypothesis, it contradicts earlier statements and is rather confusing. For there is consistency in equating ideology with world-view, despite the fact that this equation is far from Marx's conception. At least the negative character of ideology is dropped altogether. We have already seen how this conception has become more and more widespread since Lenin gave it its original form. Yet a distinction between world-view and ideology in the way in which Goldmann suggests appears a partial and unsuccessful attempt to restore the negative sense to ideology.

In effect, ideology continues to be a world-view but a distorted one, the world-view of a declining class. So, its distorted character derives from the fact that the class is doomed and not from its being ideology. Yet there is a further problem. If ideology is the world-view of a declining class, does this mean that the world-view of other classes cannot be ideological? True, Goldmann, recognizes that his criterion is limited and that, for instance, 'certain aspects of reality, visible from a reactionary point of view, which is almost always more limited, and narrow are not visible from the standpoint of the ascending class'.[96] But this is not enough to overcome the confusions which stem from this distinction. The problem remains as to whether it is possible to reduce ideology to a world-view at all, let alone a distorted world-view. In the first case ideology loses its critical character; in the second case the entire world-view of non-declining classes appears beyond ideology. Both solutions seem unsatisfactory.

Goldmann's solution to the problem of choosing between ideologies or world-views proposes their reciprocal confrontation in order to see which understands the other better. This does not seem to me a satisfactory solution either. Despite the fact that Goldmann closely associates cultural phenomena with social classes, he seems to resort to mere intellectual confrontation when the problem of truth is concerned. This certainly appears to be inconsistent with Marx's position and Goldmann's own assumptions. There is no reference to practice in this context, as if the understanding of reality were disconnected from the production of that very reality. It may be true that the reference to practice is implicit in every attempt at revealing the infrastructure of another theory, yet in order to avoid confusions with an idealist epistemology, Goldmann ought to emphasize the practical character of the problem of truth. Of course, this is not to say that practice is a self-evident criterion. Practice is also apprehended theoretically; yet this does not preclude the fact that theoretical confrontation by itself cannot produce a criterion of truth.[97]

Perhaps the most problematic aspect of Goldmann's genetic structuralism is its identification of class consciousness with the production of literary and philosophical works. True, his insistence upon the social determination of cultural phenomena belongs to the most genuine Marxist tradition. Yet his tendency to collapse cultural products into the collective consciousness of the class, without much regard for the mediation of the individual and of other cultural products, seems highly debatable. Marx recognized indeed the influence of class practice upon theories and even conceived of his own theory as an expression of the class struggle emerging in Europe. But he never thought that theories could be the automatic result of the practice of a class. Of course, Goldmann does not maintain such a position in so many words. Yet there is an unmistaken tendency in that direction.[98] Goldmann is interested in analysing texts only in so far as they express the world-view of the class. This is why not every text is in itself a significative structure.[99] Only certain privileged works which are original and coherent express the world-view. To this extent one may well ask how this can be judged. Is not Goldmann introducing arbitrary criteria which discriminate between 'authentic' and 'inauthentic' literature?

Even if this was a legitimate methodological option, it is not useful for the analysis of ideology unless one wants to restrict the scope of the concept to the world-view expressed in a few original works. But what about those products of consciousness which are not novels or philosophical texts? What about political documents, newspapers, scientific texts, etc.? Are they to be excluded from ideological analysis? Are they not also expressions of class consciousness, although not as coherent or original as a work of art? From the point of view of ideological analysis this restriction seems rather arbitrary and unnecessary. Yet more problematic than this is Goldmann's identification of ideology with class consciousness. It differs from Marx in many respects. In Marx ideology is a critical concept, showing the existence of distorted forms of consciousness which conceal contradictions in the interest of the ruling class. Class consciousness, on the contrary, is the collective consciousness of the class based upon its actual practice. There could be ideological elements in a determined class consciousness, but this is not the result of both concepts being identified nor is it a necessary phenomenon. On the contrary, if a proletarian class consciousness is to enlighten a revolutionary practice, it has to be free from ideological distortions. Goldmann's identification of world-views with class consciousness and ideologies loses the specific content of each concept and introduces a confusion between them which can only impoverish their analytical power. None the less, Goldmann's works provide stimulating insights which make a valuable contribution to the comparative study of cultural production and to the analysis of its social determination by the class struggles of the historical period in which it emerges.

5 Ideology and structural analysis

Introduction

A feature of contemporary intellectual development is the increasing importance given to the study of language as a crucial phenomenon for the understanding of consciousness and social life. Marx had already recognized, although in a very sketchy manner, the role of language in the material emergence of consciousness. According to him, consciousness originated in men's social relations, in men's need for intercourse with other men. But consciousness had to express itself in concrete forms in order to be accessible to other people. Hence, consciousness was never 'pure'. As Marx put it, 'from the start the "spirit" is afflicted with the curse of being "burdened" with matter, which here makes its appearance in the form of agitated layers of air, sounds, in short, of language'.[1] Language was therefore, practical consciousness. However, Marx did not go beyond these few remarks. In the twentieth century a new connection arises: if language is a system of signs, then not only sounds or written texts, but also all meaningful social practices and cultural phenomena may constitute particular kinds of languages.

Ideology therefore appears a crucial phenomenon to be studied in connection with language; not that ideology is necessarily a special language or that one can locate ideology in a particular kind of discourse. Ideology is rather a level of meaning which can be present in all kinds of discourses.[2] The traditional approach to ideology took language for granted and concentrated upon the basic features of ideology as found in the content of the discourse. Now attention turns to language itself, not only in the sense that ideology is found in the use of language, that is, in the selection and combination of signs, but also in the sense that the material practices which are at the basis of ideology are construed as languages, as systems of signification. Hence, several attempts have been developed to study ideology which in one way or another take into account the linguistic significance of social practices and discourses.

The common root of these analyses is the attempt to develop linguistics as a science, a task in which both Saussure's *Cours de linguistique générale* and the Prague Circle's phonological orientation are generally acknowledged as the first two landmarks. They develop a conception which supersedes genetic explanations by insisting upon the concepts of system and structure. Saussure introduces a crucial distinction between language (*langue*) and speech (*parole*) which allows him to define language as a formal system of oppositions which underlies speech. Language is a 'system which knows only its own order', a 'system where all parts can and must be considered in their synchronic solidarity'.[3] The Prague Circle propounds the concept of 'phonological system', which provides the clue to understanding the role of specific phonemes which are supposed to be structured in language. The purpose of linguistics is to study the underlying structure of phonemes, since these are no longer considered as independent entities but, on the contrary, are supposed to form part of a system which has general laws.

Hence, language constitutes a system of unmotivated or arbitrary signs which are related to one another, whereas speech is essentially an individual act of selection and actualization.[4] According to Saussure, language is constituted as an autonomous object which has a stability independent of the actual use that individuals may make of it. Furthermore, language is the condition of intelligibility of speech, a sort of logical order lying behind it which gives a basic consistency to the more contingent and changing speech.

As the language system is the foundation of actual speech, a logical corollary follows which emphasizes the importance of synchrony with respect to diachrony. A system of stable relations is bound to underline the synchronic aspects of its structure, whereas contingent speech, consisting of a succession of particular arrangements, is bound to stress the diachronic aspects. Therefore, linguistics was born as a science of synchrony, in so far as it was basically concerned with the underlying structure of language. Diachrony is confined as a sort of derivative phenomenon, dependent upon synchrony. As Ricoeur puts it, 'diachrony is intelligible only by comparison between states of former and later systems'.[5] Diachrony is conceived as an alteration of synchrony.

The consequences of these structuralist assumptions are momentous, above all when social practices or cultural phenomena are being analysed as systems of meaning or languages. History is considered a disorder of basic structures and can only be understood by reference to these structures. More than historical laws of these phenomena, then, one has to recognize structural laws; co-existential laws, as Schaff calls them, because they are concerned with the co-existence, with the systemic arrangement of things rather than with their causes.[6] This is a consequence of the fact that linguistic laws are of a morphological character: they are not the laws of speech as a human practice, but the laws of an unmotivated, arbitrary and unconscious level which consists of conventional categories which cannot be altered by any particular individual and whose finite order is not self-conscious. From here a duality emerges between unconscious system and human practice, between structure and human will, which explains the second by the first.

Starting from this structural analysis of language, different lines of development have emerged which have a bearing upon the concept of ideology. First is a semiological line, represented by the early works of R. Barthes and Greimas's structural semantic, which emphasize a synchronic analysis of language. Although the approach of these authors is different, they share the preoccupation for founding the analysis of textual meaning upon scientific and synchronic bases. Secondly, an anthropological line, represented by Lévi-Strauss and Godelier, transposes linguistic analysis into the analysis of myth and religion. Thirdly, a semiological line represented by the French journal *Tel Quel* tries to separate itself from synchronic linguistics and seeks to understand the text as a production of meaning rather than as a product with a closed significance. These three lines of development for all their differences, each draw extensively on structural linguistics. To them one can add another line, whose relation to linguistics is far less clear, but whose concern with certain aspects of structuralism and their application to Marxism is generally acknowledged. This is a line represented by Althusser, the early Poulantzas and, in Britain by J. Mepham. Their theory of ideology attempts to rid the Marxist concept of ideology of historicist and humanist interpretations in order to re-construct it upon new bases which somehow draw from structuralist assumptions.

Semiology 1: Barthes and Greimas

It is not difficult to see how the basic principles of structural linguistics could be applied to the analysis of ideology. The distinction between language and speech provides two spheres which can be transposed to express two levels of any discourse or system of signs, the manifest content and the latent content. The manifest content is analogous to speech, while the latent content represents the underlying structure of the discourse. The assumption can be made that this latent structure is equivalent to ideology; that is, ideology constitutes a sort of hidden structure in every discourse which is conveyed and received wrapped up in an external and opaque form. Hence, this ideological structure cannot be consciously noticed by the addressees.

From the point of view of linguistics therefore, ideology is a sort of second-order semiological system. Barthes has characterized this hidden second level as the level of 'connotation' (secondary language) in opposition to the level of 'denotation' (primary, ordinary language).[7] Something similar is maintained by Greimas under the terminology of 'practical level' (denotation) and 'mythical level' (connotation).[8] The denotative level expresses the primary meaning of a discourse and conceals second meanings that should be deciphered. The ideological analysis of a message, therefore, seeks to grasp the system of second meanings; it tries to decodify the denotative reading, to reveal a connotative world, a mythical level. According to this conception, if one can reach the logical model, if one can identify the structures which give coherence to the message, if it is possible to discover the principle which presides over the organization of discourse and which unifies its elements, the analysis of ideology has largely been completed.

Barthes's early semiological approach puts forward these principles in an interesting manner. Language as a system of significations comprises a plane of expression and a plane of content. These planes are also called the 'signifier' and the 'signified'. The relationship between both terms is the signification of language, that is, 'Expression related to Content (ERC) = Signification.' Now, if this system ERC becomes in turn the new expression of a second system which is more extensive than the first and which supposes a new content, one then deals with two systems of significations which are imbricated and which constitute language and ideology (myth). Graphically,[9]

| 1 | E R C | | plane of denotation — language |
| 2 | | E R C | plane of connotation — myth (ideology) |

Language becomes the vehicle, the signifier of a second structure of meaning. According to Barthes, myth is a double system, in which the signifier is already a structure of signification in itself. Myth is somehow hidden and difficult to decipher because its signification is constituted by a sort of constantly moving turn-stile which presents the expression alternately as a meaning in itself and as a form or signifier of other content.

This double capability of the ideological expression, the ubiquity of the signifier, exactly reproduces the physique of the alibi:

a sort of perpetual alibi because it is enough that the signifier has two sides for it always to have an 'elsewhere' at its disposal. The meaning is always there to present, the form; the form is always there to outdistance the meaning.[10]

Denotative language presents a permanent ambivalence between its natural meaning and the hidden latent meaning which constitutes a sort of rhetorical level. This rhetorical meaning, according to Barthes, is 'received but not read' and is characterized by its imprecision and nebulousness. The problem is to decipher, to interrupt the turn-stile of form and meaning, to get at the logical model which, lying behind, is nevertheless unclear and confused.

The answer to this problem is not clear from a theoretical point of view. In *Mythologies*, Barthes carries out several stimulating analyses in which these second-order structures appear in the turn-stile with the primary structures. The description of the holiday of a writer analyses the contrast between a brilliant spiritual vocation and everyday necessities of life. By simply describing the latter (denotation), the picture seeks to exalt the former (connotation). This is a trick of every interview which seeks to show the 'human aspects' of heroes. Likewise, in the 'Blue blood cruise', the emphasis on mundane actions by a king connotes his different origin. As Barthes puts it, 'to flaunt the fact that kings are capable of prosaic actions is to recognize that this status is no more natural to them than angelism to common mortals, it is to acknowledge that the king is still king by divine right'.[11]

The *Système de la mode* is another interesting attempt which applies the structuralist method to the exhaustive analysis of the fashion system.[12] Barthes distinguishes a denotative level or 'vestimentary code' and a connotative or rhetorical level which tries to depict the 'second-order' structures which govern the system. A most important feature of this rhetorical level is that it tries to naturalize the arbitrary character of the vestimentary signs, disguising the tyrannical decisions about fashions as if they were facts in a natural process. The more arbitrary fashion is, the more its functions appear as imperatives of an empirical world which could be verified. A series of false necessities and functions are created which appear as natural requirements which the system satisfies.

Yet these stimulating practical analyses do not provide a theoretically worked out clue as to how one can detect the double capacity of the signifier. The very analogy with structural linguistics demands, supposedly, a superior methodological precision. The discourse itself, beyond its content, should provide some clues for determining the mythical level. In this, Barthes does not seem very successful, despite the fact that he accepts that such an analysis depends upon a linguistic analysis.[13] Barthes's conclusions upon the rhetorical level of the fashion system are indeed imaginative and very much to the point. But it cannot be said that he arrives at them by linguistic analysis.[14]

Barthes himself recognizes the problem when he tries to tackle the problem of objectivity and proof concerning the rhetorical level. He maintains that

objectivity consists here in defining the rhetorical meaning as probable but not as certain; it is not possible 'to prove' the rhetorical meaning by resorting directly to the mass of users since this mass does not 'read' the connotated message but 'receives it'. There is no 'proof' of this meaning but only 'probability'.[15]

This probability can, in a way, be checked through the coherence of the construction but there is little more that can be done. According to Barthes this is inevitable when you pass from a problematic of determinism to one of meanings. So he himself retreats from any methodological claim beyond the linguistic 'coherence of a system'.[16]

Greimas's structural semantics seeks precisely to overcome some of these methodological problems, particularly when they are referred to written texts.[17] His aim is to find a scientifically rigorous way of characterizing the meaning of a text. The analysis first divides the semantic universe into micro-universes and then establishes the principles of organization, combination and permutation of these small universes so that the meaning of larger units is clarified. In other words, by starting with minimal semantic units, Greimas tries to arrive at certain rules which account for the meaning produced when these basic units combine in sentences and complete discourses.

Greimas proceeds by a series of stages which follow on one another.[18] Firstly, he starts with the constitution of the so-called 'corpus', the set of messages to be analysed. It can be said that a corpus is well constituted when it satisfies three conditions: it must be representative, exhaustive and homogenous. The corpus should be transformed into text, that is, a set of elements of signification which are located in a chosen isotopy. By isotopy he understands a set of semantic categories which are reiterative and which underly a discourse.[19] The procedure can be either elimination (exclusion of non-pertinent elements) or extraction (selection of pertinent elements). The purified corpus then takes the form of an isotopic text constituted by an inventory of messages or models. The basic structure, the minimal mode of existence of meaning, is characterized by the presence of the articulated relationship between two 'semes' (masculine/feminine, old/young, etc.). Every word manifests a certain combination of these 'semes'. The more two words have common semes, the nearer they are in meaning.

The second stage of Greimas's analysis is called 'normalization'. It consists mainly in the objectivation of the text, that is, the elimination of the parameter of subjectivity within the text and the institution of an elementary syntaxis of description. The latter is a codification which consists of: firstly, the reduction of sentences into 'Actants' and 'Predicates'; secondly, the division of predicates into qualifications and functions; and thirdly, the classification of actants into six types of roles – subject, object, sender, receiver, opponent, and helper. As Culler points out, the function of this scheme is 'to make the structure of the sentence roughly homologous to the "plot" of a text'.[20]

Finally, there follows the stage of 'construction'. It involved the building of a model which subsumes the text; that is, the transformation of the inventory of messages into a structure or model. This involves the reduction of syntactic and semiotic equivalents and the structuration as such of significative terms. Greimas develops a symbolic notation and makes some partial attempts to analysis by 'actantial models' which, he admits, are merely hypothetical. Yet it is through these models that he hints at the possibility of analysing ideology.

In effect, every text has various levels or isotopies, each of which constitute a collection of messages with its own coherence. The practical level is concerned with the denotative plane, whereas the 'mythic level' is concerned with the 'noological' or inner plane. This mythic level can be described by means of an actantial model. The scheme is very simple and it is based on a subject which desires an object which, in its turn, constitutes an object of communication between a sender and a receiver. At the same time the desire of the subject is supported by a helper and opposed by an opponent.[21] Graphically,

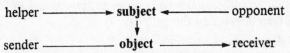

This dramatic representation of the mythic level provides, for instance, the following account of Marxist ideology: the subject is man whose desired object is the classless society; the sender is history and the receiver is mankind; the helper is the working class and the opponent the bourgeois class.[22]

As Culler has pointed out, Greimas's ambitious project of finding a scientifically rigorous way of characterizing the meaning of a text has been in vain; it seems unsatisfactory even in its more modest goals.[23] The crucial problem in Greimas's approach is the basic assumption that the 'discursive' is constituted by an aggregate of a number of minimal units. Supposing that the meanings of words could be precisely ascertained, the problem remains as to how to pass from these basic meanings to the meanings of sentences and paragraphs, and from there to the global meaning of the text. Yet even the very determination and assignment of meaning to the minimal units seems highly complicated. If one considers the immense variety of metaphorical meanings which a word can assume within a sentence, one can realize that the task of ascertaining those meanings with accuracy and exhaustiveness proves to be almost impossible.

But even if it were possible to account for every possible meaning of the basic units, one may well wonder to what extent the meaning of a text could be deduced from the meaning of its minimal units. Such a method seems inevitably to lead towards a reduction of the object of analysis. By normalization, structuration and symbolic notation, a complex text is reduced to a model of minimal enunciations which are not only arbitrary exponents of the general meaning but also the fruit of the oversimplification of the interpretive process.[24] In fact it is very difficult to know how the method works, since Greimas does not analyse any text with it in his *Semantique structurale*.

As to the so-called 'mythical level' which might correspond to the analysis of ideology, there are only a few, very general and formal remarks which make no substantial contribution. The mythic actantial model is indeed interesting but too general and formal to illuminate any analysis of ideology. Besides, it is not clear at all that ideology should be identified with a fairy tale. For that is what the mythic actantial model boils down to. One could say that, in general, fairy tales follow this pattern:

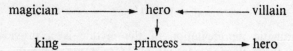

But one cannot reduce ideology to this dramatic representation without further elaboration. True, certain elements of this model could be worked out so as to coincide with a more sophisticated conception of ideology.[25] There is a basic conflict or contradiction in the fairy tale which the discourse tries to resolve. Perhaps the conflict between the hero and the villain can be made to represent a social contradiction between classes and the defeat of the villain symbolizes the solution in the mind to the contradictions which cannot be solved in practice.

Although this line of reasoning may prove promising, substantial work upon it remains to be done. For the time being, the model is too crude to represent a major advance in the analysis of ideology. Perhaps its most important contribution is to show that fairy tales and other narratives may have or may acquire a concealed ideological purpose; that is, the very structure of the fairy tale may easily adapt itself to ideological meanings. Yet this is quite different from trying to analyse ideology by starting from the model of a fairy tale. Ideology is not concerned with the general conflicts between good and bad, truth and error, and so forth. Ideology conceals historical and concrete social contradictions in the interest of a dominant class, and this is its specific level of analysis.

It seems to me that synchronic structural linguistics has contributed to the analysis of ideology with some stimulating intuitions derived from its basic distinctions between language and speech and between connotation and denotation. Yet the claim that this new method drawn from linguistics itself would be more rigorous and scientific than others does not seem substantiated by fact. In the end there is a great deal of arbitrariness when concrete analyses are attempted. Also, the location of ideology as a second-order structure underlying every text, as language is behind every speech, may convey the mistaken impression that the text is a self-supporting totality whose objective substructure is ascertainable in itself, regardless of the role of the researcher and the historical context in which the text is immersed.

Hence, the analysis of the text seems to assume the closeness of the text, the belief that its principle of intelligibility stems from its own immanence. Of course, it is impossible to deny the existence of inner organizational principles in texts. It is also true that they constitute totalities, or organic wholes. Yet as Culler has pointed out, the unity of texts, is produced ,'not so much by intrinsic features of their parts as by the intent at totality of the interpretive process'.[26] That is to say, the historical and social context, as well as the expectations, intellectual background and class origin of the analyst, play an important role in 'producing' that unity. The text is not something autonomous whose precise meaning is captured within its immanence once and for all. Every epoch, class or generation has its own interpretation. In this sense the unity of the text is a function of the meaning which is attributed to it.[27] Often structuralism tends to contemplate the objective structure of messages and to neglect the differences which are likely to arise in the operations of ciphering and of deciphering, of writing and of reading. It is a well-known fact that addressers and addressees do not always communicate upon the basis of the same code. This is why, as Eco has pointed out, the decodification process is orientated not only by the internal context and the explicit indication of the code but also by the circumstances of communication and the receiver's own code.[28]

Saussurian linguistics privileges the structure of signs to the detriment of their practical functions. The construction of basic structures allows the analysis of messages as long as the emitter and the receiver are considered to be impersonal and inter-changeable, that is, as long as they do not really count, because the message has its internal and independent structure. The approach tends to ignore the functional characteristics which every message owes to its utilization in a certain socially structured interaction. It is necessary to remember that somehow speech is a condition of language. Language cannot be grasped without speech. Every change in language is brought about through speech (*parole*). Structuralism reverses this relationship: language becomes the condition of intelligibility of speech. The primacy of practice is superseded by the blind rule of a logic order.[29]

The context which determines the meaning of a sentence in a text is wider than the other sentences of the text. The meaning of a linguistic element depends as much on extra-linguistic factors as on linguistic ones. The mere knowledge of the basic code of a text allows one to grasp very little of the linguistic interactions really performed.[30] If this is so for the normal interpretation of the text it is even more so for ideological analysis. Ideology in a text is a relationship between the textual and the extra-textual, between the content and the conditions of its production, which are external and rooted in historical and social reality. The presence of the ideological in a discourse does not consist of immanent properties of the texts, but of a system of relationships between the text and its production, circulation and consumption.[31]

Finally, a corollary of all this shows the insufficiency of a mere synchronic approach. It is not that structural linguistics does not consider diachrony in any respect; it is rather a problem of emphasis and relevance. Since it focuses on a basic underlying structure, history and change are somehow disregarded. Structuralism can do without the parameter 'time' in its search for structural laws, and these laws are thought to be superior to laws of change. Diachrony is thus subordinated; it is thought of as a disturbance in a synchrony which assumes the major explanatory role. When one challenges the explanatory primacy of pure immanent organizational principles one also undermines the role of synchrony. Of course, synchronic structures do have a role: as far as ideology is concerned the main contribution of structural linguistics is precisely the attention it pays to the level that is behind the manifest content of a text. Yet one should not confuse ideology with general and basic oppositions and systematic principles of organization. I should add two further limiting factors. First, up to now, 'there is no structuralist method such that by applying it to a text one automatically discovers its inner structure',[32] and second, the meaning of that structure does not entirely stem from the immanence of the text itself. Therefore if ideological phenomena should not be reduced to arbitrary constructions of consciousness, nor can they be reduced to a sort of underlying logic and universal pattern disconnected from history and extra-textual factors.

The structural analysis of myth: Lévi-Strauss and Godelier

Within the structuralist style of thought we have already come across the denomination 'myth' or 'mythical' to designate that underlying sphere of connotation which represents the ideological level. Up to now we have not discussed this denomination nor have we tackled the problem of the relationships between ideology and myth. Are they equivalent concepts or must we differentiate them? Lévi-Strauss's early theory of myth presents a good opportunity to come back to this subject within the framework of structuralism.

The influence of structural linguistics and Marxism are equally and explicitly acknowledged by Lévi-Strauss when he puts forward the basic premises upon which he intends to build up his theory.[33] From Marx he takes those elements which he thinks emphasize the importance of unconscious phenomena in social life. According to Marx 'men make their own history, but they do not make it just as they please; they do not make under circumstances chosen by themselves, but under circumstances directly encountered, given and transmitted from the past.'[34] This statement, frequently referred to by Lévi-Strauss, indicates for him that beyond the conscious world there is an unconscious sphere which in the end holds the clue for the explanation of human behaviour, and particularly of cultural activity.[35] As to linguistics, he claims that Troubetzkoy, father of phonology and structural linguistics, introduced a revolution into the social sciences, comparable with that which nuclear physics introduced to the physical sciences. This revolution inaugurated a shift from 'the study of *conscious* linguistic phenomena to study of their *unconscious* infrastructure'.[36] This basic premise together with the rest of structuralist principles described by Troubetzkoy, such as the introduction of the concept of system, the analysis centred on the relations between terms, and the goal of discovering general laws, are transposed by Lévi-Strauss into the study of kinship, totemism and myth.

Each of these phenomena, like a language, constitute a sort of unconscious system whose elements are meaningful only through their reciprocal relationships of opposition and are regulated by synchronic general laws. At the bottom of this transposition lies the assumption that kinship, totemism and myth are special forms of language, systems of communication, ways in which society expresses itself according to a certain universal built-in logic. And not only these phenomena but various other aspects of social life could be considered as having the same nature as that of language, even art and religion.[37] The methodological consequences of this position are obviously of great importance: whatever the social phenomenon under scrutiny, it will have to be considered as a basic system of terms (like words or phonemes in a language) which maintain certain relationships between them and whose logical connections and permutations explain the real, empirical, historical phenomenon. In the case of totemism, for instance, Lévi-Strauss proposes the following methodological operations in order to analyse it:

(1) Define the phenomena under study as a relation between two or more terms, real or supposed;

(2) Construct a table of possible permutations between these terms;

(3) Take this table as the general object of analysis which, at this level only, can yield necessary connections, the empirical phenomenon considered at the beginning being only one possible combination among others, the complete system of which must be reconstructed beforehand.[38]

This is why the phenomenon in its individuality is merely contingent, a 'possible combination'. What really explains it is the underlying structure, which is timeless and necessary.

Myth is, therefore, a language, a particular kind of language, whose purpose 'is to provide a logical model capable of overcoming a contradiction (an impossible achievement if, as it happens, the contradiction is real)'.[39] The formal similarity between Lévi-Strauss's concept of myth and Marx's concept of ideology is indeed striking and one wonders to what extent their meanings are analogous. What in Marx was a solution in consciousness to a contradiction, in Lévi-Strauss is, too, an attempt to overcome a contradiction by means of an intellectual solution. While for Marx ideology was a distorted consciousness which could not succeed in solving contradictions in so far as it was based upon an inversion of reality itself, for Lévi-Strauss, myth is a logical model which cannot succeed when it faces a real contradiction.

Being a kind of language, myth creates structures by means of its own signs, which are events, but is a prisoner of those events which it tirelessly attempts to structure. In fact, mythical structuration uses the remains and debris of events. Mythical thought uses 'fossilized evidence of the history of an individual or a society' thus reversing the relation between the diachronic and the synchronic. Science, on the contrary, creates events, changes the world by means of structures, that is, the hypotheses and theories which it constantly elaborates.[40] Yet Lévi-Strauss does not really oppose science to myth nor does he believe them to be different phases in the evolution of knowledge. For him both approaches are equally valid, and he strongly rejects Lévi-Bruhl's antinomy between logical and pre-logical mentality. The difference lies 'not in the quality of the intellectual process, but in the nature of the things to which it is applied'.[41] Mythical thought is a way of approaching events as rigorous as science, even if the two differ in their results. They apply the same kind of intellectual logic to different materials. I have already argued that Marx did not make the opposition between science and ideology his main focus of attention either. Yet would he have accepted that there is no difference in the quality of the intellectual process between science and ideology and that they only differ in the materials to which they are applied? I think not. Ideology for Marx seeks to explain the same social phenomena as science, but it inverts their terms. So ideology and science do not have the same method applied to different things, but different methods applied to the same things.

At the bottom of this problem is the concept of science which Lévi-Strauss uses. For him the form seems to count more than the content. As he puts it, a scientific explanation is always the discovery of an 'arrangement'. He stresses the search for an 'order', the cataloguing and classifying of materials as the main characteristic of science.[42] To the extent that magic and myth formally do the same – classifying, cataloguing, seeking an order or arrangement – they are similar to science. Is this formal concept of science sufficient, or must some other essential elements of content be added to it? Lévi-Strauss privileges formal intellectual requirements rather than practical results. But these requirements are so general that ultimately they seem to become a constant in every kind of thought, and it becomes difficult to differentiate common sense, science, myth, and religion. Yet the point is precisely to differentiate them, not only through external factors but in their very intellectual requirements.

It is not sufficient to find the same desire for classifying and making arrangements in every kind of knowledge. One needs to qualify these attitudes in detail: how are the arrangements arrived at? How are the materials catalogued or classified? These questions depend not only upon the things to which consciousness is applied but also upon the methodology and the intellectual tools the particular kind of knowledge possesses. Lévi-Strauss's concept of science tends entirely to substitute the discovery of an order or arrangement in phenomena for their causal explanation. These operations are not necessarily opposed, but when the emphasis lies heavily on the classificatory side without taking into account the cause-effect relationship, science becomes powerless.

Lévi-Strauss himself provides a good example of this. He argues that

the real question is not whether the touch of a woodpecker's beak does in fact cure toothache. It is rather whether there is a point of view from which a woodpecker's beak and a man's tooth can be seen as 'going together' ... and whether some initial order can be introduced into the universe by means of those groupings.[43]

There is a point of view from which an arrangement, a particular order could be found in which a woodpecker's beak and a man's tooth go together. This is precisely the mythical point of view and it undoubtedly has a logic which can be discovered. But once this is accepted, it is too much to say that that order is 'the real question'. It is only one of the possible real questions which could be raised. Another important question is whether or not there is a cause-effect relationship between toothache and woodpeckers' beaks. This is the scientific point of view. It is not necessary to return to Lévi-Bruhl's pre-logical mentality to see the differences between the two approaches. Yet these differences do not stem only from the different types of phenomena to which they are applied, as Lévi-Strauss maintains, but also from the intellectual process and method which is utilized.

Lévi-Strauss's emphasis on form rather than content casts a doubt on the equivalence of his definition of myth with Marx's concept of ideology. True, both definitions contemplate a form of consciousness which attempt at solving a contradiction. Yet the problem arises as to how this contradiction is understood. Lévi-Strauss maintains, quite rightly in my view, that nature is not in itself contradictory.[44] It becomes so only through some concrete human activity, by the mediation of man's practice. This is the reason why he criticizes the mistake of Mannhardt and the naturalist school, who think that myth seeks to explain natural phenomena. On the contrary, Lévi-Strauss propounds that these natural phenomena 'are rather the medium through which myths try to explain facts which are themselves not of a natural but a logical order'.[45] It seems to me that Lévi-Strauss's solution has avoided one pitfall only to fall in another. By trying to oppose the conception of contradictions in nature, he ends up conceiving contradictions as logical problems.

In effect, to Lévi-Strauss 'the substance of contradictions is much less important than the fact that they exist'. Their content matters much less than their form.[46] Contradiction as a social reality whose content is historically detectable makes way for a concept which emphasizes the logical, universal and non-historical character of the 'form' contradiction. The fact that this form is common to all specific contradictions underlies the fact that men very often have recourse 'to the same means for solving problems whose concrete elements may be very different but which share the feature of all belonging to 'structures of contradiction'.[47] One can see now that Lévi-Strauss's understanding of contradiction differs very much from Marx's conception. While Lévi-Strauss's concept of myth responds to a logical problem of human nature, Marx's concept of ideology responds to historical contradictions.

The consequence is not only a difference between the concept of myth and the concept of ideology, but also a difference in the very concept of myth. For although Marx distinguishes ideology from myth, the difference is not that ideology responds to historical contradictions and myth to logical conflicts. The difference is rather located in the fact that ideology tries to solve social contradictions and myth tries to solve contradictions with nature. Both aspects are imbricated yet distinguished in their emphases. For this very reason both kinds of contradictions are historical. To this extent, myth is also trying to solve a concrete, historical contradiction and not the universal conflict of the human species.

Here the whole question of the relationship between consciousness and social reality comes to the fore. Lévi-Strauss insists that the infrastructures have priority. Yet he interprets this priority not as the determination imposed by particular historical conditions, but as the determination imposed by human nature in general. To explain this he resorts to the image of a card game which men are forced to play, each deal resulting in a contingent distribution of cards. There are common rules, and individual choices in tactics that players can opt for. So men can play different games with the same hand. Yet ultimately the very card game and the rules set limits on the games which can be played with any given hand. The important thing is the general framework which conditions the game, despite the historical variability of deals and hands. Likewise, consciousness is determined more by a general logical pattern than by particular conditions. Although the social world built up through human practice does affect consciousness, the final determination, and above all, the recurrence of similar solutions, comes from the innate pattern of consciousness with which that social world is approached. Somehow, therefore, Lévi-Strauss comes back to the existence of innate cultural universals which are not dependent upon social reality.

These are the important differences between Marx's theory of ideology and Lévi-Strauss's theory of myth. Yet Lévi-Strauss explicitly relates myth to ideology. For him myth appears in modern societies to have been largely replaced by politics.[48] From a formal point of view, he maintains there is nothing more similar to myth in exotic societies than the political ideologies in modern societies. If a transposition of method were to be made, it is not modern religious traditions which must be analysed, but modern political thought.[49] It seems to me, nevertheless, that this *rapprochement* of concepts does not work well, unless one can accept the reduction of one to the other. In my view, ideology should maintain its negative connotation, as a kind of distorted knowledge which conceals contradictions. Lévi-Strauss's aim, on the contrary, is to discover a basic structure or logical pattern, irrespective of its cognitive value. The important thing for Lévi-Strauss is not that myth may distort reality, but that myth makes sense from a logical point of view. This is why the difference between science and myth is somehow blurred. The concept of ideology, on the contrary, is concerned not merely with the fact that thought 'makes sense' but also with the fact that its content may conceal real social contradictions and is, therefore, an inadequate representation of reality.

The fact that Lévi-Strauss's theory tends to conceive the contradictions as a logical problem is not easily noticeable in *Structural Anthropology* but it affirms its predominance after *The Raw and the Cooked*. As Glucksmann has put it, in the early period, up to 1962, myth 'seeks to justify the shortcoming of reality by imagining extreme solutions . . .' whereas ever since *Mythologiques* the aim is 'to examine myth as a system of logic in its own right rather than as an attempted intellectual solution to social problems'.[50] This evolution in the understanding of myth also means some changes in the methodology applied to its study. The early model is a structural analysis mainly concerned with individual myths and following closely the linguistic pattern. Since myth is a sort of language, its analysis should proceed like the analysis of language, distinguishing between language and speech, between the structural side and the sequential aspect; accordingly, it is necessary to identify the constituent units of language-myth. What in a normal language are phonemes, in myth will be 'mythemes', a sort of 'gross constituent units' as Lévi-Strauss calls them, which basically are sentences. These units present themselves as language and speech, that is, as structured bundles of related mythemes and as sequences of mythemes. The technique necessary to analyse the myth consists in 'breaking down its story into the shortest possible sentences, and writing each sentence on an index card bearing a number corresponding to the unfolding of the story'.[51] The arrangement of the cards or sentences follows the double pattern already expressed: it is necessary to find synchronic bundles of the mythemes which constitute a unit of meaning, and, at the same time, to allow the sequential reading of the story. This is achieved by ordering the cards in columns so that a vertical reading, column by column (harmony in musical scores) gives the synchronic units of meaning while a normal left to right reading (melody) provides the sequence. The musical analogy, which Lévi-Strauss likes so much, is also expressed in the form of a melody composed for several voices whose two dimensions are the horizontal melodic line and the vertical contrapuntal schemata.[52]

Just as language is the principle of intelligibility of speech, so the mythical story is made comprehensible by the basic oppositions between the bundles represented in columns. To tell the myth is a matter of diachronic speech; to understand the myth implies disregarding part of this diachronic dimension to achieve a different reading which crosses vertically through the text.[53] This vertical reading is in the end performed through four columns: two represent the terms of the contradiction to be solved; the other two are the mediating terms whose relationship is supposed to reduce the contradiction to a new logical and manageable dimension.

Many criticisms have been made of this methodological approach. M. Douglas for instance, remarks the fact that without taking into account the content and looking only for the formal structure of a myth, interpretation is rather difficult, 'just as knowing that the rhyme structure is *a, b, b, a*, does not tell us anything about the content of a sonnet'. The balance of themes like 'life' and 'death' which Lévi-Strauss finds so often at the bottom of myths (for example the Zuni emergence myth analysed in 'The structural study of myth', and some Pawnee myths) is so general that 'it might have been better to have said that it was a balanced structure of pluses and minuses or of positives and negatives'.[54] Burridge, on the other hand, doubts whether the results of structural analysis spring from the material itself or rather from the imposition of a particular mode of thought.[55]

As Culler points out, the omission of important items which are not taken into account when they do not fit in the postulated structure makes the method rather arbitrary and tautological in so far as the only logic revealed is that of the structure postulated in advance, not necessarily that of the myth.[56]

From *Mythologiques* onwards, Lévi-Strauss, without explicitly rejecting this method, abandons it. Analyses are no longer carried out for individual myths; on the contrary, it is assumed that every aspect of a myth can only be understood in relation to similar aspects in different myths. The context is then widened from the elements or mythemes of a particular myth to the system of other myths in which similar situations appear. A sort of spiral methodology is thus employed: one myth illuminates another, which in turn elucidates a third, and so forth. Every aspect is related to its homologue in other myths and the analysis aims at discovering an internal coherence, a general logic of myth. Now the emphasis is much less on the particular contradictions which myth supposedly seeks to solve in a logical manner and more on the general unconscious mental structures behind it.

In effect, if each myth refers to other myths and each structure of meanings refers to another structure, the question arises as to what final meaning these mutually significative meanings are referring to. The reply which Lévi-Strauss sees emerging from his study, *The Raw and the Cooked*, is that

myths signify the mind that evolves them by making use of the world of which it is itself a part. Thus there is simultaneous production of myths themselves, by the mind that generates them, and, by the myths, of an image of the world which is already inherent in the structure of the mind.[57]

Yalman has questioned whether the symmetry found in myths is in the natives' minds or, in fact, in the mind of the observer.[58] Lévi-Strauss gives no weight to such an argument. For him it does not matter whether his thought is affected by the real movement of natives' thought or whether their thought takes form through his thought. Both follow the same mythical way or pattern.

Despite his search for the universal synchronic logic, Lévi-Strauss is not always able to separate basic structures from specific cultural backgrounds, general forms from particular contents. This is interpreted by some authors as a methodological failure and a reversal from the stated programme, but in fact, more than anything, it shows the enormous difficulties which stem from the rigorous application of the linguistic model. As Culler has pointed out, while a linguist does not have to prove that the sentences of English should be treated as a group, Lévi-Strauss tries to prove that myths from various cultures constitute the speech (*parole*) of a general mythological language (*langue*). And that step can only be made, according to Culler, by assuming in advance that all those myths in the group have the same meaning.[59]

Ricoeur has pointed out that Lévi-Strauss's examples are all taken from the geographical area of totemism and never from the Semitic, Proto-Helenic or Indo-European world.[60] He suggests that in the former area a particular sort of savage mind may have developed which privileges synchrony as against diachrony, whereas the latter may well be an opposite world which engenders a different sort of mythical thought: 'where the structural intelligence is perhaps less important, less exclusive, and requires a more hermeneutic intelligence which seeks to interpret contents themselves'.[61] Ricoeur's point calls in question the validity of a universal methodology to analyse myth and, indeed, of a merely formal concept of myth. Ricoeur finds a solution in distinguishing two kinds of mentality, the kerigmatic Hebraic pattern and the totemic pattern, and in attributing a hermeneutical method to the former and a structural method to the latter; this, too, seems rather arbitrary. There is not only a problem of finding empirical evidence to support this distinction to the exclusion of any other, but also has not Ricoeur inadvertently come back to the same device he criticizes in Lévi-Strauss, that is, the recourse to an unconscious, though partial, pattern of mind? The analysis of myth becomes dependent upon the previous attribution of an *a priori* sort of mentality whose social determination Ricoeur does not clarify. In fact, in opposition to the totemic pattern he puts together types of thought as divergent in other respects as the Semitic and the Helenic. Hence, Ricoeur's solution does not seem to overcome completely the difficulties attributed to Lévi-Strauss.

Be that as it may, Lévi-Strauss's analysis of myth risks psychological reductionism in so far as, in the end, what seems to determine the logic of myth is the psychological structure of the mind, common to all men. Mythical logic remains unconscious, its structure is not known to men. The true nature of cultural life is its being unconscious. Lévi-Strauss conceives of anthropology as trying 'to grasp beyond the conscious and always shifting images which men hold the complete range of unconscious possibilities'.[62] Within this concept of culture, common to all theories which rely upon structural linguistics, ideology becomes an unconscious phenomenon, something whose meaning is received but not read (as Barthes put it) or (in the Althusserian formulation) a set of images, concepts and structures which impose themselves on the majority of men without passing through their consciousness. There is little difference between these formulations and Lévi-Strauss's contention that 'myths operate in men's minds without their being aware of the fact'.[63] To this extent, it becomes difficult to distinguish among superstructural phenomena, since all respond to the same unconscious pattern. Yet one may wonder in what sense culture is an unconscious phenomenon. There are several meanings we can attach to the word 'unconscious'. It certainly does not refer to a sort of Freudian unconscious, the energy and impulses which strive for discharge. Lévi-Strauss's unconscious is not an emotional content but a form empty of content.[64] This unconscious has no connection with the subject as a thinking subject; it is rather a general category which constrains the mind without being acknowledged. That is why Ricoeur calls Lévi-Strauss's theory an 'absolute formalism' or a 'Kantianism without a transcendental subject'.[65]

As we saw, Lévi-Strauss adduces in support of this conception Marx's remark that men make their own history without knowing that they are making it. But he does not realize that for Marx structures are themselves the result of man's practice. Lévi-Strauss's emphasis upon the unconscious character of culture stretches Marx's argument further than he would have accepted. Marx does identify a level in which men are unaware of the real forces of history, yet he strongly argues against those who forget that men may change circumstances through revolutionary practice. And this practice may, to a large extent, be aware of the real forces of history. There can be no doubt that ideology has an unconscious level: it is often held without conscious knowledge of its real character, and it is produced and re-produced through the reproductive practice of society, which is not aware of its own character. Yet ideology is always given in the consciousness of individuals through the process of their practice. Ideology is produced in the conjunction of subject and object; it is neither pure illusion nor pure materiality. It cannot be said that ideology constitutes a hidden structure which imposes itself upon men without passing through their practice.

Lévi-Strauss's conception, on the contrary, constitutes a sort of collective, unconscious entity which is beyond human production.

The logic of culture, with which ideology is identified, becomes an objective and external phenomenon imposed upon men. As Bourdieu has pointed out, Saussurian and Lévi-Straussian structuralism ends up conceiving of practice as the execution of an abstract model.[66] All happens as if a system of objective relations was hypostatized as a 'collective unconscious' capable of acting upon men from outside human practice. Structures and objective relations, can be found behind cultural phenomena, but they constitute models built up as part of research, which excludes their reification. It is true that men do not make history as they please and that their conscious goals do not always coincide with the actual results: but neither do they execute a pre-established order; they are not 'lived' through a basic structure which they do not know. Lévi-Strauss transforms a model of reality into the reality of the model: structures acquire a kind of hypostatized existence, an ontological essence prior to human practice and thinking. As Lefebvre remarks, this brings forward the paradox of a system of knowledge (*'pensée-pensée'*) which precedes the thinking subject (*'pensée-pensante'*). In his view this would be the hallmark of a new eleatism which contests movement in history.[67]

However, from a different perspective, *Mythologiques* contributes crucial results which may have an important bearing upon the concept of ideology. In effect, Lévi-Strauss shows kinship structures to be at the basis of the mythical world. Mythical representations about the origin of fire, food, animals, stars and so on, depict the adventures of supernatural beings whose reciprocal relationships are in terms of brothers and sisters, husbands and wives, parents and children, and so forth. In an effort to coordinate this result with a Marxist conception of ideology, M. Godelier maintains that 'if the kinship structure plays the role of organizing scheme of the mythical discourse . . . it is because in reality itself, the kinship structure constitutes the dominant aspect of the social structure within primitive societies'.[68] The correspondence between kinship structures and myths cannot be deduced from nature or from the formal principles of thought, as Lévi-Strauss would believe, but from the very social structure. Marx thought that the economic structure was determining in the last instance. Godelier maintains that this is also true in primitive societies, as the Australian natives show, because kinship relationships are the relations of production; the kinship structure constitutes the economic structure of the primitive society.

Starting from these anthropological premises and from their

confrontation with Marx's analysis of the fetishism of commodity, Godelier tries to build a general Marxist theory of ideology in which the role of religious forms would be crucial. He notes that in order to illustrate the fetishism of commodity, Marx resorts to the 'mist-enveloped regions of the religious world' in which 'the productions of the human brain appear as independent beings endowed with life and entering into relation both with one another and the human race'.[69] This contention perfectly corresponds to the findings of modern anthropology. Since the primitives cannot understand and control nature, they spontaneously represent it as the field of super-ior and mysterious powers by analogy to the human world; that is to say, they treat the forces of nature as if they were real subjects or beings endowed with consciousness and will.[70] This analogical representation is also a way of action upon the created subjects, who, are able to hear and reply to men's appeals because they possess human or superhuman powers. Religious representations are there-fore inseparable from a certain practice upon nature which, through magic and ritual, aims at propitiating the supernatural subjects which populate it.

Godelier wants to emphasize that these analogical representations have an objective fundament in the kinship structures which, by performing the function of relations of production, have a dominant role in the social life of primitive peoples. Just as in the fetishism of commodity 'it is not man who is mistaken about reality, but reality which deceives him by necessarily appearing under a form which disguises it',[71] in primitive religions and myths, the fundament of nature appearing as the kingdom of superior powers is external to consciousness. It does not matter that this fundament appears to be a non-economic structure, namely, kinship, in so far as the distinction between economic structure and superstructures is a 'distinction of functions and not of institutions'.[72] The kinship structure may have the economic function in society, as it does for Australian primitives. The ideological is not, for Godelier, a separate instance which legitimizes and reproduces the productive instance but it is the representations present in all social relations. Ideology is not produced in order to deceive. It could be used to that purpose or may have that objective result, but in itself is a necessary repre-sentation of all social relations.

Godelier's confrontation of Marx with Lévi-Strauss has produced quite a number of valuable insights and has thrown a new light on the formation of primitive consciousness within a framework which mixes in a penetrating manner the results of modern anthropology with Marx's materialism.

This interesting approach nevertheless presents problems. First, is the conflation of myth and ideology. It is true that Marx used the analogy between both phenomena, but this does not mean that he meant to fuse them. On the contrary, there are grounds to think that the analogy always kept them separate. In the fetishism of commodity, the products of work acquired life; in mythology it is nature which is invested with subjective characters. True, myth uses analogy and transposes the social world into the explanation of nature, yet its focus of attention is not directly social relations but nature. There is no need of a class system for it to exist. Myth exists largely in primitive classless societies with very simple social relations. Ideology on the contrary, emerges when the complexity of social relations has produced a system of classes. The contradiction with nature which myth seeks to explain evolves in the opposite direction to the social contradiction which is concealed by ideology. While man progressively succeeds in controlling nature and therefore the incidence of mythology tends to diminish, social relations evolve towards more complicated and abstract forms whose contradictory character assumes an increasingly deceptive appearance.

Second, some of Godelier's formulae give the impression that he confuses the necessary external referent of ideology with the contention that external reality is passively reflected upon consciousness: he maintains that it is not the subject who is mistaken about reality, but reality which misleads the subject. This is a common feature of all structuralism, which disregards the idea that reality is itself practically constructed.

Third, Godelier universalizes ideology to the point that it represents all forms of consciousness accompanying social relations. Thus, not only are the ideas which legitimize the existence order ideological, but also those which seek a return to an old order and those which look for a social order which is still to be created.[73] This extension of ideology to cover the whole spectrum of ideas, has the same consequences as the structuralist understanding of ideology as the basic structures underlying the whole of culture, namely, the dissolution of the concept into an empty form. Godelier's idea of an all-encompassing theory of ideology loses Marx's historical approach.

Althusser's 'structuralist' conception of ideology

The application of a structuralist methodology to the analysis of cultural phenomena has had vast repercussions in the field of Marxist studies. We have already seen Godelier's attempt to link the results of structural anthropology with the Marxist theory of ideology. But this is just one aspect of a wider current which tries systematically to re-interpret Marx along structuralist lines. The so-called 'structuralist' Marxist tradition starts with assumptions entirely different from those of the 'historicist' tradition. The belief in an 'epistemological break' between two stages of Marx's career, namely, the pre-scientific and the scientific, casts a doubt upon the value of works such as *The German Ideology*, which belong to the period of the break and seem to be ambiguous, destined to be surpassed by a more mature approach. Mepham claims that Marx has not achieved in *The German Ideology* a clear theoretical position on the origin of ideology. Marx appears to be struggling to discover an adequate language but has failed.[74] Poulantzas points to the 'numerous ambiguities' of such work,[75] while Althusser, more directly, calls the theory which emerges from it a 'positivist and historicist thesis'.[76]

The problem 'structuralism' tackles was advanced by Gramsci when he rejected a conception of ideology as an arbitrary and psychological creation of individuals. Structuralism wants to free Marx from a conception of ideology as 'pure speculation' or false consciousness. Historicism abets this interpretation, for it emphasizes the role of the subject-class and of consciousness in the origin of ideology. In opposition to this, 'structuralism' suggests that ideology has a material existence which determines the subject. To reject the concept of ideology as false consciousness, it has to do away with the conception of the subject participating in its origin. Ideology is not a false representation of reality because its source is not the subject but material reality itself.

By far the most important representative of this line of thought is Louis Althusser.[77] His numerous attempts at explaining ideology are not exempt from contradictions,[78] and change considerably over the years. Besides the scattered remarks which one can find in Althusser's various articles, two of them are specifically concerned with ideology. The first, 'Teoría, Práctica teórica y formación teórica. Ideología y lucha ideológica' ('Theory, theoretical practice, and theoretical formation. Ideology and ideological struggle'), was first published in Spanish in 1966 and has been ignored by most English-speaking commentators.[79] The second, 'Ideology and ideological state apparatuses',[80] is widely known and marks a change from earlier elaborations. Nevertheless, I shall try to show that this change is less fundamental than it might appear.

I think one can distinguish three different emphases in Althusser's essays. First, in his early works, he stresses ideology as an objective level of social reality, independent of individual subjectivity. Ideology is indeed a system of representations, Althusser argues,

but in the majority of cases these representations have nothing to do with 'consciousness': they are usually images and occasionally concepts, but it is above all as *structures* that they impose on the vast majority of men, not via their 'consciousness'.[81]

Men 'practise' their ideology but do not know it. Ideology is 'profoundly unconscious' and surpasses the way in which it is 'lived' by particular individuals. The essential character of ideology is only intelligible through its structure. Isolated images or representations do not make ideology; 'it is their *system*, their mode of combination and *disposition* which give them sense; it is their structure which determines them in their sense and function'.[82] Because ideology is determined by its structure, it cannot be reduced to the way in which it is 'lived' by various individuals, and can be studied as an objective phenomenon.

As to the character of this system of representations, Althusser is not very consistent. In *For Marx* he puts forward a thesis which is usually hailed as a break with the traditional conception of ideology as false consciousness:[83]

In ideology men do indeed express, not the relation between them and their conditions of existence, but *the way* they live the relation between them and their conditions of existence. This presupposes both a real relation and an '*imaginary*', 'lived' relation.[84]

In 'Theoretical practice and ideological struggle', however, Althusser seems to come back to the old formula, when he maintains that 'ideology is a representation of the real, but a necessarily false one, since it is necessarily orientated and biased . . .'.[85] Yet he does not see any incompatibility between this formula and the consideration of ideology as an objective level of society.

In effect, according to Althusser, men cannot live without a certain representation of their world and of their relations to it.

But this representation is *given* with respect to each subject. Men find it already formed, just as economic and political relations are formed before they are born. 'Ideology thus appears as a certain *representation of the world*, which links men with their conditions of existence and with other men . . .'.[86] The function of ideology is, therefore, to secure cohesion among men and between men and their tasks. Borrowing a Gramscian image, Althusser describes ideology as a 'cement' which introduces itself into all the parts of the social building, making possible the adjustment and cohesion of men in their roles. Ideology does not only allow men to execute their tasks, but also helps them to bear their situation, be it the exploited, be it the exploiter.[87]

Ideology is therefore an essential element of all societies as it secures the fulfilment of certain essential social tasks:

Human societies secrete ideology as the very element and atmosphere indispensable to their historical respiration and life. Only an ideological world outlook could have imagined societies without ideology and accepted the utopian idea of a world in which ideology (not just one of its historical forms) would disappear . . . *historical materialism cannot conceive that even a communist society could ever do without ideology.*[88]

Hence, one can affirm that ideology arises before class divisions appear, and will survive after these divisions disappear. Ideology is a structural feature of any society; its function is the cementing of its unity. But in a class society, ideology receives a further function, as a means to maintain domination of one class over the others. As Althusser puts it, 'in a classless society, just as in a class society, this function is dominated by the form which the division of labour takes in the differentiation of men in antagonic classes'.[89]

However important the general function of ideology may be, Althusser thinks that ideological representations are not true cognitions of the world. The question about the origin of the falsity of ideological representations is crucial for Althusser, and his answer shows that his structuralist leanings are more than a mere terminological 'flirtation'. In effect, he argues that

the distortion of ideology is socially necessary as a function of the very nature of the social totality, more precisely, as a function of *its determination by its structure*, which is made, as all the social, opaque for individuals who occupy a place determined by this structure. The opacity of social structure makes necessarily *mythical* the representation of the world necessary for social cohesion.[90]

In a class society, the class division over-determines the opaque character of society, so that both aspects determine the distorting and mystifying character of ideology.

In so far as ideology exists in class societies, it divides itself into various ideological tendencies which express the representations of different social classes. Thus Althusser arrives at the concept of dominant and dominated ideologies. In this he strictly follows Lenin's tenets in *What Is to Be Done?* Dominated ideologies may, under certain circumstances, give expression to the protest of exploited classes. But the dominated are always subordinate, and spontaneously formulate their grievances in the language and logic of the dominant class. That is why the working class cannot liberate itself from bourgeois ideology but needs to receive from outside the help of science. Through their simple practice, men cannot arrive at true knowledge of the social structure; they need a different practice, the 'theoretical practice' or science.[91]

This leads directly to the second emphasis, which co-exists with the first from the beginning; it can be labelled epistemological. Ideology appears in opposition to science, as a pre-scientific mode of cognition. Althusser opposes an ideological theoretical practice to a scientific theoretical practice. Yet the latter works on the results of the former in order to produce scientific concepts. Science

does not 'work' on a purely objective 'given', that of pure and absolute 'facts'. On the contrary, its particular labour consists of *elaborating its own scientific facts* through a critique of the *ideological 'facts'* elaborated by an earlier ideological theoretical practice.[92]

This ideological theoretical practice formulates false problems whose solutions are already produced outside the process of knowledge.[93] Hence, the innovation which science brings about is not just a different solution. There is a radical 'epistemological break' between ideology and science: science poses the problems in an entirely different manner, so that their solution is not prejudged and imposed in advance by ideological theoretical practice. Note how Althusser's epistemological considerations on the relationship of ideology to science correspond with Lenin's political considerations on the importation of science from without into the spontaneous consciousness of the working class.

A third emphasis in Althusser's most recent work re-formulates the problem of ideology in terms of two functional requirements. On the one hand, ideology is analysed in the context of the repro-

duction of the relations of production and of its material existence
in the Ideological State Apparatuses (ISA). On the other hand
ideology appears as a mechanism which constitutes subjects by
interpellating them. Many of the elements of this seemingly new
attempt are present in Althusser's early work, although in a different
form. In effect, in the article on ISA, Althusser formalizes a distinction foreshadowed in his first writings. There he had considered
the general function of ideology (securing cohesion among men and
between them and their conditions of existence) as different from
the particular function of ideology in class societies, where that
general function was dominated by the new function of securing
the domination of one class over the others. Now Althusser formally
distinguishes between the 'theory of ideology in general' and the
'theory of particular ideologies'.

This second theory refers to ideologies in concrete historical social
formations, which depend on a certain combination of modes of
production and on a specific class struggle. Hence, ideologies have
a history. The theory of ideology in general, on the contrary, deals
with ideology as

endowed with a structure and a functioning such as to make it a non-
historical reality, i.e. an *omni-historical* reality, in the sense in which that
structure and functioning are immutable, present in the same form throughout what we can call history. . . .[94]

Therefore, ideology in general has no history. Just as Freud's
unconscious was said to be eternal, so Althusser proposes that
'*ideology is eternal*, exactly like the unconscious'.[95] What is crucial is
that for Althusser the theory of ideologies 'depends for the most
part on a theory of ideology in general'.[96]

Just as the implicit question of the early treatment of ideology
was how men came to accept the tasks and roles allocated to them
by society, the question now for Althusser is how the skills of labour
power, and labour power itself, are reproduced in capitalist society.
His reply is, just as before, that this reproduction can only occur 'in
the forms and under the forms of ideological subjection'.[97] But in
order to fully understand this mechanism an addition should be
made to the theory of the state by distinguishing repressive state
apparatuses from ideological state apparatuses. While the former
function primarily by repression, the latter function mainly by
ideology. The reproduction of the relations of production is secured
for the most part 'by the exercise of state power in the State Appara-

tuses, on the one hand the (Repressive) State Apparatus, on the other the Ideological State Apparatuses'.[98] But while the former secures the political conditions for the operation of the latter, it is in the ISA that the ruling ideology is concentrated, thus specifically securing the reproduction of the relations of production. Among them the Educational ISA which has the predominance in capitalist society, because

it takes children from every class at infant-school age, and then for years . . . it drums into them . . . a certain amount of 'know-how' wrapped in the ruling ideology . . . or simply the ruling ideology in its pure state. . . .

Each mass ejected *en route* is practically provided with the ideology which suits the role it has to fulfil in class society: the role of the exploited . . . the role of the agent of exploitation . . . of the agent of repression . . . or of the professional ideologist.[99]

As far as ideology in general is concerned. Althusser now solves the problem of its definition. Of the two early alternative formulations – ideology as a representation of the world and ideology as representation of man's 'lived' relation to the world – he reaffirms the one contained in *For Marx*, and thus he asserts that 'ideology is a representation of the imaginary relationship of individuals to their real conditions of existence'.[100] Ideology is not produced because a small group of men invent falsified representations of reality or because men express the alienated character of their conditions of existence. Ideology projects not the real world but the relationship between man and their reality. Ideology has not an ideal existence but a material existence, it always 'exists in an apparatus, and its practice, or practices'.[101] Individuals 'live' in ideology by participating in certain practices within specific ideological apparatuses. Hence, 'there is no practice except by and in an ideology'. Althusser's final aim is to show that 'there is no ideology except by the subject and for subjects'.[102] In effect, he presents the central mechanism of ideology as an interpellation of individuals which constitutes them as subjects. Ideology thus appears duplicated into an imaginary Subject and subjects. Ideology is the Subject who holds 'speculary' relationships with individual subjects. They recognize themselves as free subjects in the Subject, and are therefore subjected to It. Individual subjects are thus constituted as such by submitting to the Subject; they act in so far as they are acted by ideology.

Althusser's distinction between the theory of ideology in general and the theory of particular ideologies is highly problematic for a Marxist approach. It entails the pretension of constituting ideology as an immutable object of study across the various modes of production. One can formulate and use some abstract concepts applicable to various modes of production. Yet they cannot be the object of a general theory, and even less can they be assumed the basis upon which regional and class ideologies depend. Marx proceeded the other way around. If he accepted the existence of abstract categories – labour, production, consumption and so on – which are valid for all epochs, it was with the clear consciousness that they 'are nevertheless, in the specific character of this abstraction, themselves likewise a product of historic relations, and possess their full validity only for and within these relations'.[103]

For Marx, ideology in general, just as production or labour in general, have no substance or validity, such that, by themselves, they could explain the way in which they appear in specific situations. Abstract concepts do not 'manifest' or 'realize' themselves in concrete situations. Even when Marx analyses the labour process in general and recognizes that, as such, it is common to every social phase of its existence, he adds: 'as the taste of the porridge does not tell you who grew the oats, no more does this simple process tell you of itself what are the social conditions under which it is taking place'.[104] There is no possible connection between the abstraction of ideology in general and concrete ideologies such that by starting from the general one can deduce the conditions of the concrete.

Althusser's contention that the theory of particular ideologies depends on the theory of ideology in general is clearly mistaken and borders on idealism. In a related situation, Marx criticizes Proudhon precisely because he considers abstract categories as primary causes. According to Proudhon, Marx says, 'they, and not men, make history. The *abstraction*, the *category taken as such*, i.e. apart from men and their material activities, is of course, immortal, unchangeable, immutable, it is simply an entity of pure reason . . .'.[105] A dualism is then introduced between practical life and abstract categories as if the former were the application of the latter.

Between Althusser's first writings and *Lenin and Philosophy*, a change has occurred. At the beginning the general function of ideology was applicable even to classless societies; now the functioning of ideology is said to be immutable, present in the same form throughout the history of class societies. Yet this change does not really amount to considering class struggle. In defining ideology and the process of reproduction, class contradictions are not taken into account, either as specific to each mode of production or as an abstract general mechanism. The impression is given that ideology in general as much as the ideology of the ruling classes are unproblematically realized in certain apparatuses and imposed upon society even against, and precisely by means of, the efforts of a conscious minority. This is why Althusser apologizes to progressive teachers: 'so little do they suspect it that their own devotion contributes to the maintenance and nourishment of this ideological representation of the School . . .'.[106]

In a belated Post-Scriptum to his article on ISA,[107] Althusser recognizes the abstract character of his former analysis. He now accepts that the point of view of the class struggle must be introduced for the analysis of ideologies and their 'realization' in ISAs. Yet this does not solve the problem. As Hirst has argued, the general mechanism of ideology and the 'concrete' conditions are merely brought together and they are not shown to relate theoretically.[108] Class struggle appears a foreign addition to a general mechanism of ideology constituted outside its influence. Class struggle cannot be introduced from without as a mere 'overdetermining' factor. To avoid a dualism Althusser should do away with the theory of ideology in general, not merely supplement it. In so far as ideology in general can subsist as the object of a theory which of itself does not consider class struggle, the objective role of such a theory will be the concealment of that struggle. In Marx's terms, the theory of ideology in general is an ideological theory.

Even more, ideology in general has the characteristics of a hypostatized transcendental subject, which, by interpellating individuals, constitutes them as subjects. To challenge humanism and historicism, Althusser rejects the notion of the constitutive subject and propounds instead, the constitution of the subject by ideology. Hirst has shown how this inversion has not really displaced the concept of subject and its identification with the human subject. Yet the subject appears now not as an essence, but as an effect. In this way, Hirst maintains, the subject is not hypostatized as in the humanist tradition.[109] Hirst does not however, consider whether, in pursuing the concept of a non-hypostatized subject, Althusser may have hypostatized ideology itself. The subject becomes an effect at the cost of ideology becoming constitutive, as a new essence. One might see in this inversion the elements of a Hegelian conception in which historical class ideologies and human subjects become manifestations and instruments by means of which ideology in general (the Idea, one may say) unfolds itself.

In criticizing Althusser's first writings on ideology, Rancière has pointed out that they try to reconcile the general function which structural-functionalism assigns to the 'value system' of every society and the function which Marx assigns to ideology. They appear to compromise between the necessity of social cohesion 'in general' and class domination 'in particular', between Durkheimian sociology and historical materialism.[110] Apparently, Althusser has presented the problem under a different light when, instead of social cohesion, he proposes the question about the reproduction of the relations of production. Yet this is a mere terminological illusion. As Hirst has shown, this question, too, is equivalent to the functionalist inquiry: how is it possible for capitalist social relations to exist? Rightly enough, Hirst points out that 'no general answer can be given to this question which is not functionalist'.[111] Indeed Althusser's new context of the reproduction of relations of production does not differ from his early concern about social cohesion and the acceptance of social roles by individual subjects. As Hirst shows, Althusser equates the relations of production with the functions assigned to economic agents understood as human subjects.[112]

Just as ideology in general loses its historical character, science also appears stripped of its connection with social contradictions. In Althusser's Leninist formulation, science came from without to rescue the spontaneous ideological consciousness of the working class. In his theoretical formulation, science constitutes itself by breaking with ideological knowledge at the moment of its inception. In both cases, science appears located above class struggle. At least in the Leninist formula, spontaneous consciousness appeared as ideological as the result of the domination of bourgeois ideology. In the second formula, however, ideology is just the material basis for the emergence of science; the opposition between ideology and science becomes an abstract confrontation between truth and error. Althusser is at least consistent in linking the overcoming of ideology with the emergence of science, as he conceives both phenomena to exist beyond historical contingencies. But the picture one gets is similar to a battle in heaven between two non-historical and transcendent actors, ideology and science, which are engaged in a permanent struggle. The reality of the concrete historical ideological struggle between classes would be just a reflection, a secondary and relative one, of the real transcendent world.

In his *Essays in Self-Criticism*, Althusser revises his conception of the relation between science and ideology. He recognizes that

Marx was able to break with bourgeois ideology 'because he took inspiration from the basic ideas of proletarian ideology, and from the first class struggles of the proletariat . . .'.[113] Yet there is no explicit disavowal of his distinction between the theory of ideology in general and the theory of particular ideologies; the seeds of an ahistorical concept of ideology remain unchallenged. True, there has been a change. In the first writings the source of the distorted character of men's representations of their conditions of existence is the natural opacity of the social structure; in *Lenin and Philosophy*, Althusser abandons that explanation. For a start, he rejects the idea that the imaginary representation reflects the conditions of existence; rather it reflects men's relation to those conditions of existence. So, he argues, the question of the 'cause' of the distortion disappears. The new question is why the relation represented by ideology is necessarily an imaginary relation. As Hirst shows, this new question is left unanswered.[114] In other words, the abandonment of the question about the cause of distortion and its structuralist answer is carried out at the cost of failing to answer the new question; the imaginary relation is left without fundament.

For Marx, the justification of the distortion of ideology lies in the fact that men cannot solve in their minds the contradictions they are unable to solve in practice. By putting forward the idea of a revolutionary practice capable of practically solving contradictions, Marx can conceive the fundament of a non-ideological consciousness. Althusser's theory of ideology, on the contrary, is the theory of the necessary domination of ideology. Ideology is a functional requirement of society, which constitutes subjects in their imaginary relations to their world as if their minds were just helpless and passive. Althusser's theory overlooks the very essence of the origin of ideology in class contradictions and thus cannot conceive a way out, other than resorting to the precarious solution of science.

Yet as ideology is a functional requirement of society, the challenge presented by science is necessarily a never-ending battle; it cannot be won. Ideology can be unmasked by science, but cannot be overcome in its source; it will always subsist. Althusser cannot envisage a defeat of ideology because its theoretical approach leaves no role for a revolutionary practice which may change the source of ideology. True, Marx, also accepts the unmasking role of science. Yet his point was not just the understanding or unmasking but the change of circumstances. Marx accepts that science could not be automatically derived from a transforming practice, yet it cannot be separated from it either.[115] Althusser does not consider class contradictions in the origin of ideology; science also appears detached from class contradictions. Althusser has substituted a functional requirement for the origin of ideology in contradictions and has consequently substituted 'theoretical practice' for revolutionary practice. In this he is indeed consistent but it cannot be said to represent Marx's theory.

True, ideology may appear to protect the interest of the dominant class, and science to represent the interests of the dominated classes. But one can hardly find a rigorous justification for this allocation if class struggle is absent from the very concepts of ideology and science. As Rancière has shown, this is a kind of metaphysical articulation by means of which the pair science–ideology introduces class struggle and vice-versa.[116] Furthermore, the conception is contradictory with Althusser's early distinction between dominant and dominated ideologies. One wonders how ideology can be necessary for social cohesion or reproduction and simultaneously express protest from the exploited classes. If ideology can express protest, then it cannot serve social cohesion. It may be argued that cohesion or reproduction is not affected by a protest spontaneously made in the language and with the logic of the dominant ideology. What Lenin showed in the case of the spontaneous working-class consciousness, Althusser tries to show in the case of the few progressive educators. This may be so. But the problem remains: why can protest arise and take any expression whatsoever if ideology is really performing its functional role?

Summing up, there are two main criticisms to Althusser's theory of ideology. Firstly, its non-historical character leads to its being the theory of the social necessity of ideology. Secondly, its incorrect, though consistent, solution to the relations between ideology and science leads to the over-rating of the role of science and the disregarding of revolutionary practice. Althusser's structuralism sets out to curb the idealism of 'historicism' which lays too much emphasis on the false consciousness of the subject. However, by going to the other extreme it makes of ideology an objectified functional requirement of all societies and falls into another form of idealism. The epistemological idealism of the false consciousness has been superseded by the transcendental idealism of the eternal ideology.

Semiology 2: *Tel Quel*

A number of problems besetting structuralism and linguistics have also been noticed and criticized by some French intellectuals grouped around the journal *Tel Quel*. While still considering language as the key to understanding social reality and ideology, they try to set a new direction to semiology. Among them one could mention J. Kristeva, P. Sollers, J. L. Baudry and even Barthes himself, who has moved towards a similar outlook since *S/Z*. In England, R. Coward and J. Ellis represent the same line of thought.[117]

This particular position within semiology attempts to bring together linguistics, Althusserian Marxism and Lacanian psychoanalysis. It starts from a critique of the early semiological analyses, which concentrated too much on a synchronic approach and disregarded the conception of meaning as production. The relationship between signifier and signified was unilaterally taken to mean a given correspondence within a system, without realizing that the signifier could also have a role in producing the signified. For Kristeva the sign can be approached both as a product and as a process of production. In the first case it is possible to make a structural description of a system of relations. But this does not suffice. Semiology must go beyond to find how meaning is produced in the text itself: the text appears as a process of production of meaning.

While the early semiological analyses were content to study the structuration of signs within a system, Kristeva proposes now a different analysis she calls 'Semanalysis', a

theory of textual signification which considers the sign as a specular element which secures the representation of this begetting – this process of germination – which is internal to it but also encompasses it, and whose laws it is necessary to define. In other words, without forgetting that the text presents a system of signs, 'Semanalysis' opens inside that system a different scene: that which the screen of the structure conceals, and which is the meaning as operation....[118]

Before a work or book was taken as a closed message, as a product; now the work is presented as a text, as a meaningful production. Semanalysis proposes a theory of texts as producers of meanings; it is concerned with how the text means, not so much with what it means. Yet every text, is in turn, produced by other texts; the production of meaning is a form of *intertextuality*, that is, the way in which a text works other texts, in order to produce a new text:

> In order to analyse the structuration of the novel rather than the structure, we shall situate it within the totality of previous or synchronic texts ... so as to study the structuration of the text as transformation, we shall picture it as a textual dialogue or, better, as inter-textuality.[119]

For Kristeva, a text is not a structured meaning, present in a linguistic corpus, it is rather its begetting. Of course, this begetting is inscribed in a linguistic corpus, but this is just a 'pheno-text', the printed text, which is intelligible only by the 'geno-text', its genesis. The pheno-text is the surface, the signified structure, whereas the geno-text is the foundation, the significant productivity.[120] The ideological phenomenon appears precisely in the process of production of meaning. While structural linguistics had collapsed ideology into language, Semanalysis finds ideology in the textual production of meaning. Thus, for instance, Barthes, in his early writings, had identified ideology with a connotative second system which took over an innocent language (denotation). *Tel Quel* questions this separation. Ideology is present in the process of constitution of every sign and operates by closing the meaning of the text. As Barthes himself puts it after his change of mind,

> denotation is not the first sense, but pretends to be; under this illusion, it is ultimately only the *last* of connotations (that which seems at once to found and close the reading), the superior myth by which the text pretends to return to the nature of language, to language as nature.[121]

So ideology is no longer conceived as a connotated level but as the reduction of the production of meaning to only one signification which seems natural.

This fixing of meaning is accomplished in relation to the subject. But while structural linguistics implicitly assumed that both meaning and subject were given, now both appear to be 'produced' in the discursive work of the text. Even the author of the text acquires a new character. As Baudry puts it, 'in this perspective, the subject, the cause of the writing, vanish himself and the author, the "writer" with him. . . . It is not an author that signs a work *but a text that signs a name*.'[122] If this is so for the author, it is even more so for the reader. The subject is specifically constructed for a certain meaning. In Coward's and Ellis's terms, 'ideology is conceived as the way in which a subject is produced in language to represent his/herself and therefore able to act in the social totality, the fixity of those representations being the function of ideology'.[123] The analysis of how these fix representations are produced for/in the subject, they argue, can only be carried out by a special kind of psychoanalysis which incorporates linguistic theory, that is, Lacanian psychoanalysis, the only theory which can scientifically analyse the subjective processes of the construction of the subject and can account for the positioning of the subject in language.

According to Coward and Ellis, the problem of the subject is crucial for Marxism. Aware of the shortcomings of both extreme structuralism and historicism, they contend that 'Marxism cannot conceive of a subject who remains outside the structure, manipulating it or acting as a mere support, if it did so, it would cease to be a revolutionary philosophy'.[124] In close dialogue with Althusser's theory of ideology they criticize the traditional Marxist conception of ideology as a 'system of ideas' or 'false consciousness': it is not the subject that produces distorted ideas, but it is rather ideology that produces the subject. Ideology is, therefore, 'a practice of representation, a practice to produce a specific articulation, that is, producing certain meanings and necessitating certain subjects as their supports'.[125] The subject appears as the place of crystallization of certain practices and of a certain horizon which naturally and unconsciously control the way he acts and feels. To the extent that subjects are produced for certain representations, in an unconscious process, they are led to believe that they are the producers (Althusser). But this is an ideological effect.

Ideology has a material character, not only because it is expressed in material apparatuses and practices as Althusser puts it, but also because 'it works to fix the subject in certain position in relation to certain fixities of discourse'.[126] To this extent, Coward and Ellis believe that Althusser's theory is limited and gives insufficient credit to the family as the main ideological apparatus where the subject is produced in relation to a certain meaning. The character of this meaning is its closure, the fact that it delimits the mental horizon, thus fixing the individual. Althusser' also fails to see that the subject thus produced is traversed by contradictions and is not homogeneous. In this sense, the work of ideology produces the continuity of the ego; 'it puts in place the contradictory subject, puts him in positions of coherence and responsibility for his own actions so that he is able to act'.[127] This is why the subject appears to be the origin of his own activity. By closing off contradictions, ideology gives to the subject the appearance of unity.

Only Lacanian psychoanalysis can provide an account of how this process actually happens. Although Althusser has produced the most advanced Marxist formulations on the subject, he still cannot show how the subject is constructed in contradiction and thus cannot explain the ideological crisis of the subject in conflict with ideology. So it appears as if the dialectical process in society, which is based upon contradictions, leaves man 'untouched as a unity, in conflict with others but never with himself'.[128] *Tel Quel* proposes, on the contrary, the existence of a subject which, like society, is 'in process', a subject whose identity is in crisis. As Kristeva puts it,

the logical expression of objective processes, negativity can only yield a subject in process, the subject which constitutes itself according to the law of negativity, that is, according to the laws of objective reality: it can only be a subject crossed over by this negativity, opened onto by a non-subjected free objectivity in movement. A subject immersed in negativity ceases to be 'external' to objective negativity, a transcendent unity, a monad to specific rules, but rather places itself at the moment which is the 'most interior', the most objective in the life of the spirit' (Lenin).[129]

Many of the criticisms which *Tel Quel* levels against the early practice of semiology and structural linguistic seem pertinent. They show problematic areas which have either received unsatisfactory solutions or been entirely disregarded. Yet its own solutions, which bravely draw from sources as different as Marxism and psychoanalysis, run into even more serious problems. In effect, *Tel Quel* wants to found its theory of texts on an articulation of Marx with Freud; it seems to contend, further, that their articulation is the only means to avoid both idealism and mechanical materialism. Freud without Marx leads to idealism; Marx without Freud leads to mechanical materialism. This is why Sollers sees in the attempt to separate them the work of bourgeois ideology.[130] A genuine materialism would require the integration of both. A first problem arises from the fact that this current openly identifies Marxism with Althusser and Freudianism with Lacan. As Sollers puts it, Althusser and Lacan 'have profoundly transformed, in a rapport of productive difference with the University, the field of knowledge. What is at stake here is decisive: it is the problem of the articulation of Marx and Lenin with Freud.'[131] Not only are these identifications assumed without major discussion or justification, but also there is the consequent tendency to impute the shortcomings of interpreters to the original authors, thus conveying a misleading and confusing impression.

A typical example is provided by Coward and Ellis. First, they expose Althusser's arguments against humanism and conclude that man is not the origin of society but, on the contrary, society is the origin of man. From here, they misleadingly derive that 'Marxist analysis of society treats men, real concrete men, as the bearers, the supports of these relations which determine them,'[132] even worse, by basing themselves on this account (which is in fact Althusser's) they conclude that 'clearly, there is something missing in the Marxist analysis of the subject'.[133] The point is not whether there is something missing in Marx's analysis – which in principle could be the case – but is that the argument has been concerned not with Marx's statements but with Althusser's. Another example, this time about the interpretation of Lacan, is mentioned by D. Adlam and A. Salfield.[134] Coward's and Ellis's account of Lacan is based on Laplanche's and Leclaire's article entitled 'The unconscious: a psychoanalytic study' whose interpretation has been repudiated by Lacan himself.[135] The problem is not so much the repudiation itself as the question it poses about the nature of the unconscious in Lacanian theory and its relation to Freud's conception. As Adam and Salfield put it, the question is thus: is the unconscious,

as *Language and Materialism* seems to assert, to be conceived as the site of plurality and diversity *in general*? or is it to be conceived as in some sense closer to the Freudian concept as the site of repressed, unspeakable but *definite* representations?[136]

A second problem concerns the meaning of 'genuine materialism'. We have already seen that for Coward and Ellis this means mainly an analysis of the process by which the subject is produced for/in fixed relations of predication. Their insistence that this analysis can only be met by psychoanalysis makes them disregard what Marx saw as the essence of materialism: the determining character of historical material practice.[137] Content with analysing and criticizing Althusser for not being sufficiently psychoanalytic, they forget to mention what Marx considered the premises of materialist method. Marx argues that the mode of production is a definite form of activity of individuals:

as individuals express their life, so they are. What they are, therefore coincides with their production, both with *what* they produce and with *how* they produce. The nature of individuals thus depends on the material conditions determining their production.[138]

In *Capital* he basically recognizes the same, that man by 'acting on the external world and changing it, he at the same time changes his own nature'.[139] To use Coward's and Ellis's own image, the subject is produced by/in its material practice.

This is a long way away from holding, as Coward and Ellis do, that genuine materialism mainly entails the production of the subject for/in ideological representations. True, like Althusser, they take ideology as a material force. But one wonders whether this is not a conflation of ideology with its material base. For Marx, the fact that ideology has a material base is not to be confused with ideology *being* the material base. This is why he argues that his conception of history does not explain practice from the idea but explains the formation of ideas from material practice.[140]

I am not denying the active role of ideology in society. It is just that its so-called 'relative autonomy' has become in this account an absolute autonomy. Ideology appears as constitutive of the subject, and its own determinacy has been consistently obscured. There can be good arguments for proceeding in this way, but it is surely too much to maintain that this is *the* 'genuine' materialism.[141]

By this transposition, ideology, as articulations which constitute subjects as support for their meanings, is inflated and extended to the point that it acquires the crucial determining character within society. What is more, its main function of fixing the subject for/in a certain meaning can only be challenged at the level of the individual. This is why Marxism on its own would not be able to account for the struggle between the closure of ideology and subjective processes. In other words, Marxism would not have the elements, the instruments for analysing the dynamic force of change which supposedly springs from the divided individual. Psychoanalysis can do this. Consequently, the only possibility of revolutionary action is the psychoanalytic break of the imaginary unity and closeness which ideology imposes upon each individual. As Coward and Ellis put it 'until Marxism can produce a revolutionary subject, revolutionary change will be impossible'.[142]

This is a complete inversion of what Marx asserts, that 'the coincidence of the changing of circumstances and of human activity or self-changing can be conceived and rationally understood only as *revolutionary practice*',[143] and that this practice is conditioned by material forces in society. Two consequences follow. First, the change of the subject is not prior to the change of circumstances; on the contrary, it can be achieved only by means of that revolutionary practice. Second, this practice is not dependent upon the free will or psychological forces of individuals, but is conditioned by material forces. The psychoanalytical account, on the contrary, transfers the basis of revolution to the individual. Just as ideology produces the subject for a reactionary meaning, psychoanalysis produces the subject for a revolutionary meaning. There is nothing really materialist in this conceptualization. It is just a return to idealism: meanings and discourses become constitutive while the subjects become passively 'acted' by them.

6 Ideology and science: Marx and the contemporary debate

The problem

The relationships between science and ideology are not easy to sort out. The complexity of the matter is due, to a great extent, to the many meanings which each concept may assume and the distinctions and different characteristics bestowed upon each by various authors and currents of thought. To tackle some of the problems involved in this complex relationship I shall outline a possible scheme within which they may be better understood. First of all, we can take the viewpoint of ideology and its comprehension. Here we have two possible broad meanings which have already been mentioned; ideology understood in a positive way, and ideology understood as having a negative content.

Ideology with a positive meaning refers to a system of opinions, values and knowledge which are connected with certain class interests and whose cognitive value may vary. Distortion is not of the essence of the concept of ideology. Thus there may be ideologies based upon scientific premises and ideologies based upon pre-scientific or non-scientific assumptions. Within the Marxist orthodox tradition initiated by Lenin, for instance, the scientific or non-scientific character of ideology is determined by the specificity of class interests which condition knowledge. This allocation of cognitive value is sometimes supported by a distinction between ascendant and descendant classes.[1] This allows a proletarian ideology to be called 'scientific', whereas bourgeois ideology is considered non-scientific.

The important thing here is that ideology in itself is not a concept to be distinguished from science. Ideology could be 'scientific'. If it is not scientific, this is not due to its being ideology but, rather, due to its being developed within the scope of certain specific class interests. Ideology is non-antithetical to science – it could also be a science: the distinction between science and ideology is blurred. The most important consequence of this conception is the loss of the concept of ideology as a critical notion.

When the concept of ideology is taken in its negative meaning, the differences between ideology and science come to the fore. Ideology is distorted knowledge, whereas science is true knowledge. While ideology remains trapped in the appearances, science manages to penetrate the phenomenal forms of reality, uncovering the laws and the real relations beneath the surface. Yet the distinction between a negative concept of ideology and science can be construed in two different ways.

First of all, ideology can be seen as the opposite or antithesis of science, and the distortions of ideology as mere cognitive errors. The relationship between science and ideology is the opposition between truth and error. In so far as true knowledge appears the only means to surpass error, science appears as the way to overcome ideology. Ideology and science assume opposite characteristics which are irreducible to one another. Science involves a kind of cognition entirely different from ideological cognition.

This way of understanding the relationship is typical of certain traditions of positivist origin, like the Vienna school, and can also be said to encompass some Marxist theories linked with structuralism like Althusser's. These traditions are very much concerned with the criteria of demarcation between science and ideology. The differences between these two concepts are not a matter of degree; they involve a qualitative distinction which allows science to overcome ideology.

Second, ideology can be interpreted as different from science, though not its antithesis. Despite their differences, science cannot possibly defeat ideology, as ideology is rooted in social contradictions. Ideology is not simply a cognitive error which can be overcome by a more adequate cognition. Nor does science exhaust the concept of truth. There are errors which are not ideological, and there are truths which may be found beyond the actual cognition of society as it is. The specificity of the ideological error is the fact that it conceals contradictions. The only truth which may successfully defeat this particular error is the practical solution of those contradictions. Ideology cannot be dispelled by simple theoretical means because its roots are beyond the boundaries of mere intellectual mistakes. This position, I think, can be attributed to Marx.

If we now take the viewpoint of science, the second term of the relationship we are analysing, further distinctions can be introduced which in some respects overlap those detected from the viewpoint of ideology. If we consider the relationships between social sciences and natural sciences relevant to the analysis, we may arrive at a new three-fold scheme. A first possibility is to consider science as having a universal identity which recognizes no fundamental difference between social and natural sciences. This position is held by the various positivist traditions and is also implicitly accepted by Althusser.

In general, the positivist viewpoint accepts that the method of science is basically unitary, although there may be peculiarities between individual sciences. Thus, this conception does not regard social sciences as a particular case more prone to ideology. Science in general is antithetical to ideology: consequently, scientific knowledge of society is opposite to ideology in that it accounts for objective facts, is verifiable and studies its object through a particular method whose logic is public and common to all sciences. The gap between ideology and science is not diminished when the object under study is society.

The Althusserian formulation, bearing Bachelard's influence, describes this gap as an 'epistemological break'. The ideological problematic may be overcome by science only when its terms are replaced. A mere refutation or falsification of past theories does not suffice if the same terms of the problem are maintained. The overcoming of ideology implies new terms, a new problematic. This epistemological break is as strong a criterion of demarcation as that which the Vienna school conceived between science and metaphysics. In general, this first position is characterized by its rationalism, which makes scientific knowledge the paradigm of all worthwhile cognition and which confronts ideology as the 'total other' to be overcome by the advance of that very scientific knowledge.

A second possibility arises when social sciences are forcefully distinguished from natural sciences. Here are some traditions of romantic and idealist origin which do not accept the existence of only one valid pattern of knowledge; they introduce a sharp distinction between the methods and contents of social sciences (*Geisteswissenschaften*) and those of natural sciences (*Naturwissenschaften*). The hermeneutical tradition, for instance, considers that causality, empirical verification and experiment are not applicable to human sciences, where a kind of 'intuition' (an 'understanding' or *Verstehen* is necessary to support meaningful assertions. Human history is not predictable as a physical phenomenon according to certain causes and verifiable laws. Historical knowledge is in need of 'understanding', of a particular kind of comprehension which starts with the personal experience of the analyst.

This distinction between two kinds of knowledge has its direct antecedent in the Kantian distinction between phenomenon and noumenon. The phenomenal world of nature is subjected to causal laws whereas the noumenal world of spirit lacks that determination and can be grasped only by a special kind of understanding. Stedman Jones has argued that hermeneutics not only maintains this Kantian tradition but goes further to affirm the superiority of historical knowledge over scientific knowledge.[2] This is the origin of a certain distrust of science as practised in the world of nature. The human world should be excluded from the positive ascription of causes in so far as that method seeks to manipulate, to secure dominion over things. And this manipulation of nature impoverishes and dehumanizes man.

From the anti-positivist and rather conservative position of hermeneutics, other equally anti-positivist but progressive positions developed. Marxism and its critique of bourgeois society presents a good vehicle to continue the anti-scientist line of thought. If science and technology have served the bourgeoisie to exploit the working class, it is indeed tempting to identify the class-orientated manipulation of men with the instrumental manipulation of nature, an identification which leads to the comprehension of science as ideology.

Lukács started by studying reification in capitalist society and soon found a suspicious harmony between capitalist society and 'science'. In accepting the immediacy of data as a basis for scientific work, science falls into the typical bourgeois reification which accepts the given as the unalterable foundation of society. The Frankfurt school follows with a critique of the instrumental and subjective rationality which permeates scientific industrialization. The dominion over nature has transformed itself into the basis of the dominion over man. Marcuse and Habermas are perhaps the most explicit representatives of this line of thinking today. Both insist on technology and instrumental practice as the new source of ideology in advanced capitalism.

This tradition, which separates natural sciences from human sciences, ends up by introducing the idea of science as ideology. While the positivist-orientated tradition believes that ideology is actually defeated by science, the German school of Kantian origin asserts that science itself may be ideological. The former believes in science as the paradigm of knowledge; the latter gives no special character to science with respect to other kinds of knowledge. On the contrary, it is ready to see fetishization or reification in science. The former thinks that ideological critique is carried out by science and its method; the latter affirms that it is carried out by 'critical theory' or the 'critique of ideologies'.

There is still a third way of understanding the relationships between social sciences and natural sciences. This position follows a different approach which rejects both total identification and sharp separation between human and natural sciences. The relationships between them derive from the more basic relations existing between historical society and nature, which are not to be opposed. The history of society is a part of natural history: natural history, in turn, is only conceivable with reference to human society. Yet neither aspects can be reduced to the other. They maintain a set of relationships which, as Schmidt has put it, could be called a 'differentiated unity'.[3]

This differentiated unity is ultimately justified by the fact that men are themselves part of nature while nature itself is mediated by human practice. In this conception science is neither the antithesis of ideology nor a mere form of ideology. Ideology, in turn, is not a simple cognitive error nor is it founded upon scientific rationality. Yet science is not a separated sphere, excluded from ideological penetration. Ideology may try to present itself as science. The differential character of human mediation in nature and society means that this danger affects more decisively the comprehension of society than that of nature. This, I believe is again Marx's viewpoint.

I think three main positions deserve attention: the position which holds science against ideology; the position which understands science as ideology; and, finally, Marx's dialectical position. I therefore concentrate upon these three viewpoints.[4]

Science and ideology in Marx

Marx's ideas on science underwent an evolution along with his own intellectual development. This evolution, on the one hand, deepened Marx's critique of current conceptions, and on the other it added new elements and completed some of his fundamental earlier intuitions. Although I do not think that one can possibly find dramatic leaps or even one decisive 'epistemological break' in his intellectual development, it is natural that certain moments condense the process of introduction of a new emphasis or the finding of a new perspective or dimension to the problem in question.[5]

The *Theses on Feuerbach* may be considered as one of these representative moments. Before Marx's critique of abstract materialism in 1845, no concept of ideology had been yet thoroughly developed but Marx's ideas on science, nevertheless, take a more distinct form. The basic intuition – one which will remain throughout Marx's work – is the unity between natural science and the science of man. 'History itself is a *real* part of *natural history* and of nature's becoming man. Natural science will in time subsume the science of man just as the science of man will subsume natural science; there will be *one* science'.[6] Hence for Marx it is possible to speak of 'the social reality of nature' as much as of 'the natural science of man'.

Marx's emphasis upon the unity of science does not mean that he thinks it already an accomplished fact. Philosophy has remained alien to the natural sciences just as these have remained alien to philosophy. But now the real foundation of the unity has been found. And it is Feuerbach who gets the honours for having accomplished the task: 'Feuerbach's great achievement is . . . to have founded *true materialism* and *real science* by making the social relation of "man to man" the basic principle of his theory'.[7]

The foundation of the unity of science is the human essence, human nature. 'The whole of history is a preparation, a development, for "*man*" to become the object of *sensuous* consciousness . . .'[8]; up to now the history of industry 'has not been grasped in its connection with the *nature* of man . . .'.[9] Industry is therefore the 'exoteric revelation of man's essential powers', an open book where one can find man's psychology in tangible form'.

The importance Marx concedes to this notion of human essence – whose Feuerbachian origin should not be disregarded – is further shown in the fact that both philosophy and natural science are criticized for failing to conform to it. Natural science has an 'abstractly material, or rather idealist orientation' because it has not grasped its own history in connection with the nature of man. Likewise, philosophy and religion are seen – following Feuerbach – as a form of the estrangement of man's nature.

Marx's insistence upon the unity of science being based on human essence leads him to detect, at this early phase, the double character which the independent development of natural science has had for human life. Natural science has intervened practically through industry and 'has prepared the conditions for human emancipation, however much its immediate effect was to complete the process of dehumanization'.[10] This liberating and simultaneously dehumanizing character of science is a feature Marx will also uphold in his mature writings.

With the *Theses on Feuerbach* Marx explicitly separates himself from abstract materialism. In the concept of science there is a change of perspective. The idea of a unified science is kept but on a different basis, one which replaces human nature by history:

> We know only a single science, the science of history. One can look at history from two sides, and divide it into the history of nature and the history of men. The two sides are, however, inseparable; the history of nature and the history of men are dependent on each other so long as men exist.[11]

True, the priority of external nature remains unassailed,

> but this difference has meaning only insofar as man is considered to be distinct from nature. For that matter, nature, the nature that preceded human history, is not by any means the nature in which Feuerbach lives. . . .[12]

Even the most pure natural science is mediated by man's practice, by industry.

As is evident, the unity of science is now based upon historical practice, and no longer upon the essence of man. The concept of practice has become central. Feuerbach resolved religion into the human essence as an abstraction inherent in each individual. Thus he was compelled to abstract from the historical process.[13] Now Marx proposes to understand the 'earthly core' of religion in history. If Marx previously criticized natural science for not having grasped its own history in connection with man's nature, now he criticizes the Feuerbachian foundation of science for accepting an abstract conception of human nature and excluding the historical process. Marx previously endorsed Feuerbach's endeavour to discover the earthly core of religion by analysis and his conclusion that religion was man's alienation; Marx now thinks that the earthly core of religion should be both 'understood in its contradiction and revolutionized in practice'.[14]

Later on, in *Capital*, Marx will synthesize this change of perspective when he affirms that it is, in reality, much easier to discover by analysis the earthly core of the misty creations of religion, than, conversely, it is, to develop from the actual relations of life the corresponding celestialized forms of those relations. The latter method is the only materialistic, and therefore, the only scientific one.[15]

Science should be founded on the historical analysis of social relations, and no longer on the analysis of philosophy or religion. The real character of philosophy and religion can be derived from social relations, which cannot be derived from philosophical principles. That is why Marx asserts that 'when reality is depicted, philosophy as an independent branch of knowledge loses its medium of existence'. 'Where speculation ends – in real life – there real, positive science begins . . .'.[16]

The concept of ideology is born out of this context; therefore it emphasizes, at this stage, the inversions of German philosophy which 'descends from heaven to earth', not explaining the formation of ideas from material practice but explaining practice from the idea. Ideology appears the inversion in the order of determination, as if ideas could rule over material life. Marx criticizes the Young Hegelians, for they attribute an independent existence to the products of consciousness.[17] A similar criticism is later made of Proudhon, who, as a true philosopher, sees 'things upside down, sees in the real relations only the incarnation of these principles . . .'.[18] These inversions thwart the sight of material social relations and therefore conceal the real contradictions. The problems of men are reduced to the sway of certain wrong ideas over them.

This is why Marx's new historical science of social relations is not to be construed as the antithesis of ideology. If mere ideas were the real chains of men, as the Young Hegelians believed, then a critique of those illusions would suffice to dispel them. But ideas cannot be detached from the material conditions of their production. Only by revolutionizing these conditions can ideology be destroyed. Marx concludes that the products of consciousness cannot be dissolved by science or mental criticism but only by the practical overthrow of actual social relations, 'that not criticism but revolution is the driving force of history . . .'.[19] Therefore, from the very beginning the concept of ideology does not oppose the concept of science as error opposes truth.

None the less, science does contribute to the understanding of ideology. By studying real social relations science can show how ideas are spiritualized forms of these material relations, how the various categories are the theoretical expressions, the abstractions, of social relations. That is why Marx says to the utopian theoreticians that 'they no longer need to seek science in their minds; they have only to take note of what is happening before their eyes and to become the mouthpiece of this'.[20]

Now it is evident that in showing the new point of departure of science Marx has emphasized the change from human essence and other philosophical principles to the historical social relations which are empirically verifiable. Yet this new point of departure still appears unproblematic, as though it was simply a matter of turning towards reality, allowing empirical observation to bring out the inner connections of that reality.[21] When Marx involves himself more deeply in the study of these social relations his concept of science receives its final formulation. The *Grundrisse* seems to have been a turning-point in these studies, for it concorporates a re-reading of Hegel's *Logic*, to which Marx conceded a great importance.[22] It can be considered another crucial moment in Marx's intellectual development.

Now the study of social relations no longer appears the simple task of taking note of what is happening before one's eyes.[23] A double dimension of reality is now definitively and explicitly taken into account, one which distinguishes between the 'surface process' and the processes which go on beneath, 'in the depth'. Science should seek the essence of relations behind their appearances. Circulation, for instance, appears as that which is immediately present on the surface of bourgeois society; but its immediate being is pure semblance. 'it is the phenomenon of a process taking place behind it'. Profit is a phenomenal form of surplus-value which has the virtue of obscuring the real basis of its existence. Competition is a phenomenon which conceals the determination of value by labour-time. The value-relation between commodities disguises a definite social relation between men. The wage-form extinguishes every trace of the division of the working-day into necessary labour and surplus-labour, and so on.

Marx adopts a vocabulary of Hegelian origin which assumes different though equivalent expression such as essence-appearance, law–phenomenon, real relations–phenomenal forms, etc. Science is concerned with discovering the essence, the law, the real relations behind the appearances. As Marx puts it, 'scientific truth is always paradox, if judged by everyday experience, which catches only the delusive appearance of things'.[24] Science would be superfluous if the outward appearances and the essence of things directly coincided.[25]

Within this context the concept of ideology can be both expressed in a new form and extended to cover other phenomena beyond philosophy. The inversions of German philosophy which explained social relations from ideas can now be expressed in terms of an appearance which gives ideas a seeming autonomy.[26] But of course, there are other kinds of appearances such as those mentioned above with respect to circulation, competition, wage-form, profit, and so on. These may lead to economic ideological forms. The general requisite for ideology to exist continues to be the concealment of contradictions in the interest of the dominant class. But this is now expressed in the form of a consciousness which fixes phenomenal forms, thus concealing the real contradictory social relations.[27]

Science aims to uncover the inner connections by penetrating through appearances; yet it is not the direct antithesis of ideology, or the power which may overcome ideology. Marx insists on this point again:

The recent scientific discovery, that the products of labour, so far as they are values, are but material expressions of the human labour spent in their production, marks, indeed, an epoch in the history of the development of the human race, but, by no means, dissipates the mist through which the social character of labour appears to us to be an objective character of the products themselves.[28]

Although science has discovered its real essence, this appearance, Marx argues, remains for the producers as real and final as the fact that the atmosphere remains unaltered after the scientific discovery of its component gases. One may dispel the deceptive appearances only by practically changing the social relations which support them.

Although ideology cannot be defeated by theoretical arguments, science makes an important contribution to its comprehension by unmasking its contradictions and deceptions. Yet science in itself is not, to Marx, a substitute for revolutionary practice. Even more, science can be the subject of ideological penetration in so far as it is produced and developed by human practice in a historical and contradictory society. Science does not constitute a special sphere exempt from the contingencies of class contradictions.

In effect, science is seen from a double perspective. From one view it has a liberating effect and plays an essential role in human emancipation. Science transforms the production process and subjugates the forces of nature by compelling them to work in the service of human needs.[29] Yet from the other view science realized *in the machine* appears as *capital* in relation to the labourers. And in fact all these applications of science, natural forces and products of labour on a large scale, these applications founded on *social labour*, themselves appear only as *means for the exploitation* of labour. . . .[30]

Science under capitalism becomes a productive force for the use of the capitalist; an instrument of class rule which 'does not exist in the worker's consciousness, but rather acts upon him through the machine as an alien power, as the power of the machine itself'.[31]

Ultimately, however, Marx considers science, together with the rest of the productive forces, a progressive element for the liberation of mankind. The circumscription of science within capitalist social relations is transitory. Science's fate is the same as that of machinery; while it is 'the most appropriate form of the use value of fixed capital, it does not follow that therefore subsumption under the social relation of capital is the most appropriate and ultimate social relation of production for the application of machinery'.[32]

As I have said, this positive balance does not prevent Marx from appreciating the possibility of ideological shortcomings in science:

The weak points in the abstract materialism of natural science, a materialism that excludes history and its process, are at once evident from the abstract and ideological conceptions of its spokesmen, whenever they venture beyond the bounds of their own speciality.[33]

The disregard of history is the main source of ideological distortions, in so far as the understanding of society may transform itself into the unqualified acceptance of the present system of social relations. Marx's interest in the discovery of the inner laws of these relations does not prevent him from detecting the danger of absolutizing these laws.

None the less the error of excluding history, which spokesmen for the natural sciences may incur, leaves the field of their own speciality aside. Here Marx hints at a difference within the scope of science which qualifies its basic unity. Although nature and society cannot be dissociated, Marx recognizes that nature is an object for mankind, an object which possesses autonomous laws whose theoretical discovery allows its subjugation to human needs.[34] These natural laws work independently of men's consciousness despite the fact that men become aware of them historically. The ultimate external character of nature with respect to society explains why science may discover the laws of nature while at the same time it fails to understand how society works. True, both nature and society are mediated, and thus unified by human practice. Yet an essential difference survives. While a natural world is still conceivable without the intervention of practice, society has no consistence and permanence beyond that practice.

A non-historical method applied to nature could discover its laws, in so far as they do not ultimately depend upon practice. The same method, applied to society, produces ideological deceptions in so far as it could only reduce social relations to the state of autonomous nature facing men from without. Of course, with respect to individual existence and consciousness, the social world can be conceived as externally given and independent, like the natural world. Marx does not abandon for a moment the position already reached in *The German Ideology*, that the 'fixation of social activity', the 'consolidation of what we ourselves produce into an objective power above us', is one of the chief factors in historical development.[35] Yet he does not absolutize this fact to make it unchangeable like a natural law. The ideological illusions of a non-historical approach creep in:

Nature does not produce on the one side owners of money or commodities, and on the other men possessing nothing but their own labour-power. This relation has no natural basis, neither is its social basis one that is common to all historical periods.[36]

In regard to society, natural laws seem abstract and incapable of accounting for the richness of history. This is why history cannot be expressed in terms of natural laws. Marx mocks Mr Lange for his great discovery, that

the whole of history can be brought under a single great natural law. This natural law is the *phrase* . . . 'struggle for life'. . . . Thus, instead of analysing the 'struggle for life' as represented historically in various definite forms of society, all that has to be done is to translate every concrete struggle into the phrase 'struggle for life.'. . . [37]

Science does not consist of asserting this kind of abstract generalization. The verification of the universal necessity of certain phenomena like 'production', 'distribution and social labour', 'struggle for life' and so on, does not suffice for science. Science consists precisely of demonstrating how these laws assert themselves in historically different forms.[38]

Therefore, in looking at society, science cannot proceed in exactly the same way as when dealing with nature. It is not that an essential difference between social sciences and natural sciences should be established, nor is the distinction between free, historical, lawless men and given, natural things subject to immutable laws. Natural laws are not arrived at in an entirely different way from social laws. What unifies these two kinds of law is the fact that both are historically detected through human practice. The history of both natural and social sciences is determined by the development and contradictions of that practice. Yet a difference remains: within a set of conditions, the necessity of natural laws can be said to be 'absolute' as compared with the 'historical' necessity of social laws. As Marx points out, the fact that the objective conditions of labour occur as a process of appropriation of alien labour from the standpoint of capital is merely a 'historical necessity', 'a necessity for the development of the forces of production solely from a specific historic point of departure, or basis, but in no way an absolute necessity of production; rather a vanishing one . . .'.[39]

This is crucial to understanding how science can unveil the essence behind the appearances. For it means that the essence of reality is not to be construed as a fixed and given object apprehended once and for all after dispelling appearances. The essence of reality is historical and therefore is constituted by two closely related aspects which condition one another. One is the way the real social relations work in their necessity. The other is the historical character of that necessity, which means that those social relations are transitory (because contradictory) and thus destined to vanish.

These two aspects do not always have the same weight. At the beginning of their historical evolution, social relations show very little of any of the contradictions which will finally destroy them. As contradictions in the mode of production are initially not apparent, but latent, science tends to grasp social relations in their necessity without entirely envisaging their historical temporariness. This does not prevent science from surpassing the level of outer appearances in order to establish the way in which those relations work. However, the impossibility of grasping the inner contradictions limits that science to an imperfect knowledge of the essence. When contradictions come to the surface, science can no longer avoid their explanation. Either it deals with them, or it conceals them and becomes riddled with ideology.

This is why Marx thought that political economy could remain a science only so long as the class struggle was latent or manifested itself in isolated and sporadic phenomena.[40] The very development of political economy and of the opposition to which it gives rise 'keeps pace with the real development of the social contradictions and class conflicts inherent in capitalist production.'[41] This development goes from the beginnings of the rising bourgeoisie in its struggle against feudalism to the appearance of new contradictions with the proletariat. The intellectual representatives of the initial stage Marx regards as 'scientifically honest', even ruthless. Ricardo, its last great representative, did not mind 'whether the advance of the productive forces slays landed property or workers'; all he was concerned with was the productive development of human labour.[42]

Yet Ricardo did not know anything of crises arising out of the production process itself. He could explain the few crises he witnessed as accidental phenomena originating in external, political pressures. 'Later historical phenomena, especially the almost regular periodicity of crises on the world market, no longer permitted Ricardo's successors to deny the facts or to interpret them as accidental'.[43] Ricardo had set foot on the threshold of this new period by making the antagonism of class interests, of wages and profits and so on, the starting point of his investigations. But he thought these antagonisms were a social law of nature.[44]

From then onwards, the strikes in Lyons and Silesia, the revolts of the English country proletariat, the appearance of socialist writers like Owen, Fourier and Saint-Simon and other manifestations of the new emerging contradictions with the proletariat, determined the emergence of the vulgar economists.[45] With them scientific achievements were lost. They refused to investigate the nature of the conflicts which confronted them and apologetically falsified the simplest economic relations: 'In place of disinterested inquirers, there were hired prize-fighters; in place of genuine scientific research, the bad conscience and the evil intent of apologetic'.[46]

The ideological character of vulgar economy is beyond doubt and shows how Marx acknowledged that the name of science could be used to legitimate ideology. But how are we to interpret the achievements of classical political economy? Are they also ideological because they understand capitalist social relations as an absolute necessity, misreading the historical essence of these relations? It seems to me evident that Ricardo remains trapped in appearances in a way quite different from the way vulgar economists do. For instance, Ricardo did not arrive at the distinction between surplus-value and profit, yet he did not fall into the vulgar version which construes profit as a mere addition over and above the value of the commodity. He conceived capitalist production to be absolute, yet he did not remain entangled in circulation and competition as the vulgar economists did. The limitations of classical political economy did not prevent it from penetrating appearances. This is what constituted it as a science.

Marx is very clear in this regard. He thinks Ricardo shows the real movement of bourgeois production, which is value:

Ricardo's theory of values is the scientific interpretation of actual economic life. . . . Ricardo establishes the truth of his formula by deriving it from all economic relations, and by explaining in this way all phenomena, even those . . . which at first sight seem to contradict it; it is precisely that which makes his doctrine a scientific system.[47]

Referring to the 'trinity' formula 'capital–land–labour' as the sources of wealth, Marx states that

it is the great merit of classical economy to have destroyed this false appearance and illusion . . . this personification of things and conversion of production into entities, this religion of everyday life.[48]

A last example clearly shows that Marx considered Ricardo's theory to be scientific because it surpassed appearances:

. . . to examine how matters stand with the contradiction between the apparent and the actual movement of the system. This then is Ricardo's great historical significance for science.[49]

Yet Ricardo and, in general, classical economy, are clearly shown to be insufficient by Marx's critique. Despite a basically correct theory of value, Ricardo did not distinguish profit from surplus value. He confused labour with labour-power, constant capital with fixed capital, and variable capital with circulating capital. His definition of rent was deficient and he held mistaken views on money. He was unable to examine the connection of labour with money, and so forth.[50] Besides these criticisms Marx shows the more substantial and general shortcomings which stem from Ricardo's failing to conceive of the possibility of a crisis of over-production. Even more, Ricardo thought that the bourgeois mode of production was the absolute mode of production.

According to Marx, Ricardo could not admit that bourgeois social relations were to transform themselves into barriers to the development of productive forces. Ricardo was unable to grasp the specific form of bourgeois production; he was obsessed with the idea that bourgeois production was production as such.[51] In short, Ricardo, and likewise the whole of classical economy, failed to interpret capitalist social relations as a historical necessity. They regarded economic categories 'as eternal laws and not as historical laws which are valid only for a particular historical development, for a definite development of the productive forces'.[52] Classical economy surpassed the level of appearances so as to constitute a science, but it did so imperfectly.

Now, these scientific inadequacies are not necessarily ideological. Ricardo's lack of precision and most of his errors and confusions result from his method, which, despite being deficient, is historically justified.[53] Ricardo did not see the relative character of the bourgeois mode of production because the contradictions and crises which could bring about a change of the mode of production were not apparent. Hence, Ricardo's errors did not originally result in the objective concealment of contradictions. On the contrary, classical economy wanted at that moment to exacerbate the existent contradictions against the remnants of feudalism. Thus, in so far as the concealment of contradictions is essential to ideology, many of Ricardo's tenets were not ideological, although erroneous or insufficient: there are sources of errors other than ideology. Of course, there were ideological distortions in Ricardo's theory. In so far as he confronted certain new contradictions, even the first of them like the crises between 1800 and 1815, and explained them away, he fell into ideology.[54] In sum, classical economy as a science did have some ideological distortions, but not all of its errors were ideological.

The ideological character of distortions in science is not a kind of immanent attribute of the error in question. Ideology is historically referred to practice, to the evolution of contradictions in society. Knowledge has to be judged not only in relation to the social contradictions present at the moment of the production of such knowledge, but also in relation to the contradictions present at the moment of passing judgement. A piece of knowledge, be it correct or erroneous, but not at first ideological, can perfectly well become ideological if certain new contradictions come into existence and are consequently objectively concealed by that knowledge.

Ricardo's idea that there can be no crises of over-production cannot be said to be ideological before these crises first appeared. After 1825, this idea objectively conceals social contradictions that the evolution of society has brought to the fore. So, in this new context, the idea becomes ideological. In general, it can be said that by the time Marx was writing on economy, the inability of classical economy to conceive of capitalist social relations as a mere historical necessity is already ideological. The difficulty in interpreting Marx with respect to the relations between political economy and ideology originates in the fact that sometimes he judges political economy in the context of its epoch and at other times in the context of the state of society in Marx's own time.

None the less, the scientific value of political economy is not to be disputed. A difference should be made between it and vulgar economy, which only translates the common consciousness – deceived by superficial appearances – of capitalists into a doctrinaire language. The approach of vulgar economy is, therefore, apologetic and 'very different from the urge of political economists like the Physiocrats, Adam Smith and Ricardo to grasp the inner connection of the phenomena'.[55] The difference is one between a science (which may have some ideological distortions) and mere ideology pretending to have scientific status.

To Marx, science stands in a set of complicated relationships with ideology. Science is not the total opposite which may overcome ideology by mere intellectual criticism; it does not oppose ideology as truth opposes error. It may, however, contribute to its understanding. Science itself is not a special sphere exempt from ideological penetration. Science's self-understanding as a supra-historical phenomenon unaffected by social contradictions is erroneous and may play an ideological role. None the less, not all scientific errors are ideological. Those which conceal social contradiction in the interest of the dominant class can be considered ideological errors. This ascription, nevertheless, should be historically understood, according to the evolution of these contradictions.

In dealing with nature, the specific content of science is, in principle free from ideology (not from errors, though) in so far as its object possesses autonomous laws and can be ultimately conceived as independent from human mediation. However, as the knowledge of nature and its laws is historically acquired through practice and as the goals and methods of science are mediated by human activity and industry, opportunities for ideological distortions arise, above all, in the 'abstract conceptions' of natural scientists in regard to all that which has to do with the relationship between science and society.

In dealing with society, science also differs from ideology. Yet as the object necessarily reflects human mediation, the possibility of ideological distortions increase. In so far as social science in dealing with its object takes into account its historical character, and in so far as it penetrates appearances and discovers the real relations, then it is as free from ideology as any other science. A different matter is the existence of ideologies which take the form of science, but which are not really science, as Marx shows in the case of vulgar economy. Ideology resorts to the name of science to cover up its distortions, an operation typical of capitalism. While in feudal times ideology legitimated itself in religion, in capitalism ideology seeks to do it in science.[56] So although social science is different from ideology, ideology has selected the field of social science in order to legitimate itself.

Science against ideology

As I said above, this position is mainly held by a tradition of positivist origin. It is difficult to define this broad current of thought, as the great variety of authors commonly associated with it do not all agree on essential points. The best general and comprehensive description is Kolakowski's definition of positivism: 'a collection of prohibitions concerning human knowledge, intended to confine the name "knowledge" or "science" to the results of those operations that are observable in the evolution of the modern sciences of nature'.[57]

The way in which the operation of natural sciences is understood determines the features ascribed to its privileged knowledge and the criteria of its demarcation from other kinds of knowledge. The most commonly mentioned are three. First, that which is not based upon experience as directly manifested is not real scientific knowledge (there is no difference between 'essence' and 'phenomenon'). Second, judgements of value and normative statements are not science, as there is no empirical basis for testing their validity. Third, there is a fundamental unity of the scientific method, so the methods employed in natural sciences must be applied in social sciences.

From the outset, positivism understands science as the antithesis of a mythical world. The process of rationalization introduced by the new scientific attitude of the modern times has achieved the disenchantment of nature. The metaphysical world of objective and hierarchical essences corresponded to a period in which man's inability to appropriate nature was the outstanding feature of society; now it is superseded by the scientific approach, which enables man to break that immovable world and appropriate it as a means for his own ends. Reason is no longer orientated towards an immutable world of essences but is now based on the operation of natural sciences.

Scientific reason is concerned with means and ends, with the technical procedures to achieve an end, but not primarily with the rationality of the end itself. It is an instrumental reason.[58] This instrumental reason, without itself denying the existence of an objective rationality of ends in reality, tends to overlook it as delusive and, at any rate, considers it beyond scientific assessment. What is not scientifically verifiable constitutes an altogether different world, which is not governed by instrumental rationality. That world which is not accessible to scientific reason appears as irrational or mythical and in this sense is equated with ideology.

Bacon's search for a new methodology capable of overcoming the deficiencies of medieval thought offers one of the first examples of this opposition. The Baconian tradition accentuates the observational character of science, and therefore its inductive methodology as against the meaninglessness of metaphysical pre-notions or speculations. Bacon recognized that there existed in human thought more than objects and reason: there was also a quota of irrationality or a subjective contribution which implied distortions and deformations, against which some precautions were necessary. The source of these distortions were what Bacon called 'idols', 'false notions which are now in possession of the human understanding', that 'beset men's minds that truth can hardly find entrance', and that 'in the very instauration of the sciences meet and trouble us'.[59] As I have already shown, the elements of a conception of ideology are already present in these idols, which as pre-notions perturb the production of real science.

This problematic was developed under different forms by several authors and currents of thought. We may remember Condillac's and Destutt de Tracy's transposition of Baconian idols into 'prejudices' which obstructed the true science of ideas. Comte, in his turn, wanted to base science on observation and saw imagination as the main obstacle for its development. Hence he opposed metaphysics to the rigorous science of facts. The evolution from the metaphysical stage to positive science was still to be carried out for sociology, and this was precisely the task he set himself to accomplish.[60] Durkheim analysed the problems which sociology faced in constituting itself as a science, thus abandoning the situation of 'ideology'. Durkheim too wanted a science of facts as opposed to ideology, but he was critical of Comte's failure to eliminate the pre-notion of progress.[61]

More or less in the same spirit, as is widely known, the Vienna Circle fought against metaphysics, which was supposed to contaminate the purity of science with nonsensical propositions. The key factor in this combat was the logical analysis of language and the attempt to create an artificial language of science. Like Baconian idols or Durkheimian pre-notions, metaphysics appears as the opposite of science. Yet now it may be purged by means of logical analysis. This analysis proves that philosophies of value, normative theory and metaphysics in general are entirely meaningless.

The difference between this position and the latter two is that logical positivists do not regard metaphysics as mere speculation or fairy tales (which are false but meaningful), but as nonsense. In effect, they think that significant propositions can be exhaustively divided into two classes: formal or tautological propositions, and factual propositions. The latter require that they should be empirically verifiable.[62] As metaphysics is not tautological nor does it express something which could be empirically tested, it is nonsensical.

What explanation do they give for the existence and widespread use of nonsensical pseudo-propositions? Carnap proposes the hypothesis that metaphysics originated from mythology. It arises, as does poetry, from the 'need to give expression to a man's attitude in life, his emotional and volitional reaction to the environment'. Its negative character for science arises not so much from its being a natural expression of man, as from the fact that 'it pretends to be something that it is not'[63] – it pretends to be cognitive and true when it is meaningless. As opposed to ideology or metaphysics, science appears as knowledge which is verifiable through the objective observation of facts.

As Habermas has pointed out,[64] the big difference between the positivist philosophy of science and the traditional epistemology which goes from Kant to Marx is that to the former the knowing subject is no longer the system of reference. Objective science as a system of propositions and procedures is now the main reference: subjective aspects of the knowing person must be avoided or can logically be avoided if the subject proceeds according to objective rules and procedures. Personal values, attitudes or goals do not matter any more; method does. The scientific method guarantees in a precise manner that knowledge comprehends reality, a reality made of objective facts.

All that is beyond this world of facts is ideological. The difference between ideology and science is in the criterion of verifiability, which in general terms is identified with two requirements. The first is empirical observation or experimentation. The second is the application of a method which guarantees certainty, that is, a commonly accepted procedure which secures the accuracy of the gathering of empirical evidence.

Popper represents a different and more critical tradition within positivism. He does not accept a naïvely inductive approach which supports science on a simple observational basis. He shows how modern science is deductive and highly speculative and proposes refutability as the criterion of demarcation. This means, in his own words, that 'a system is to be considered as scientific only if it makes assertions which may clash with observations; and a system is, in fact, tested by attempts to produce such clashes, that is to say by attempts to refute it'.[65] According to Popper, there are 'degrees of Testability', metaphysics being an example of 'non-testable' theories which are of no interest to empirical scientists. But he refuses to conclude that non-testability is the same as meaninglessness. Arguing against Carnap, he insists that falsifiability is a criterion not of meaning but of demarcation.[66]

Popper refuses to be called a positivist and, indeed, rejects many common assumptions of positivism. However, though he overcomes a crude empiricism and replaces verifiability by falsifiability, he is still concerned with only one particular mode of knowledge and experience. Refutation is still based upon sense experience organized by experimental or analogous procedures. Popper maintains that the common language in natural sciences is achieved 'by recognizing experience as the impartial arbiter', which means 'experience of a public character, like observations and experiments, as opposed to experience in the sense of more private aesthetic or religious experience; and an experience is public if everybody who takes the trouble can repeat it'.[67]

Yet, as Popper himself argues, all this does not make him a positivist.[68] So far we can agree. The problem appears when he deals with social science. For Popper social science cannot avoid the same approach since 'methods are fundamentally the same in all sciences', that is ,'methods of trial and error, of inventing hypotheses which can be practically tested, and of submitting them to practical tests'. As a consequence, 'a social technology is needed whose results can be tested by piecemeal social engineering'.[69] Here Popper simply transposes the method of natural sciences into the social sciences without making allowance for the historical and contradictory character of society. Under the guise of a fight against sociological relativism and the defence of objective truth,[70] a presupposition creeps in which tends completely to assimilate society to nature, overlooking the historical and thereby transitory character of these objective social truths. Popper is right to assert that it is a mistake to assume that the objectivity of science depends upon the objectivity of the scientist. But he disregards the particular character of social objectivity. When he attempts to rehabilitate an 'absolute' concept of truth as the correspondence between a proposition and the facts, he simply equates social facts with natural facts in the Durkheimian fashion. Positivism is, therefore, still present in Popper.

As far as ideology is concerned the positivist tradition has a choice. It can pass a judgement of the sort 'what is non-testable is ideology, but this does not tell us anything about its meaningfulness'. Or the judgement it passes can imply that 'only what is verifiable is meaningful; therefore ideology is meaningless'. This second position is nearer to logical positivism whereas the first is nearer to Popper. An obvious weakness of the second choice is that its identification of meaningfulness with verifiability is in turn unverifiable and constitutes an *a priori* which is by no means self-evident.

Yet both versions share a more important weakness: in equating social facts with natural facts they tend to absolutize the existent structure of society as though it was a natural law. In other words, they disregard the historical character of social reality and thus can easily become an apology of the *status quo*. As Habermas has pointed out 'the critique of ideology, which for the sake of resolving dogmatism and asserting technologically rational behaviour insistently separates reason from decisions of commitment, in the end automates the decisions according to the laws of the rationality thus made dominant'.[71]

The decisive feature of the positivist treatment of the relationship between ideology and science is the fact that ideology appears as pure 'otherness', the antithesis of the latter. Even when the validity of ideology is not judged, science appears to confront it with an absolute character or, at least, with an entirely different nature which permits it to supersede ideology. Science appears a special sphere of knowledge exempt from ideological distortions as long as it complies with its method. Science assumes an abstract and non-historical character which insulates it from the actual economic and social organization of society. The relationship between science and society is lost or distorted, and science acquires a self-supporting special status, immune to historical contingencies.

Kuhn and Feyerabend have contributed substantially to dispelling these rationalist conceptions and have shown how ideology can operate within the common self-understanding of science. For historians of science, Kuhn claims that it is no longer possible to distinguish the 'scientific' component of past observations from 'error' and 'superstition'. 'If these out-of-date beliefs are to be called myths, then myths can be produced by the same sort of methods and held for the same sort of reasons that now lead to scientific knowledge'.[72] Out-of-date theories are not unscientific because they have been discarded. However, science textbooks tend to 'refer only to that part of the work of past scientists that can easily be viewed as contributions to the statement and solution of the texts' paradigm problems'.[73]

This is why science can see itself as a discipline which develops linearly in an endless accumulation, unaffected by social problems and internal ruptures. This rationalist self-understanding contends that observation and experience are the only factors which determine scientific knowledge.[74] Kuhn shows, on the contrary, that historical accidents and arbitrary elements always form part of science. Feyerabend goes so far along this line that he finally seems to dissolve all boundaries between science and other forms of knowledge such as religion and mysticism.[75] Despite this evident exaggeration, many of Feyerabend's historical examples show that Kuhn's assertions are correct.

Most interesting is Kuhn's account of how scientific evidence is structurally affected by what he calls 'normal science'. The criterion of validity is not the adequacy of theory to an objective reality, but rather, its adequacy to an approved way of doing things which is fixed by a paradigm.[76] Kuhn propounds a conception of the history of science similar, *mutatis mutandi*, to the way Marx understands the evolution of economic modes of production with its sequence of revolutions and normal periods. One is tempted to call it a theory of scientific modes of production. However, neither Kuhn nor Feyerabend attempt to link structurally the evolution of the economic mode of production to that of the scientific mode of production.[77]

This line is explored by people like Hilary and Steven Rose, J. M. Levy-Leblond, G. Ciccotti, M. Cini and M. de Maria.[78] They emphasize the ideological penetration of science which arises from its being closely tied up with the development of capitalist industry. They talk of an 'industrialization of science' and of scientific institutions. Typical of the contemporary way of doing science is its integration into the productive process: science becomes another commodity. All these authors reject an anti-scientific pessimism and do not believe that the specific contents of science are ideologically distorted. Yet they try to show that scientific activity bears the marks of the dominant ideology in many ways – the military orientation of science, the encouraging of an image of pure objectivity which hides exploitation behind rational and technical necessities, the emphasis on specialization and elitism which restricts everyone to a small sector while a seemingly objective general plan is not discussed, and so forth.

A shortcoming which affects large sections of the positivist tradition is the inability to relate the phenomena of knowledge to social relations in society. Ultimately it is possible to find an underlying epistemological assumption that knowledge is autonomous, with its own rules and rationality, disconnected from historical social reality as far as its validity is concerned. Indeed, the positivist struggle against relativism justifies to a certain extent the stress laid upon the difference between truth and the social genesis of knowledge. However, the danger arises of absolutizing this difference so as to make of validity and rationality a separate sphere. As Adorno has pointed out, genesis and validity cannot be separated without contradiction; 'objective validity preserves the moment of its emergence and this moment permanently affects it'.[79]

Besides, positivism petrifies what is rational and non-rational into autonomous separate entities, given once and for ever. The boundaries between science and ideology are fixed and the relationships between these two phenomena are external: science overcomes ideology as truth overcomes error. Their spheres are perfectly well demarcated and the relationships are presented as the hypostatized opposition of self-sufficient totalities, the positive and the negative, the rational and the irrational. One can see underlying this the old antithesis between myth and logos which Enlightenment philosophy brought to the fore.

It is roughly along these lines that Althusser interprets Marx's distinction between ideology and science. The influence of Lenin's conception of the importation of science into the working-class movement from without has an important bearing upon Althusser's interpretation. The spontaneous ideology of the working class can give expression to protest and criticism, but only in the language and the categories of bourgeois ideology. Spontaneous working-class ideology is therefore subordinated and uses the logic of the dominant class. That is why the working class cannot liberate itself from bourgeois ideology, but needs to receive from without the help of science, which is capable of unmasking such ideology. The spontaneous working-class ideology needs to be transformed 'under the influence of a new element, radically different from ideology: precisely science'.[80]

Hence, science acquires a crucial role in the Althusserian conception as the only means to combat ideology and thus liberate the proletariat. Science is 'radically different'; it is the antithesis of ideology, although it can never defeat it completely. Science lives in a permanent struggle against the socially necessary existence of ideology. Like Baconian idols, Durkheimian pre-notions and Carnapian metaphysics, ideology does not cease to trouble science, as it is a condition of all societies. Yet its social necessity does not weaken its opposition to science.

Marxist science has two main features in Althusser's version: the reduction of the phenomenon to the essence; and the consideration of that essence as a totality in which the 'internal connections' of all phenomena are linked.[81] However, this reduction of the phenomenon to the essence should not be understood as though the essence was abstracted from real objects. Althusser calls this an 'empiricist' deviation, quite apart from Marx's intention. Marx would have rejected the 'Hegelian confusion which identifies the real object with the object of knowledge'; on the contrary, he would have maintained that the object of knowledge is produced entirely in knowledge.[82]

In this conception Althusser is following Bachelard rather than Marx. For Bachelard science has no object outside its own activity. The object of science has no 'direct realistic value in ordinary experience', it has to be designated as a *'secondary object'*.[83] Knowledge working on its 'object', then, does not work on the real object, but on a peculiar raw material which could be called 'ideology', 'intuition' or 'representation', as against the 'scientific concept' which is the outcome of the process.

The acquisition of science appears, therefore, as a process of labour based upon three generalities. Generality I is the ideological material, knowledge already produced, not the real object, but distorted knowledge about it. To this basis, a 'work', 'theoretical practice', or Generality II is applied in order to arrive at the scientific concept, Generality III. The path thus traversed is from the abstractions of ideology to the concreteness of science. The result is radically different from the original material.[84] Following Bachelard's concept of break, Althusser describes the gap between them as an 'epistemological break'. In Lecourt's words, this is the moment when 'the tissue of pre-existing ideology is torn and scientificity is installed'.[85]

It seems to me that this Bachelardian philosophy of science which Althusser incorporates into Marxism is in the best tradition of positivism and opposes science to ideology in the same way as the rational opposes the irrational. It is striking, therefore, that Lecourt should present Bachelard and Althusser as the antithesis of positivism. He characterizes positivism as a tendency concerned with the 'value of science'. Bachelard, on the contrary, only 'poses' the thesis of the objectivity of science and does not seek to guarantee it like Popper, Kuhn, Feyerabend and others. Following the Spinozian dictum, *'veritas norma sui'*, which Althusser also quotes, Lecourt claims that Bachelard is in the authentic materialist position when he propounds the thesis that 'the truth of a scientific truth imposes itself by itself'.[86]

As truth is not only its own measure but also the measure of what is false (*'veritas norma sui et falsi'*), it therefore devalues what is anterior and exterior to it. The history of science appears as an 'irreversible' demarche which continuously bars the way of irrationalities. 'The history of the sciences is the history of the defeats of irrationalism. But the fight is without end . . . .'[87] One can notice the affinity of this statement with Althusser's permanent confrontation between ideology and science. Lecourt thinks that Bachelard sets aside the idealist philosophy concerned with the 'problem of knowledge' by just posing the truth of science.

Hence, for this interpretation, positivism of the Popperian or 'Kuhnian'[88] kind appears trapped in an idealist problematic. It seems to me that Lecourt has completely inverted the terms of the problem. Neither Bachelard nor Althusser think it necessary to prove the value of science and only 'take cognizance' of it; yet this does not make them anti-positivist, nor does it prevent them from assuming the idealist premises which they want to avoid. On the contrary, one of the features of positivism is precisely its postulate that scientific knowledge is the paradigm of valid knowledge, a postulate that indeed is never proved nor intended to be proved. So what Bachelard and Althusser consciously propound, in the sense that scientific truth imposes itself by itself, is precisely and nothing less than the *a priori* of positivism.

Moreover, the idea that science conceives its object as a 'result'

(secondary object) and not as a 'thing' leads to the idealist foundation of scientific knowledge upon itself. For Marx the object was a
'result', not a mere external thing, because it was mediated by
human practice. But it was the only real object of knowledge. For
Bachelard and Althusser, on the contrary, the object is a 'result',
because it is different from the real object. So the object is a
'result' not because it is mediated by practice but because as object
of knowledge it is produced by knowledge itself. Knowledge is
conceived as constituting its own object as in the idealist tradition.[89]

In a self-critical work, Althusser recognizes some of the problems
which stem from this position; in particular, he identifies a 'theoreti-
cist deviation' in his conception of the relationships between ideology
and science.[90] He finds the source of the problem in the identification
of the pair science–ideology with the pair truth–error, as if the
break from ideology to science was just the immanent result of the
scientific procedure of replacing the error by the truth. He recognizes
that he did not pay attention to class influence at the break, nor
explain the class basis of that break. As a consequence, he accepts
that he theorized a difference between science and ideology in
general which led him to a one-sided insistence on theory and to the
overlooking of practice. In sum, he recognizes a rationalist deviation.[91]

These elements of self-criticism seem quite appropriate. Yet Althusser reverts to the same errors in the very process of self-critique.
In arguing against John Lewis, Althusser describes the 'break' as
'this *irruption* of a new science in a still "ideological" or pre-
scientific universe'.[92] In equating ideological with pre-scientific, he
actually upholds his past theory; that is, he denies the status of
science to the universe previous to the irruption of science and he
confuses ideology with all kind of errors. In fact, science for
Althusser continues to be the antithesis of ideology. Science is
elevated to a special sphere from which there is no return. Like
Bachelard, Althusser conceives of science as an irreversible process
which discovers and acquires the truth and definitively breaks with
errors.

So, Althusser reaffirms a rather rationalist concept of science
which puts it beyond any contradiction. How does he solve then
the problem of class intervention which he had recognized as lacking
in his earlier formulations? By transposing the problem to a different
sphere, that of philosophy. Philosophy is the theoretical field of class

struggle. While science has an irreversible history and is exempt from any ideological dispute, philosophy has no history and nothing is radically new for her. Old theses take up a new form and return to the philosophical debate. The epistemological break is then restricted to science; in philosophy there are only 'philosophical revolutions'. From the epistemological break there is no way back. From philosophical revolutions there is always a way back. Nothing in philosophy is ever settled definitively; there is always the struggle of antagonistic tendencies. Thus, the class intervention which may be said to inaugurate Marx's scientific break is due to a previous philosophical revolution and not to the fact that class may interfere with science. As Althusser puts it, 'Marx's philosophical revolution preceded Marx's "epistemological break". *It made the break possible*'.[93]

Althusser's solution, therefore, tries to safeguard the epistemological break by restricting it to the field of science. Simultaneously he juxtaposes the problem of class struggle but in the separate sphere of philosophy. Althusser takes this scholastic distinction so far as to contend that one may only speak of 'errors' in science, because it is there that the truth can be achieved. In philosophy there are no errors or truths. There are 'deviations', which are a function of class theoretical positions. Equally, there are not 'true propositions' but only 'theses' which are 'correct'. Truth can be predicated of science; correctness can be predicated of philosophy.[94]

The price Althusser pays for this arbitrary solution is the elevation of science to an even more mythical status above all contingencies. Consequently, the class problematic can only be juxtaposed to science through a different theoretical sphere. The sharp demarcation which results between science and philosophy is even more puzzling when one realizes that they are supposed to co-exist in a single thought. Althusser necessarily has to make both spheres co-exist in Marx (historical materialism the science, dialectical materialism the philosophy), in order to keep both class struggle and science. But in doing that he drives a wedge between them as if it was possible to distinguish Marx as a philosopher engaged in class struggle from Marx as a scientist, detached and concerned with the objective truth. Ultimately, Althusser introduces a dualism which continues to oppose the reign of scientific truth to that of class ideologies, as in the best rationalist tradition.

Science as ideology

As I said in the introduction, there are two possible ways of under-standing science as ideology. The first derives from the evolution of the concept of ideology towards a positive meaning which connects it with a class outlook, without necessarily entailing a negative character immanent to the concept itself. Thus, ideology could be distorted or scientific depending upon the class with which it is connected. In this sense science may assume an ideological character without any negative implications. The ideological character of science would only signify the special relationship that science holds with a certain class.

The second way of understanding science as ideology derives from a negative concept of ideology; it maintains that scientific rationality may be ideological not merely in the sense of being related to a class, but in the sense of being the source and justifi-cation of domination in society. In the former ideology could be either scientific or distorted; in the latter science itself appears as the source of distortion. The first position dilutes the concept of ideology whereas the second affects more profoundly the concept of science.

The second position has its origin in the anti-positivist tradition of German historicism which was developed by the hermeneutic school.[95] The influence of this tradition can be detected in different, and sometimes opposite, viewpoints; from Weber and Simmel to Gramsci, Korsch and Lukács. In their view of ideology, Mannheim and Goldmann as much as Gramsci and Lukács share a common root in hermeneutics. In one way or another the four of them rely on a concept of *Weltanschauung* (the world-view or spirit of an epoch) as a central unifying principle of analysis. Yet I am particu-larly interested here in detecting those theories which are suspicious of the role played by natural sciences in society and that, conse-quently, arrive at considering them as a form of ideology in the negative sense.

From this point of view Gramsci, Korsch, Mannheim and Gold-mann seem less pertinent than Lukács, Habermas and Marcuse. While all these authors accept a more or less clear distinction between the social and the natural sciences, the first group share a common belief in the emancipatory character of natural sciences whereas the second has a more negative view. For instance, Lukács in *History and Class Consciousness* gives little consideration to the liberating effects of natural sciences.[96] On the contrary, some of the expressions used suggest that science, being a part of the bourgeois world-view, is contaminated to the core by bourgeois ideology. Thus, Lukács can describe the methodology of natural sciences as 'the methodological ideal of every fetishistic science and every kind of Revisionism'. This methodology deserves such a treatment because it 'rejects the idea of contradiction and antagonism in its subject matter'.[97] By basing itself upon specialization, science is caught up in the same immediacy and cannot have a vision of the whole.[98]

For Lukács, each class ripe for hegemony develops a coherent world-view in its attempts to achieve control of society. This world-view includes a theory of economics, politics and society, in short, a comprehensive viewpoint which encompasses science and its method. 'We can clearly observe the close interaction between a class and the scientific method that arises from the attempt to conceptualize the social character of that class together with its laws and needs.'[99] Science acquires a subjective character, like other ideological forms. In the case of the bourgeoisie this world-view is necessarily contradictory in so far as it cannot face the question of totality. As bourgeois rule is particularistic, in favour of a minority, any awareness of the question of totality is fatal because it leads to self-destruction.

Hence, bourgeois science is necessarily a false consciousness. Of course, not all its results are equally false. 'When the ideal of scientific knowledge is applied to nature it simply furthers the progress of science. But when it is applied to society it turns out to be an ideological weapon of the bourgeoisie'.[100] On the other hand, as the proletariat is a universal class and represents the general interest, it gains from the consciousness of totality, and thus its world-view may count on truth as one of its weapons. Because proletarian subjectivity is universal, it is objective and, therefore, scientific.

So, in Lukács's thought, the class character of science affects its validity to a much larger extent than in Marx. There is no mention, for instance, of the fact that Marx considered classical political economy to be a science. Even more, inasmuch as the method of natural sciences forms part of the bourgeois world-view, it is treated as yet another expression of capitalist reification. Lukács perceives that 'there is something highly problematic in the fact that capitalist society is predisposed to harmonize with scientific method'. In idolizing 'facts' as they present themselves, this method 'takes its stand simply and dogmatically on the basis of capitalist society'.[101]

I think Lukács is right to stress the historical character of social facts, but in identifying the method of natural sciences with capitalist reification he risks throwing out the baby with the bath-water.

Hence, in the young Lukács the first seeds of a conception of science as ideology make their appearance. The Frankfurt school goes further along this line and provides an extensive critique of the kind of reason with which science operates. Horkheimer describes how reason has been subjectivized in the attempt to dominate nature in the interests of man.[102] With science reason becomes an instrumental reason, concerned with the manipulation of means and no longer with the question of whether the ends are reasonable. Horkheimer distinguishes an objective reason, which used to be the basis of great philosophical systems and which affirms reason as a reality in the objective world, from a subjective reason, which exists in and for men.

It is true that scientific instrumental reason displaced a mythical belief in the reasonability of a hierarchical system of essences in reality (religion and metaphysics); yet its pervasive influence has brought about a progressive inability to determine the desirability of any goal in itself. Self-interest has become dominant. Reason is no longer autonomous but has become an instrument which is measured only by its role in the domination of nature and, consequently, of men. Subjective reason conforms to anything; 'the more the concept of reason becomes emasculated, the more easily it lends itself to ideological manipulation and to propagation of even the most blatant lies'.[103]

By destroying the theoretical basis of mythology, science has become the only authority in society; yet it cannot decide whether 'justice and freedom are better in themselves than injustice and oppression'. 'The functions once performed by objective reason, by authoritarian religion, or by metaphysics have been taken over by the reifying mechanisms of the anonymous economic apparatus.'[104] Horkheimer believes it is no good saying that it is possible to make a constructive or destructive use of science. Science is above all an auxiliary means of production; its value is positive or negative according to its role in economy. And economy is the field of manipulation and reification. Domination of nature involves domination of man. Hence, in subjective reason 'domination becomes "internalized" for domination's sake'.[105] Industrialism has brought about the subjection of all life to rationalization and planning. Individuals should 'adujst' themselves to the system if they want to survive. The more elaborate the system for dominating nature, the more must men serve such a system of domination.

The same argument is taken up by Adorno and Horkheimer in *The Dialectic of Enlightenment*. The price that men have to pay for liberating themselves from the constraints of nature, is a new kind of submission: Enlightenment is totalitarian and, in dominating nature, has subjected man to the impersonal rule of reified relationships. Technological reason in industrial society compels men to conform. 'What appears to be the triumph of subjective rationality, the subjection of all reality to logical formalism, is paid for by the obedient subjection of reason to what is directly given'.[106]

Thus the process of disenchantment of the world is associated with a new alienation, the reification of the industrial world. But this reification is no longer explained in terms of the bourgeois world-view as in Lukács. Lukács had upheld the Weberian process of rationalization as the typical product of bourgeois capitalism, and had spoken of a 'relative irrationality of the total process'.[107] With Adorno and Horkheimer the irrationality becomes of paramount importance and is not related to any particular class thinking. Enlightenment appears as a vast process which subsumes all of Western thought, including Marx. Scientific rationality appears as an alienating ideology disconnected from class analysis. In fact, as Jay has noticed, after the mid-forties, Adorno and Horkheimer no longer seek answers to cultural questions in the material substructure of society.[108]

Ultimately, therefore, science is ideological not as bourgeois science, but as science itself. The problem is no longer the framing of the relationship between men and nature in class relations, but rather, the very attitude of men towards nature. The problem is in the mentality of man as master, in his effort to dominate nature. The subjugation of nature acquires a repressive character which is prior to, and the origin of, the repression of man. But this repression of man appears quite unmediated by social relations. Thus Horkheimer can speak of a 'revolt' of nature which expresses itself in social rebellions. Yet these are not interpreted as class revolutions which could introduce a substantial change in the way nature is subdued. The rebellions appear as rather aimless explosions which do not change the basic attitude of man towards nature.

That is why civilization as 'rationalized irrationality' is capable of integrating these revolts of nature as another means or instrument,

The basic contradiction of society is not in the social relations within which men face nature, but in the human condition itself:

> On the one hand, the social need of controlling nature has always conditioned the structure and forms of man's thinking and thus given primacy to subjective reason. On the other hand, society could not completely repress the idea of something transcending the subjectivity of self-interest.[109]

One can notice that this contradiction has no history in so far as it 'has always conditioned' mankind.

Marcuse is the final stage in this demotion of science. For him

> the very concept of technical reason is perhaps ideological. Not only the application of technology but technology itself is domination (of nature and men) – methodical, scientific, calculated, calculating control.[110]

Yet Marcuse not only focuses on domination as such, but also distinguishes the fact of domination from its oppressive character: in advanced capitalism domination has lost its oppressive character and has become legitimate, because it constantly increases production permitting widespread consumption. Domination, therefore, does not appear as irrational or as political, but rather 'as submission to the technical apparatus which enlarges the comforts of life and increases the productivity of labour. Technological rationality thus protects rather than cancels the legitimacy of domination'.[111]

Technology and science have furnished advanced capitalism with everything to conceal class differences and legitimate political power. Domination no longer requires political repression; the manipulation of needs suffices. Industrial society creates necessities and satisfies them. The very freedom of choice between commodities, new brands and modes of relaxation is transformed into an instrument of domination. Hence, 'individuals identify themselves with the existence which is imposed upon them and have in it their own development and satisfaction'.[112]

Consequently, ideology has become absorbed into reality. It appears a practically unassailable force in the process of production itself. So, rationality and oppression, technology and domination have become finally fused. Technological rationality appears as a progressive stage of alienation in which the products indoctrinate and manipulate. The special characteristic which the domination of products brings about, is the fact that 'they promote a false consciousness which is immune against its falsehood'.[113] This happens because the vehicle of ideology is rationality itself, which successfully conceals the irrationality of the whole. Taking Lukács's intuition to its extreme, Marcuse claims that technology is the great vehicle of reification, reification 'in its most mature and effective form'. 'The web of domination has become the web of Reason itself, and this society is fatally entangled in it'.[114]

It is only natural, therefore, that Marcuse should think that the alternative to this society should transcend reason itself. Although he is very careful in pointing out that dialectical theory cannot be positive and offer remedy, he hints at a different context where 'science would arrive at essentially different concepts of nature and establish essentially different facts'.[115] The very structure of science would be changed in a rational society, the very idea of reason would be subverted and replaced by the notions of another rationality.

Science and the productive forces have lost the progressive character which Marx used to assert so strongly. Instead of leading society to a more rational organization, they constitute themselves into vehicles of alienation. A more rational society, therefore, should do without technological rationality as we know it. In other words, the social revolution should be necessarily accompanied by a revolutionary transformation of science itself.

As Habermas has pointed out, an alternative new science would also require a new technology and it is difficult to envisage how, as long as men have to survive through labour and with the aid of material means, present technology could be renounced in favour of a qualitatively different one.[116] Even if this was possible, one must wonder what the force would be that could move society towards a more rational future. For if relations of production and productive forces are both in themselves intrinsically tied up with domination, the conditions for a change in society seem rather dubious. In effect, despite the irrationality of the system as a whole, contradictions seem to disappear from the surface of society in Marcuse's analysis. As ideology has become absorbed into reality, domination is effectively legitimated. Where is the impulse for a change to come from? The working class, in Marx's analysis the force for revolution, is no longer revolutionary since it identifies itself with the consumer society and finds there its satisfaction. Therefore, revolutionary activity, if at all possible, loses its social source and becomes an act of free will whose agents, radical students, are essentially indeterminate. Marcuse's concept of ideology appears the concept of the necessary domination of ideology. It is difficult to see not only how science could be changed, but also what would impel academics to change it.

Habermas locates himself in the tradition represented by Marcuse, but is critical of some of its results and seeks to change the basis of the argument. His main objection is that Marcuse oscillates between the corruption of scientific rationality and the political innocence of the forces of production without being able to reconcile both aspects. Habermas wants to show that 'neither the model of the original sin of scientific technical progress nor that of its innocence do it justice'.[117] The peculiarity of scientific rationality lies in its simultaneous double function, as a progressive force of production and as ideology. To account for this double character he proposes to reformulate Weber's concept of rationalization upon a new basis, the distinction between *work* (purposive–rational action) and *interaction* (communicative action). Capitalism brought with it an extension of the 'system of purposive-rational action' at the expense of the 'system of communicative action or symbolic interaction'. Accordingly, ideological domination was founded on the market economy and the principle of equal exchange. Domination could thus be legitimated 'from below' rather than from above as in the traditional society.

Nevertheless, the evolution of capitalism in the twentieth century brought about two new factors, the increase in state intervention on the one hand, and the interdependence of research and technology on the other hand. The change from liberalism to a welfare state destroyed in practice the ideology of just exchange, and the need for a new legitimating ideology arose. It is found in technology and science which have become fused and increasingly manipulative. They provide the ideological basis to justify decisions as if they were merely 'technical', not 'political'. Therefore ideology in advanced capitalism means technocratic consciousness and depolitization, the concealing of communicative interaction and its replacement by a scientific manipulative system.[118]

In liberal capitalism, the consensual norms of interaction – freedom, equality, and so on – were seen to operate as ideological forces which stemmed from the free exchange economy. With the arrival of large-scale industrial capitalism, consensual norms are replaced by the logic of scientific–technical progress and the purposive–rational actions. The model for this new legitimating basis is systems analysis. Technocratic ideology blurs the difference between symbolic interaction and purposive–rational action, and for this reason is 'more irresistible and farther-reaching than ideologies of the old type'.[119] It is less vulnerable to criticism because it is not only ideology. Productive forces have been the motive force of social evolution. Yet

they do not appear, as Marx supposed, *under all circumstances* to be a potential for liberation and to set off emancipatory movements – at least not once the continual growth of the productive forces has become dependent on scientific-technical progress that has *also* taken on functions of *legitimating political power*.[120]

Scientific rationality would be liberating only in so far as it does not encroach upon rationalization at the level of the institutional framework; that is, only if the restrictions on the system of communicative interaction are lifted. Public discussion and repoliticization of decision-making processes are the necessary condition for scientific rationality not to be ideological. In so far as advanced capitalism may secure the loyalty of the working class through rewards, class antagonism has become latent. Technocratic consciousness has depoliticized the masses. Thus the struggle against this ideology cannot be the fruit of class conflict. Like Marcuse, Habermas is unable to determine, structurally, a group which may carry out the protest and struggle for the repoliticization of decisions. For the present he sees some potential in certain groups of university, college and secondary school students.

For Horkheimer the problem was not the way men used technology but the domination which technology intrinsically entailed. He points towards a problem in the human attitude to nature. Marcuse, although asserting that technological rationality is not only ideological but also immune against its falsehood, envisaged the possibility of a new approach to nature and the development of a new scientific rationality. Habermas is both more realistic and less pessimistic: he does not accept the feasibility of a new technology and recognizes the partially progressive character of scientific rationality. Yet although Habermas's position is more moderate than Marcuse's, it leads to three similar basic conclusions: that science and technology appear as the source of legitimating ideology; that they do so independently of class struggle which is supposed to have disappeared or become permanently latent; and that radical academics and students seem the only potential force which can challenge techno-cratic ideology.

Although Habermas, unlike Marcuse, believes that technocratic ideology is not practically unassailable, his conclusions about the latency of class conflicts and the impossibility of a 'system crisis' in advanced capitalism[121] put him within what Mandel calls the ideology of 'technological rationality'. This ideology, Mandel argues, 'proclaims the ability of the existing social order gradually to eliminate all chance of crises, to find a "technical" solution to all its contradictions, to integrate rebellious social classes and to avoid political explosions'.[122] Curiously enough, this ideology is shared by those like Daniel Bell, who talk about the end of ideology.[123] Of course, Marcuse and Habermas are certainly not talking about the end of ideology but rather about the new character of ideology and, at least in the case of Habermas, there is a firm belief in the liberating possibilities of critical theory; but their scepticism about system crises and class conflicts only conceals the reality of growing social contradictions.

Mandel tries to show how this tradition totally overlooks the fact that advanced capitalism has not solved all the contradictions of society; on the contrary, the irrationalities of the capitalist system increasingly emerge to the surface, allowing people to become aware of them.[124] The total integration of the working class is far from a consummated fact. On the contrary, as the economic crises grow worse, the militancy of the working-class movement increases. The typical contradictions and wastages which Marx foresaw in his time are still the hallmark of advanced capitalism with its recessions and crises of over-production. The facts do not support the alleged Marcusian immunity or Habermasian increased irresistibility of technocratic ideology.

As another argument against the ideology of technological rationality, Mandel contends that 'the notion of capitalist ration-ality developed by Lukács, following Weber, is in fact a contradictory combination of partial rationality and overall irrationality.[125] But this may lend itself to a misunderstanding. It may imply that this tradition only recognizes the reign of rationality. In fact Marcuse recognizes the 'overall irrationality' of the system. His argument against Weber is precisely that the so-called process of 'rationaliza-tion' does not realize rationality.[126] The real contention of the Marcusian approach is that such irrationality of the whole is successfully covered up by technological rationality and thus cannot reach consciousness. It is against this contention that the argument should be addressed, and indeed, it is a help to show, as Mandel does, the emergence of unmanageable contradictions in advanced capitalism which effectively reach the consciousness of vast sectors. If the irrationalities of the system have access to the people's consciousness, Habermas's nightmare of the robot society where all decisions conform to a merely technical pattern can never come true.

Yet this is not enough, for it only affirms that technological rationality as ideology is not perfectly successful. It implicitly accepts without discussion that technological rationality is the new source of ideology. And this, it seems to me, is the most important problem which arises in this tradition, namely, a tendency to collapse the source of ideology into science. One may question whether science itself is the basis of depoliticization and the belief that the system cannot be challenged, or whether the main factor responsible for depoliticization is rather an ideology about science. It might be contended that this is exactly what Habermas is arguing, that technocratic ideology is an ideology which uses the name of science to hide itself. Yet there is a clear-cut difference. While Habermas affirms that the basis of that ideology is scientific–technical progress itself,[127] one could argue against this that the basis of technocratic ideology is class contradictions and the appearance of scientificity just a new ideological form which conceals those contradictions.

I think one ought to distinguish science from ideology about science. The latter, not the former, is the basis upon which depoliticization arises. This ideology conveys the image of science as an all-powerful force which holds men in chains, precisely by stripping science of its connections with class decisions. This is exactly the procedure which Marx criticized in the Young Hegelians. They considered the products of consciousness, 'to which they attribute an independent existence, as the real chains of men',[128] forgetting to combat the real contradictions in material reality. Similarly, science is made responsible for an abstract domination which cannot reach consciousness, except that of the most enlightened academics, and thus, the concreteness of class domination in society is concealed. It is not that science is itself entirely neutral but usable for ideological purposes. As Marx thought, there is the possibility of ideological penetration in science in so far as it is produced by human practice within a contradictory society. But this is quite different from maintaining that science as such is the source of ideology.

Habermas's contention that advanced capitalism has entirely changed the basis upon which ideology stands is not accurate. Indeed capitalism has evolved since Marx's time. Yet the mode of production is basically the same. Hence the basis of ideology cannot possibly have changed so completely as to make science the new source of ideology. One can accept that there is something new in the emergence of the ideology of technological rationality. The cybernetic dreams concerning society are certainly a new ideological development. But this does not necessarily entail that technological rationality itself has become the new source of ideology. For Habermas the novelty of advanced capitalism is the disappearance of the importance of class struggle for ideology; the truth may be on the contrary, that the ruling class has succeeded in camouflaging itself by using the name of science. Science has not replaced class contradictions as the source of ideology, but the dominant class has instrumentalized the name of science to pretend it has.

Conclusion

The relationships between science and ideology cannot be simplified to make them relations of pure opposition or relations of identity. Against the relations of pure opposition one should remember that science is not a special sphere of knowledge which may escape from the contradictions of society and the determinations of the economic base; also that ideology is not a simple error of knowledge which can be corrected by true knowledge or criticism. The social determination of scientific knowledge does not make it an ideology, but opens the possibility for ideological penetration.

However, not all the accidents and errors which accompany the development of science are necessarily ideological. The resistance of Kuhn's 'normal science' or Lakatos's 'research programmes'[129] to change is certainly not the mere result of abstract methodological decisions, but neither is it necessarily ideologically biased.

For ideology to be present, the two conditions which Marx laid down should be satisfied: the objective concealment of contradictions, and the interest of the dominant class. Ideology is not a simple error. It is a particular kind of distortion, dependent upon real contradictions, which demands their solution in practice before it can be overcome. Science itself cannot overcome ideology. Yet it is through science that ideology can be understood in its mechanism.

Against the relations of identity one should remember that

science is not the opposite of ideology, but that it is different from ideology. While science penetrates the appearances of reality to reach the inner connections, ideology remains trapped in the former and conceals the latter. The difference is not in the claim that ideology is class-orientated knowledge whereas science is neutral knowledge; nor in the pretension that ideology is bourgeois knowledge while science is proletarian knowledge. All knowledge is socially determined: the mere class character of knowledge does not discriminate between ideology and science. One has to accept, as Marx did, the existence of a bourgeois science like classical political economy. At the same time it is also true that the proletarian consciousness could be ideological.

The difference between ideology and science does not preclude the fact, already recognized by Marx, that ideology may dress itself up as science. Marx came across this phenomenon when he criticized vulgar economy. Of course, this meant that it could not be considered to be a science. Yet the occurrence of this phenomenon may not be disconnected from the very essence of bourgeois ideology. As Poulantzas has shown, it is a feature of bourgeois ideology to try and hide its presence by explicitly presenting itself as science.[130]

Social sciences appear as a privileged place for this operation of legitimating ideology. It is not that social sciences are ideological whereas natural sciences are exempt from ideology. In so far as they are sciences, neither is ideological. The problem is that, by the nature of its object, social science appears better suited than natural science to be used by ideology. In feudal society ideology resorted to religion in order to justify class domination; in capitalist society ideology tries to appear as science so as to conceal all trace of class domination. As we know, ideology is the negation of the inverted character of social relations in reality. To be effective, though, it has to negate that negation; it has to justify it by resorting to an unimpeachable criterion which is found in science.

Hence, it is not science itself that provides the basis for ideology. It is bourgeois ideology which invests itself with the appearance of science. Here lies the fundamental mistake of the tradition which presents science as ideology. It sees the basis of ideology in scientific rationality itself, but in doing so, it suppresses class contradictions as the real basis of ideology. It is thus itself ideological. Science is not in itself ideological; but it may be ideological to claim that it is.

Notes

1 Historical origins of the concept of ideology

1 Kurt Lenk, 'Problemgeschichtliche Einleitung', in K. Lenk (ed.), *Ideologie, Ideologiekritik und Wissenssoziologie*, H. Luchterhand, Berlin, 1970, p. 17.

2 N. Machiavelli's opinion of the 'gentry' is indicative of the new bourgeois critical spirit: '. . . I would point out that the term "gentry" is used of those who live in idleness on the abundant revenue derived from their estates, without having anything to do either with their cultivation or with other forms of labour essential to life. Such men are a pest in any republic and in any province. . . .' *Machiavelli, Discourses*, B. Crick (ed.), Penguin, 1970, pp. 245–6.

3 Machiavelli, p. 268.

4 Machiavelli, p. 278.

5 Machiavelli, p. 311.

6 N. Machiavelli, *The Prince*, G. Bull, (trans.), Penguin, 1974, pp. 100–1.

7 F. Bacon, *The New Organon and Related Writings*, O. Piest (ed.), Liberal Arts Press, New York, 1960, Book i, Aphorism XLI, p. 49.

8 Bacon, Aphorism LXVI, p. 50.

9 See on this Hans Barth, *Truth and Ideology*, F. Lilge (trans.), University of California Press, 1976, pp. 24–5. Barth treats superstition as different from the four classes of idols.

10 Bacon, Aphorism XLIX, p. 50.

11 Bacon, Aphorism XLIII, p. 49.

12 See Barth, pp. 20–1.

13 K. Marx and F. Engels, *The Holy Family*, R. Dixon and C. Dutt (trans.), Progress Publishers, Moscow, 1975, p. 150. However, Marx also acknowledges the shortcomings of this incipient materialism: 'In Bacon, its first creator, materialism still holds back within itself in a naïve way the germs of a many-sided development. On the one hand, matter, surrounded by a sensuous, poetic glamour, seems to attack man's whole entity by winning smiles. On the other, the aphoristically formulated doctrine pullulates with inconsistencies imported from theology' (p. 151).

14 George Lichtheim, *The Concept of Ideology and Other Essays*, Random House, New York, 1967, p. 9.

15 T. Hobbes, *Leviathan*, C. B. Mcpherson (ed.), Penguin, 1975, p. 99.
16 Hobbes, pp. 166, 169 and 167–8.
17 Marx and Engels, p. 152.
18 Hobbes, p. 177.
19 Hobbes, p. 260.
20 Lenk, p. 21.
21 P. H. Th. D'Holbach, *Système de la nature*, Georg Olms, Hildesheim, 1966, vol. 1, pp. xxix–xxxii.
22 Helvetius, *De l'Esprit*, Éditions Sociales, Paris, 1959, chapter xiv, pp. 103–11.
23 Helvetius, p. 110.
24 D'Holbach, vol. 1, pp. 332–3.
25 D'Holbach, p. 347.
26 Barth, pp. 33–4. Helvetius believes that 'if under a liberal regime men are generally open, loyal, and industrious, but under a despotic one, deceitful, base, lacking in genius and courage, this difference in character is due to the different types of education they have received under the two types of government' (Helvetius, *De l'homme*, in *Oeuvres complètes*, London, 1977, vol. ii, p. 333; quoted by Barth, p. 34).
27 K. Marx, *Theses on Feuerbach*, in K. Marx and F. Engels, *The German Ideology*, C. Arthur (ed.), Lawrence & Wishart, 1970, p. 121, thesis III.
28 See L. Goldmann, *Marxisme et sciences humaines*, Gallimard, Paris, 1970, p. 177.
29 Marx and Engels, p. 147, passim.
30 See for instance E. Condillac, *Traité des Systèmes*, in tome 33, *Oeuvres Philosophiques de Condillac*, Presses Universitaires de France, Paris, 1947, vol. 1, pp. 119–217.
31 Cassirer has made the point that 'the strongest intellectual forces of the Enlightenment do not lie in its rejection of belief but rather in the new form of faith which it proclaims' (*The Philosophy of the Enlightenment*, F. Koelln and J. Pettegrove (trans.), Princeton University Press, 1951, p. 135). Besides he finds Helvetius' work *De l'esprit* rather weak and unoriginal in comparison with Condillac and other philosophers of the Enlightenment (Cassirer, p. 25). This is a point which is contested by H. Barth (see Barth, p. 29) and which should also be contrasted with Marx's opinion that in Helvetius materialism assumed a really French character (see Marx and Engels, p. 153). Be this as it may, the influence of Helvetius upon his century was enormous, something which even Cassirer acknowledges.
32 Destutt de Tracy, *Éléments d'idéologie*, Chez Madame Lévi Libraire, Paris, 1827. For accounts of its contents in relation to ideology, see M. Horkheimer and T. Adorno, *Aspects of Sociology*, J. Viertel (trans.), Heinemann, 1973, pp. 185–6, also Barth, pp. 1–16, and Lichtheim, pp. 4–11.

33 Destutt de Tracy, Preface to the 1801 edition, pp. xx–xxi.

34 De Tracy, chapters 1, 2, and 3.

35 De Tracy, Preface to the 1801 edition, pp. xviii–xix.

36 De Tracy, pp. xxvii–xxix.

37 In 1795 the Convention entrusted a group of intellectuals with the management of the Institute of France, an institution of high studies committed to the ideas of the Enlightenment. Among them was Destutt de Tracy. The Institute helped Bonaparte to get his accession to power. In 1797, Bonaparte became a honorary member of the Institute. See Lichtheim, pp. 4–5.

38 Lichtheim, p. 5. After the defeat in Russia, Napoleon blamed the '*idéologues*': 'It is to ideology, that sinister metaphysics, that we must attribute all the misfortune of our beloved France. Instead of adapting the laws to knowledge of the human heart and the lessons of history, ideology seeks to base the legislation of nations on those first principles into which it so subtly inquires,' (cited by Hippolyte Taine, *Les Origines de la France contemporaine: le régime moderne*, 5th edition, Paris, 1898, vol, 2, pp. 219–20 and quoted by Barth, p. 13).

39 G. Hegel, *Werke*, vol. 15, pp. 387, 474, quoted by Barth, p. 15.

40 Auguste Comte, 'Plan of the scientific operations necessary for reorganizing society' (Third Essay 1822), in G. Lenzer (ed.), *Auguste Comte and Positivism, the Essential Writings*, Harper & Row, New York, 1975, p. 34.

41 Auguste Comte, *Cours de philosophie positive*, in Lenzer (ed.), p. 71.

42 Comte, *Cours . . .*, p. 83.

43 Comte, *Cours . . .*, p. 213.

44 Comte, *Cours . . .*, p. 215.

45 See É. Durkheim, *The Rules of Sociological Method*, G. Catlin (ed.), Free Press of Glencoe, Chicago, 1964, pp. 18–20. See also pages 91–9 of this book.

46 F. Engels, letter to F. Tonnies of 24 January 1895, in K. Marx and F. Engels, *Selected Correspondence*, I. Lasker (trans.), Progress Publishers, Moscow, 1975, p. 453.

47 K. Marx, letter to F. Engels of 7 July 1866, in Marx and Engels, *Selected Correspondence*, p. 169.

48 See on this Barth, pp. 38–47, and F. Copleston, *A History of Philosophy*, Image Books, New York, 1965, vol. 7, part 1, chapters 9, 10 and 11.

49 L. Feuerbach, *The Essence of Christianity*, G. Eliot (trans.), Harper & Row, New York, 1957, pp. 29–30.

50 Feuerbach, p. 13.

51 Marx, *Theses on Feuerbach*, p. 122, theses VI and VII.

52 K. Marx, 'A contribution to the critique of Hegel's *Philosophy of Right*: Introduction,' in K. Marx, *Early Writings*, Penguin, 1975, p. 243.

53 Lenk, p. 24.

54 Marx, 'A contribution to the Critique . . ., p. 244.

55 Marx and Engels, *The Holy Family*, p. 128.

56 The historical importance which the critique of religion has had for the concept of ideology should not be underestimated. However, in evaluating the relationship between religion and ideology from a global point of view, it must be borne in mind that although religion has an ideological dimension, it would be hasty and without a firm basis to pretend that it can be reduced to that dimension. Religion certainly is a historical phenomenon related to social contradictions; yet this does not necessarily preclude the possible existence of other dimensions in it. None the less, as far as the scientific study of ideology is concerned these other possible dimensions are not pertinent and their eventual positing must certainly not hinder the analysis of the ideological dimension. In this respect I entirely agree with Schmidt's contention that 'only the realized utopia can decide, in its *practice*, whether the intellectual constructions he denounced as ideological are mere appearances which will vanish along with the false society, or whether religion is absolutely posited by the being of man, as Christian apologetics would have us believe'. See A. Schmidt, *The Concept of Nature in Marx*, New Left Books, 1971, p. 141. Furthermore, even from a purely sociological point of view, it cannot be affirmed that the relation of religion to social contradictions has always been in the sense of concealing and negating them in the interest of the ruling class. There are many historical examples that show religion playing the opposite role, that is, unmasking and revealing social contradictions.

2   Marx's theory of ideology

1 See K. Marx, *Theses on Feuerbach*, in K. Marx and F. Engels, *The German Ideology*, C. Arthur (ed.), Lawrence & Wishart, 1970, p. 123. theses XI: 'The philosophers have only *interpreted* the world in various ways; the point is to change it.'

2 On the two strands of Marx's thought, materialist and Hegelian, and their influence upon the Marxist tradition see T. Bottomore, *Marxist Sociology*, Macmillan, London, 1975; G. Lichtheim, 'On the interpretation of Marx's thought', in N. Lobkowicz (ed.), *Marx and the Western World*, University of Notre Dame Press, 1967, and R. Aron, *Main Currents in Sociological Thought*, R. Howard and H. Weaver (trans.), Penguin, 1974, vol. 1.

3 See, for instance, A Wellmer, *Critical Theory of Society*, J. Cumming, (trans.), Herder & Herder, New York, 1971. Wellmer develops J. Habermas's critique of Marx in *Knowledge and Human Interests*, J. Shapiro (trans.), Heinemann, 1972.

4 L. Althusser, N. Poulantzas and M. Godelier belong to this tradition. In England one may cite J. Mepham as a representative with a special interest in the theory of ideology.

5 Marx, thesis I, p. 121.

6 This idea has been emphasized by A. Schmidt, *The Concept of Nature in Marx,* B. Fowkes (trans.), New Left Books, 1971, p. 114. A similar position could be found in C. Arthur's introduction to *The German Ideology,* Lawrence & Wishart, 1970, p. 22.

7 K. Marx and F. Engels, *The German Ideology,* C. Arthur (ed.), Lawrence & Wishart, 1970, p. 47.

8 Marx and Engels, p. 51.

9 K. Marx, Preface to *A contribution to the Critique of Political Economy,* in K. Marx and F. Engels, *Selected Works* in one volume, Lawrence & Wishart, 1970, p. 181.

10 Jakubowski has remarked that if in *The German Ideology* thought appears strongly dependent on being, it is because Marx and Engels took it for granted that the dualist Kantian version of this thesis had already been overcome. See F. Jakubowski, *Ideology and Superstructure,* A. Booth (trans.), Allison & Busby, 1976, p. 15.

11 Marx and Engels, p. 62.

12 Marx, *Theses on Feuerbach,* thesis VIII, p. 122.

13 Marx and Engels, p. 42.

14 Marx and Engels, p. 48.

15 Marx and Engels, p. 42.

16 K. Marx, *Capital,* F. Engels (ed.), Lawrence & Wishart, 1974, vol. 1, p. 174.

17 Marx and Engels, p. 42.

18 For Aristotle praxis was immanent activity whereas poiesis was activity whose end was external. Marx unifies both aspects so that practice appears as activity which produces an external object and simultaneously expresses the subject itself.

19 Marx and Engels, p. 50.

20 K. Kosik distinguishes a 'labour aspect' and an 'existential aspect' in practice. The former alludes to human activity in the sphere of necessity, whereas the latter refers to the formation of human subjectivity. See *Dialéctica de lo concreto,* A Sanchez (trans.), Grijalbo, Mexico, 1967, p. 243. There is an English translation under the title *Dialectics of the Concrete,* Reidel, Boston, 1976. As I said in note 18, Marx unified these two aspects in the same concept of practice. Marx's point is now to show that practice as labour, which includes technical and existential elements, does not exhaust the concept of practice.

21 Marx and Engels, p. 54. See also p. 69.

22 Marx and Engels, p. 54.

23 K. Marx, *The Eighteenth Brumaire of Louis Bonaparte,* in *Selected Works,* p. 96.

24 Marx and Engels, p. 55.

25 Marx, *Theses on Feuerbach*, thesis III, p. 121.
26 Marx and Engels, p. 115.
27 Marx and Engels, p. 56.
28 See on this Kosik, pp. 247–60.
29 Marx and Engels, pp. 117 and 56–7. The distinction and reciprocal relationship between revolutionary and reproductive practice discards any unilateral understanding of the concept. Some historicist interpretations stress man's ability to transform the world by his practical activity but forget to take sufficiently into account the conditions of such practice. This can be seen, for instance in Habermas's treatment of symbolic interaction. On the contrary, some structuralist interpetations emphasize practice as totally determined by structure so that both labour and revolution appear as the automatic result of structural factors. This can be seen, for instance, in Althusser and Godelier.
30 Marx and Engels, p. 43.
31 Marx and Engels, p. 116.
32 Marx and Engels, p. 116. The concept of contradiction is one of the most difficult and slippery in Marx's thought. It is never carefully defined, although it is profusely used in various contexts. There is little doubt about its Hegelian origin and it is certainly crucial to the concept of dialectic. In very general and simple words one can say that contradiction refers to the development of social phenomena as a movement of opposite tendencies which, in spite of being mutually interdependent, are also mutually exclusive and struggle with each other. Engels (see *Anti-Dühring*, Lawrence & Wishart, 1967), Lenin (see *Philosophical Notebooks, Collected Works*, vol. 38, Moscow, 1960) and Mao-Tse Tung (see 'On contradiction', in *Four Essays on Philosophy*, Peking, 1968), developed the concept but went beyond Marx by extending its scope to the separate field of natural forces. More recently, Althusser (see 'Contradiction and Overdetermination', in *For Marx*, New Left Books, 1977) attempts to separate the Marxist concept of Contradiction which, he argues is, 'overdetermined', from the Hegelian concept which is 'simple'. Godelier (see *Rationality and Irrationality in Economics*, New Left Books, 1972) is concerned with the same problematic and tries to solve it by means of a distinction of two kinds of contradictions in *Capital*. (See on this note 88 below.) In a recent article, L. Colletti has drawn attention to the distinction between 'dialectical contradiction' (which would be a merely logical opposition) and 'real opposition' or 'contrariety' (which would be the mutual struggle of incompatible opposites) ('Marxism and the dialectics', *New Left Review*, no. 93, 1975). Colletti argues that science can only work with the principle of no-contradiction and that if Marx applies the concept of contradiction to social reality, it is only from a philosophical point of view. However interesting these new approaches

may be, it seems to me that the above-mentioned definition is near to Marx's idea, with three provisos: that the concept was applied to social phenomena and not separately to the forces of nature; that Marx always referred to contradictions in social reality and that consequently he was not concerned with 'logical contradictions'; and that Marx did not make an essential difference between the various kinds of contradictions, although he recognized different phases in their historical evolution. It has to be accepted nevertheless, that Marx's use of the concept was far from being consistent and that it is possible to find variations in the meaning attached to it which depend upon the context of the discussion. One can only refer here to the more general sense of the concept.

33 Marx, Preface to *A contribution* . . ., p. 182. Marx had arrived at a similar conclusion in *The German Ideology*, p. 117: 'In the present epoch, the domination of material conditions over individuals, and the suppression of individuality by chance, has assumed its sharpest and most universal form, thereby setting existing individuals a very definite task. It has set them the task of replacing the domination of circumstances and of chance over individuals by the domination of individuals over chance and circumstances.'

34 Marx and Engels, p. 47.

35 See on this R. Echeverría and F. Castillo, 'Elementos para una teoría de la ideología', *Cuadernos de la Realidad Nacional*, no. 7 (March 1971), Santiago.

36 N. Poulantzas, *Political Power and Social Classes*, T. O'Hagan (trans.), New Left Books and Sheed & Ward, 1973, p. 207.

37 Marx and Engels, *The German Ideology* (large version), Lawrence & Wishart, 1965 (passage crossed out).

38 Marx and Engels, *The German Ideology*, pp. 58–9.

39 Marx and Engels, *The German Ideology* (large version), p. 52.

40 Marx and Engels, *The German Ideology* (large version), p. 41.

41 Marx and Engels, *The German Ideology* (large version), pp. 65–6.

42 Marx and Engels, *The German Ideology* (large version), p. 66. See also the marginal note where Marx affirms that in the beginning the illusion of the common interest is true.

43 Consciousness as a body of structured ideas or theory transcends the conditions in which it is produced, so that its validity cannot be confined to the situation in which it first arises. Yet this transcendence is not only the result of inner qualities of the theory in question, but also the result of men bestowing new meanings upon it as new situations come about. See on this, Kosik' sexcellent analysis on the validity of works of arts, in Kosik, pp. 152–68.

44 Marx and Engels, *The German Ideology*, p. 87.

45 Marx and Engels, *The German Ideology* (large version), pp. 316–17.

46 Marx and Engels, *The German Ideology* (large version), pp. 316–17.

47 A. Schmidt, *The Concept of Nature in Marx*, New Left Books, 1971, p. 121.

48 Marx and Engels, *The German Ideology* (large version), p. 317.

49 Marx and Engels, *The German Ideology* (large version), p. 417.

50 Marx, Preface to *A contribution . . .*, p. 181.

51 Marx, *The Eighteenth Brumaire . . .*, p. 117, and *The German Ideology*, p. 57 (my emphasis).

52 Marx and Engels, *The German Ideology*, p. 64.

53 K. Marx, *Theories of Surplus-Value*, Lawrence & Wishart, 1969, (my emphasis), vol. 1, p. 285.

54 Marx and Engels, *The German Ideology*, p. 53. See also K. Marx, *The Poverty of Philosophy*, Martin Lawrence, 1966, pp. 146–7: 'political power is precisely the official expression of antagonism in civil society'.

55 Marx and Engels, *The German Ideology*, p. 80. Poulantzas has convincingly criticized a conception of the state as the monolithic fortress of the ruling class. Yet he blames the Third International for it and does not trace its origin back to some of Marx's own formulations. See N. Poulantzas, *L'État le pouvoir, le socialisme*, Presses Universitaires de France, Paris, 1978, passim.

56 The unity of the political superstructure should not be understood as homogeneity. As Poulantzas has shown, the state itself is internally crossed by class contradiction. See Poulantzas, passim.

57 Marx and Engels, *The German Ideology*, p. 65.

58 See M. Nicolaus, 'Introduction' to K. Marx, *Grundrisse*, Penguin, 1973, pp. 24–44. I thank R. Echeverría for drawing my attention to the importance of this turning point in Marx's development. For a detailed analysis see his unpublished doctoral thesis, *Marx's Concept of Science*, Birkbeck College, London, 1978.

59 See Marx's letter to Engels, 14 January 1858, in K. Marx and F. Engels, *Selected Correspondence*, I. Lasher (trans.), Progress Publishers, Moscow, 1975, p. 93, in which he points out that he is discovering some nice arguments. 'For instance, I have overthrown the whole doctrine of profit as it has existed up to now. The fact that by a mere accident I again glanced through Hegel's *Logic* . . . has been a great service to me as regards the method of dealing with the material.'

60 See Marx, Preface to *A contribution . . .*, p. 180: 'I am omitting a general introduction which I had jotted down because on closer reflection any anticipation of results still to be proved appears to me to be disturbing, and the reader who on the whole desires to follow me must be resolved to ascend from the particular to the general.'

61 Marx, Letter to Engels, 30 April 1868, in Marx and Engels, *Selected Correspondence*, p. 195.

62 See Kosik, p. 201. Kosik argues that both Marx's *Capital* and Hegel's *Phenomenology of Spirit* are structured around a symbolic motive current to the cultural atmosphere of their epoch, which is the *Odyssey*. The subject must go on a pilgrimage through the world in order to come to know himself. The subject's self-knowledge is only possible upon the basis of his activity on the world. In Hegel's *Phenomenology* the subject is consciousness which recuperates itself through its pilgrimage, whereas in Marx's *Capital* the subject is historical practice.

63 Kosik, p. 210.

64 Marx, *Capital*, vol. 1, p. 76.

65 Marx, *Capital*, vol. 1, p. 82.

66 Marx, *Capital*, vol. 3, p. 44.

67 Marx, *Capital*, vol. 3, p. 168.

68 Marx, *Capital*, vol. 3, p. 168.

69 Marx, *Capital*, vol. 1, p. 227.

70 K. Marx, *Critique of the Gotha Programme*, in Marx and Engels *Selected Works*, p. 324.

71 Marx, *Capital*, vol. 1, p. 503.

72 Norman Geras distinguishes between real appearances and false appearances. The fetishism of commodity and the fetishism of capital belong to the former whereas the wage form belongs to the latter. It seems to me that this distinction is not quite clear. Why should not the wage-form be a real appearance? If appearances could be so different from the essence as to constitute mere illusions, their internal bond with the essence would be lost and thus it would be impossible for them to conceal it. See N. Geras, 'Marx and the critique of political economy', in R. Blackburn (ed.), *Ideology in Social Science*, Fontana, 1972, p. 291.

73 Marx, *Capital*, vol. 3, p. 209 (my emphasis).

74 K. Marx, *Grundrisse*, M. Nicolaus (trans.), Penguin, 1973, p. 831.

75 Marx, *Capital*, vol. 3, p. 45.

76 Marx, *Capital*, vol. 1, pp. 505–6.

77 Marx, *Theories of Surplus-Value*, vol. 3, p. 453.

78 Marx, *Theories of Surplus-Value*, vol. 3, p. 265.

79 Marx, *Grundrisse*, p. 164.

80 Geras, p. 297.

81 Marx, *Capital*, vol. 1, pp. 93–4.

82 Marx, *Theories of Surplus-Value*, vol. 3, p. 296.

83 Marx, Letter to Kugelmann, 11 July 1868, in Marx and Engels, *Selected Correspondence*, p. 197.

84 Marx, *Capital*, vol. 1, p. 79.

85 Marx, *Capital*, vol. 1, pp. 80–1.

86 Marx, *Theories of Surplus-Value*, vol. 3, p. 467. Marx does not really analyse the relationship which exists between the inversion of real

relations and the fact of their being contradictory. There is no doubt that inversion and contradiction are closely related. Yet there seems to be no relationship of causality between them. In principle there is no compelling reason why the inversion of real relations should determine their being contradictory or why contradictory relations should determine their being inverted. It seems to me that contradiction and inversion of real relations must be understood as two aspects of the same phenomenon. Real relations could be said to be inverted when looked at from a static point of view, that is, when the point is to define their ultimate content. On the other hand, the same real relations could be said to be contradictory when looked at from a dynamic point of view, that is, from the standpoint of their actual development towards a solution. In this sense to say that ideology conceals contradictions could be made equivalent to saying that it conceals or negates a real inversion.

87 On the contradictions inherent in commodities see Marx, *Capital*, vol. 1, p. 115.

88 Godelier distinguishes two kinds of contradictions in *Capital*. First he mentions contradictions internal to the structure of relation of production (class contradictions), which are original but do not contain in themselves the conditions for their solution. Second, he mentions contradictions between two structures, that is, between productive forces and relations of production, which are not original and develop, not in connection with any will or purpose, but as a result of the system. See M. Godelier, *Rationality and Irrationality in Economics*, B. Pearce (trans.), New Left Books, 1972, pp. 77–104. One has to point out that although this classification is attractive, Marx himself did not draw it. The problem I see in it is the fact that class contradictions assume an almost intentional character without any possible internal solution, whereas contradictions between structures are entirely non-intentional but successful in bringing about a solution. Subject and object are thus sharply split off. Class contradictions seem disconnected from structural contradictions. It is forgotten that for Marx's 'the conditions under which definite productive forces can be applied are the conditions of the rule of a definite class of society' . . . and that therefore 'every revolutionary struggle is directed against a class' (Marx, *The German Ideology*, p. 94). By reducing the terms of the so-called fundamental contradiction to unintentional structures, Godelier devoids it of all practical meaning and makes of its solution a sort of blind, natural process.

89 Marx, *The Poverty of Philosophy*, p. 66.

90 Marx, *Theories of Surplus-Value*, vol. 3, p. 491.

91 This terminology is used by Marx in the Preface of the German edition of *Capital*, vol 1, p. 24 and also in *Theories of Surplus-Value*, vol. 2, p. 512.

92 Marx, *Capital*, vol. 3, p. 249. See also *Theories of Surplus-Value*, vol. 2, p. 500.
93 Marx, *Theories of Surplus-Value*, vol. 1, p. 285.
94 Marx, *Theories of Surplus-Value*, vol. 3, pp. 491–2.
95 Marx, *The Poverty of Philosophy*, p. 105.
96 See Marx, *Theories of Surplus-Value*, vol. 2, pp. 117–18: 'Ricardo's conception is, on the whole, in the interests of the *industrial bourgeoisie*, only *because*, and *in so far as*, their interests coincide with that of production or the productive development of human labour. Where the bourgeoisie comes into conflict with this, he is just as *ruthless* towards it as he is at other times towards the proletariat and the aristocracy.'
97 Marx, *Theories of Surplus-Value*, vol. 1, p. 285.
98 See on this F. Castillo, *El problema de la praxis en la Teología de la Liberación*, Wilhems Universität, Münster, 1976, p. 258.
99 Jakubowski, pp. 38 and 59.
100 Kosik, p. 141.
101 Quoted by Schmidt, p. 50, as printed in F. Mehring, *Aus dem literarischen Nachlass von Karl Marx und Friedrich Engels*, vol. 2, Stuttgart, 1920, p. 456.
102 See R. Williams, *Marxism and Literature*, Oxford University Press, 1977, pp. 77–8.
103 Jakubowski, pp. 46 and 56.
104 See R. Rossanda, 'Mao's Marxism', *The Socialist Register*, Merlin, 1971, p. 40. Rossanda associates these errors with political deviations. Thus the autonomy of the superstructure appears as a 'revisionist' deviation, whereas the subordination of the superstructure appear, as a 'Stalinist' deviation.
105 Aron, vol. 1, p. 160.
106 Marx, *Grundrisse*, p. 694: 'The accumulation of knowledge and of skill, of the general productive forces of the social brain . . .'; also p. 699: 'science too is among these productive forces'.
107 S. Timpanaro, 'Considerations on materialism', *New Left Review*, no. 85, 1974, p. 17.

3 From Engels to Durkheim: the continuing debate on ideology

1 Besides Paul Barth, Dühring, Buckle and other positivists with whom Engels took issue, one could also name Max Weber as propounding a kind of theory of factors. He was concerned with demonstrating that the economic factor was not the only important one. Thus he distinguished three more or less autonomous spheres: economy, power and social position. His point about the protestant ethic as a decisive factor in the production of capitalist economy is also well known.

2 F. Engels, Letter to J. Bloch, 21–2 September 1890, in K, Marx and F. Engels, *Selected Correspondence*, I Lasher (trans.), Progress Publishers, Moscow, 1975, p. 394.

3 F. Engels, Letter to C. Schmidt, 5 August 1890, in Marx and Engels, p. 292.

4 See Engels, Letter to Borgius, 25 January 1894, in Marx and Engels, p. 442. See also letter to C. Schmidt, 27 October 1890, p. 402: 'What these gentlemen all lack is dialectics. They always see only cause here, effect there. . . . This is an empty abstraction.'

5 Engels, Letter to F. Mehring, 14 July 1893, in Marx and Engels, p. 435: 'connected with this is the fatuous notion of the ideologists that because we deny an independent historical development to the various ideological spheres which play a part in history we also deny them any *effect upon history*. The basis of this is the common undialectical conception of cause and effect as rigidly opposite poles, the total disregard of interaction.'

6 F. Engels, *Anti-Dühring*, Lawrence & Wishart, 1969, p. 25.

7 See Engels, *Ludwig Feuerbach and the end of Classical German Philosophy*, in K. Marx and F. Engels, *Selected Works* in one volume, Lawrence & Wishart, 1970, pp. 588 and 609. One might argue that it is necessary to give Engels the same allowances which are given to Marx. In criticizing idealism, it is very easy to overstate the opposite point of view without really meaning to accept the traditional mechanical materialism. In any case, the use of the terms 'reflex' and 'reflection' is rather unfortunate.

8 See G. Lukács, *History and Class Consciousness*, Merlin, 1971, particularly p. 3 passim and pp. 199–200.

9 K. Korsch, *Karl Marx*, Russell & Russell, New York, 1963, p. 224.

10 Korsch, p. 221. Korsch is referring to Marx's analysis in the 1857 Introduction, see K. Marx, *Grundrisse*, M. Nicolaus (trans.), Penguin, 1973, pp. 94–100.

11 G. Stedman Jones, 'Engels and the end of classical German philosophy', *New Left Review*, no. 79, 1973, p. 32.

12 K. Kosik, *Dialéctica de lo concreto*, A Sanchez (trans.), Grijalbo, Mexico, 1967, p. 137.

13 Korsch, p. 229.

14 Antonio Labriola published his *Essays on the Materialistic Conception of History* in 1896; a year later, Plekhanov, reviewing the book, adhered to most of its tenets as far as the role of the economy was concerned. See A. Labriola, *Essays . . .*, C. Kerr (trans.), Monthly Review Press, New York, 1966, particularly chapters 6 and 7. Also G. Plekhanov, *The Materialist Conception of History*, International Publishers, New York, 1969.

15 Plekhanov, pp. 108–10.

16 Labriola, p. 113.

17 Labriola, p. 152.

18 Labriola, p. 216–17.

19 Plekhanov, p. 115.

20 As Rossanda opportunely remarks, Marx, in the *Preface to a Contribution to the Critique of Political Economy*, in Marx and Engels, *Selected Works*, referred to the economic structure as being formed not just by the property of the means of production but by the 'sum total of relations'. See R. Rossanda, 'Mao's Marxism', *The Socialist Register*, Merlin, 1971.

21 As Kosik has pointed out, if the economic structure is disconnected from practice, it could degenerate into an economic factor. See Kosik, pp. 127 and 141.

22 See V. Lenin, *What the 'Friends of the People' Are and How They Fight the Social Democrats*, in *Collected Works*, Foreign Languages Publishing House, Moscow, 1960, vol. 1, specially part 1. For a good account of Lenin's views see T. Moulian, 'La idolatría de la ciencia y las maladanzas de la teoría de la ideología', Manuscript, Santiago, 1976.

23 Lenin, p. 138.

24 Lenin, pp. 140–1.

25 Lenin, p. 141.

26 Lenin, p. 177–8.

27 See V. Lenin, *What Is to be Done?*, Foreign Languages Press, Peking, 1975, p. 37.

28 Lenin, *What Is to be Done?*, p. 50.

29 V. Lenin, *Philosophical Notebooks*, in *Collected Works*, vol. 38, pp. 212–13.

30 Lenin, *Philosophical Notebooks*, p. 182.

31 Lenin, *Philosophical Notebooks*, p. 171.

32 Engels, Letter to C. Schmidt, 27 October, 1890, in Marx and Engels *Selected Correspondence*, p. 400.

33 See F. Castillo, *El problema de la praxis en la Teología de la Liberación*, Wilhelms Universität, Münster, 1976, p. 266.

34 See the abundant use of 'socialist ideology' in opposition to 'bourgeois ideology' in Lenin, *What is to Be Done?*.

35 Thus for instance is treated by N. Poulantzas, *Political Power and Social Classes*, T. O'Hagan (trans.), Sheed & Ward, 1973, p. 197.

36 See on this G. Stedman Jones, 'The Marxism of the early Lukács: an evaluation', *New Left Review*, no. 70, 1971. See also I. Meszaros, *Lukács' Concept of Dialectic*, Merlin, 1972.

37 Lukács, p. 200.

38 G. Lukács, *Writer and Critic*, Merlin, 1978, p. 73.

39 Lukács, *History and Class Consciousness*, pp. 202–3.

40 Lukács, *History and Class Consciousness*, p. 204.

41 Lukács, *History and Class Consciousness*, p. 257.

226 Notes to pages 79–83

42 Lukács, *History and Class Consciousness*, p. 205. Eleswhere Lukács
states: 'The now emerging self-consciousness of mankind announces
as a perspective the end of human "prehistory". With this, man's
self-creation acquires a new accent; now as a trend we see the emergence of a unity between the individual's human self-constitution and
the self-creation of mankind. *Ethics is a crucial intermediary link*
in this whole process' (quoted in Meszaros, p. 77). This quotation is
taken from a lecture in 1947. As Meszaros rightly remarks, its failure
as an assessment of a particular historical situation cannot be explained by Lukács's political inexperience. It strikingly resembles
Lukács's early formulae, but thirty years later.

43 Lukács, *History and Class Consciousness*, p. 262.

44 Lukács, *History and Class Consciousness*, p. 263.

45 Lukács, *History and Class Consciousness*, p. 257.

46 For Lukács a class ripe for hegemony is that whose 'interests and
consciousness enable it to organize the whole of society in accordance
with those interests' (Lukács, *History and Class Consciousness*, p. 52).

47 Lukács, 'Introducción a los escritos . . .', p. 7.

48 A. Gramsci, *Prison Notebooks*, Q. Hoare (trans.), Lawrence &
Wishart, 1971, p. 366.

49 Gramsci, p. 376.

50 Gramsci, p. 164. These quotations are quite obviously anti-histori-
cist in character and show, as in Lukács's case, that Gramsci's thought
is far more balanced than the 'structuralists' would have us believe.
See on this S. Hall, B. Lumley, G. McLennan, *Politics and ideology:
Gramsci*, Working Papers in Cultural Studies, no. 10, Centre for
Contemporary Cultural Studies, University of Birmingham, 1977.

51 Gramsci, pp. 376–7.

52 Gramsci, p. 328.

53 Gramsci recognizes that the strength of religions and of the Catholic
church in particular, lies in this unifying character which for instance
'immanentist philosophies' (Croce, Gentile) are unable to produce.

54 Gramsci, p. 404.

55 Gramsci, p. 405.

56 Gramsci, pp. 366–7. On the comparison between Lenin and Gramsci
see Moulian.

57 Gramsci, p. 367. See also Marx, *Capital*, vol. 3, p. 820.

58 See on this J. M. Piotte, *La Pensée politique de Gramsci*, Anthropos,
Paris, 1970, p. 204.

59 P. Anderson, 'The antinomies of Antonio Gramsci', *New Left
Review*, no. 100, November 1976–January 1977, p. 28.

60 In one version hegemony pertains to civil society and coercion to the
state. Another version divides hegemony into civil and political
hegemony so that the state itself becomes an apparatus of hegemony.
Still a third version presents the state as including both political

society and civil society so that the distinction between state and civil society disappears.

61 S. Freud, 'Draft H. Paranoia' (24 January 1895), *The Standard Edition of the Complete Psychological Works of Sigmund Freud*, vol. 1, Hogarth Press, p. 209

62 S. Freud, 'Notes on a case of paranoia', *Standard Edition . . .*, vol. 10, p. 66.

63 S. Freud, 'Notes upon a case of obsessional neurosis', *Standard Edition . . .*, vol. 10, p. 192.

64 W. Reich, *The Mass Psychology of Fascism*, Penguin, 1978, p. 17. See also p. 64: 'Man's authoritarian structure – this must be clearly established – is basically produced by the embedding of sexual inhibitions and fear in the living substance of sexual impulses', and p. 118: '. . . The core of the Fascist race theory is a mortal fear of natural sexuality and of its orgasm function.'

65 Reich, p. 16.

66 Reich, p. 52.

67 For a critique of Reich's psychological approach to Fascism see E. Laclau, *Politics and Ideology in Marxist Theory*, New Left Books, 1977, chapter 3.

68 S. Freud, *The Future of an Illusion*, Hogarth Press, 1928, pp. 22–3.

69 Freud, *The Future of an Illusion*, p. 24.

70 Freud, *The Future of an Illusion*, p. 52.

71 Freud, *The Future of an Illusion*, p. 30.

72 Freud, *The Future of an Illusion*, p. 42.

73 Freud, *The Future of an Illusion*, p. 68.

74 Freud, *The Future of an Illusion*, p. 76.

75 Freud, *The Future of an Illusion*, p. 89.

76 Freud, *The Future of an Illusion*, p. 95.

77 S. Freud, *Civilization and Its Discontents, Standard Edition . . .*, vol. 21, pp. 112–13.

78 Freud, *Civilization and Its Discontents*, p. 113.

79 V. Pareto, *Treatise on General Sociology, Sociological Writings*, D. Mirfin (trans.), Blackwell, 1976, p. 184.

80 Pareto, p. 179.

81 Pareto, p. 185.

82 Pareto, pp. 216–17.

83 Pareto, p. 194.

84 Pareto, p. 196.

85 Pareto, p. 187.

86 Pareto, p. 188.

87 Pareto, p. 172.

88 Pareto, pp. 174 and 194.

89 Pareto, p. 189.

90 Pareto, p. 244.

91 Pareto, p. 245.

92 Pareto, p. 201. See also p. 171 on Comte, Spencer and others.

93 É. Durkheim, *The Rules of Sociological Method*, S. A. Solovay and J. H. Mueller (trans.), Free Press, New York, 1964, p. 15. For a good exposition of Durkheim's concept of ideology in *The Rules* see P. Q. Hirst, *Durkheim, Bernard and Epistemology*, Routledge & Kegan Paul, 1975, pp. 83–9.

94 Durkheim, p. 14.

95 Pareto, p. 171.

96 Durkheim, p. 20.

97 Durkheim, p. 17.

98 Durkheim, p. 32.

99 Durkheim, p. 15. Note the similarity between this idea and Pareto's distinction between the social utility of ideas and their logico-experimental truth.

100 Durkheim, p. 18.

101 Durkheim, p. 16 (my emphasis).

102 Durkheim, p. 31 (my emphasis).

103 The latter seems to be the position of Paul Q. Hirst – see Hirst, p. 89. For a good exposition of Durkheim's sociology of religion and its connections with the sociology of knowledge see Steven Lukes, *Émile Durkheim*, Penguin, 1975, pp. 435–84.

104 É. Durkheim, *The Elementary Forms of Religious Life*, J. W. Swain (trans.), Allen & Unwin, 1976, p. 10.

105 Durkheim, *The Elementary Forms . . .*, p. 225.

106 Durkheim, *The Elementary Forms . . .*, p. 423.

107 Durkheim, *The Elementary Forms . . .*, p. 226.

108 Durkheim, *The Elementary Forms . . .*, p. 427.

109 Durkheim, *The Elementary Forms . . .*, p. 419.

110 Durkheim, *The Elementary Forms . . .*, p. 429.

111 Durkheim, *The Elementary Forms . . .*, p. 417.

112 Durkheim, *The Elementary Forms . . .*, p. 4.

113 Durkheim, *The Elementary Forms . . .*, p. 421.

114 Durkheim, *The Elementary Forms . . .*, p. 421.

115 Durkheim, *The Elementary Forms . . .*, p. 422.

116 Durkheim, *The Elementary Forms . . .*, p. 423.

117 Durkheim, *The Elementary Forms . . .*, p. 423.

118 Durkheim, *The Elementary Forms . . .*, p. 444.

119 Durkheim, *The Elementary Forms . . .*, p. 435.

120 Durkheim, *The Elementary Forms . . .*, p. 437. The same line is taken when Durkheim argues that religion 'cannot rest upon an error and a lie' (p. 2) and when he affirms that a collective representation cannot be 'wholly inadequate for its subject' (p. 438).

121 Durkheim, *The Elementary Forms . . .*, p. 444.

122 Durkheim, *The Elementary Forms . . .*, p. 437.

123 Durkheim, *The Elementary Forms . . .*, p. 445.

4 The historicist tradition: Mannheim's sociology of knowledge and Goldmann's genetic structuralism

1 K. Mannheim, *Ideology and Utopia*, L. Wirth and E. Shils (trans.), Routledge & Kegan Paul, 1972, p. 238.
2 K. Mannheim, 'On the interpretation of Weltanschauung', in K. Mannheim *Essays on the Sociology of Knowledge*, P. Kecskemeti, (ed.), Routledge & Kegan Paul, 1968, p. 73.
3 Mannheim, 'On the interpretation of Weltanschauung', p. 42.
4 Mannheim, 'On the interpretation of Weltanschauung', p. 61.
5 'On the interpretation of Weltanschauung', (1921–2) can be considered as the main work of the first 'interpretative' period. The second period could be said to start with the publication of 'The problem of a sociology of knowledge' (1925) and 'The ideological and the sociological interpretation of intellectual phenomena' (1926).
6 See Mannheim, *Ideology and Utopia*, p. 240. *Ideology and Utopia* (1929) expounds in detail some of Mannheim's basic intuitions already present in 'The problem of a sociology of knowledge'.
7 Mannheim, 'Competition as a cultural phenomenon', in *Essays on the Sociology of Knowledge*, p. 192.
8 Mannheim, *Ideology and Utopia*, p. 2.
9 Mannheim, *Ideology and Utopia*, p. 4.
10 Mannheim, *Ideology and Utopia*, p. 26. Further below Mannheim adds 'precisely because knowing is fundamentally collective knowing (the thought of the lone individual is only a special instance and a recent development) it presupposes a community of knowing which grows primarily out of a community of experiencing prepared for in the subconscious' (p. 28).
11 Mannheim, 'Competition as a cultural phenomena', pp. 193–4.
12 Mannheim, 'The problem of a sociology of knowledge', in *Essays on the Sociology of Knowledge*, p. 135.
13 Sometimes Mannheim also uses the terms 'commitment' or 'perspective' to refer to a *Weltanschauung*.
14 Mannheim's concept of social class differs from Marx's in that the sphere of production is not considered to be ultimately determinant. He accepts that the class-position is a common location which individuals hold in the economic and power structure of a given society, yet he adds 'one is proletarian, *entrepreneur*, or *rentier*, and he is what he is because he is constantly aware of the nature of his specific "location" . . .' ('The problem of generations', in *Essays on the Sociology of Knowledge*, p. 289). So the subjective perception of individuals seems crucial for class determination.

15 Mannheim, 'The problem of a sociology of knowledge', p. 184.

16 See on this Mannheim, 'The ideological and the sociological inter-
    pretation of intellectual phenomena', in *From Karl Mannheim*, K.
    Wolff (ed.), Oxford University Press, New York, 1971.

17 Mannheim, 'The ideological and the sociological interpretation . . .',
    p. 121.

18 See Mannheim, 'Competition as a cultural phenomenon', and 'The
    problem of generations'.

19 Mannheim, 'The problem of generations', p. 291.

20 Mannheim, 'Competition as a cultural phenomenon', pp. 198–210.

21 Mannheim, 'The ideological and the sociological interpretation . . .',
    p. 124. If in order to analyse a theory one does not relativize it
    through a process of functionalization but, instead, only debates its
    intrinsic meaning, one may well be caught in its ideological sphere,
    even if in the end one rejects it. In this case, according to Mannheim,
    we make not a proper sociological interpretation but an ideological
    one.

22 Mannheim, 'The ideological and the sociological interpretation . . .',
    p. 125. It seems to me that the terms of Mannheim's distinction are
    not clear from a logical point of view. The main alternative should
    have been between those who emphasise the union of immanent and
    functional meaning and those who stress their incommensurability.
    In this way the latter could have been properly divided into those
    who emphasise immanent meaning and those who emphasise func-
    tional meaning to the exclusion of the contrary. As it stands, the
    distinction starts with those who stress the relevance of functional
    meaning and those who maintain that it can be neglected altogether.
    As a consequence, Marx may appear as a sub-group within the latter,
    which is, of course, not the case at all.

23 Mannheim, 'The problem of a sociology of knowledge', p. 137.

24 Mannheim, 'The problem of a sociology of knowledge', p. 140.

25 Mannheim, 'The problem of a sociology of knowledge', p. 140.

26 Mannheim, *Ideology and Utopia*, p. 256.

27 Mannheim, *Ideology and Utopia*, p. 255.

28 Mannheim, 'Competition as a cultural phenomenon', p. 194.

29 Mannheim, *Ideology and Utopia*, p. 254.

30 Mannheim, *Ideology and Utopia*, p. 70.

31 Mannheim, *Ideology and Utopia*, p. 71.

32 Mannheim, *Ideology and Utopia*, p. 49.

33 Mannheim, *Ideology and Utopia*, pp. 49–50.

34 Kant's philosophy contributed the idea that the 'world exists only
    with reference to the knowing mind, and the mental activity of the
    subject determines the form in which the world appears'. Hegel and
    the historical school added the historical dimension so that the unity
    of consciousness was seen as a process of continual historical trans-

formation. Finally Marx replaced 'folk' by class as the bearer of the historically evolving consciousness. The concept of *'Volkgeist'* is superseded by class consciousness or class ideology. See Mannheim, *Ideology and Utopia*, pp. 58–60.

35 Mannheim, *Ideology and Utopia*, p. 66.

36 Mannheim points out that the total concept of ideology entails 'the courage to subject not just the adversary's point of view but all points of views, including his own, to the ideological analysis' (*Ideology and Utopia*, p. 69).

37 Mannheim, *Ideology and Utopia*, p. 83.

38 Mannheim, *Ideology and Utopia*, p. 84.

39 Mannheim, *Ideology and Utopia*, p. 86.

40 Mannheim, *Ideology and Utopia*, p. 86.

41 Mannheim, *Ideology and Utopia*, p. 238.

42 Mannheim, *Ideology and Utopia*, p. 239. Notwithstanding this, Mannheim propounds elsewhere to use the concept of ideology as 'the outlook inevitably associated with a given historical and social situation, and the weltanschauung and style of thought bound up with it' (p. 111).

43 Mannheim, 'Conservative thought', in *From Karl Mannheim*, p. 134. Outhwaite rightly points out that there seems to be an ambiguity as to whether what is at issue is the interpretation of *Weltanschauungen* as such or the interpretation of other cultural phenomena in terms of *Weltanschauungen*. At any rate, as he suggests, the two are related in the 'hermeneutic circle'. See W. Outhwaite, *Understanding Social Life, the Method Called Verstehen*, Allen & Unwin, 1975, p. 77.

44 See on this Mannheim, *Ideology and Utopia*, pp. 276–7.

45 Mannheim, 'Conservative thought', p. 136.

46 Mannheim, *Ideology and Utopia*, p. 277.

47 Mannheim 'Conservative thought', p. 177.

48 Mannheim, *Ideology and Utopia*, pp. 277–8.

49 Mannheim, 'Conservative thought', p. 180. One can see here the extent to which Mannheim pioneered the method which Goldmann will popularize later on. See on this, pages 122–9 of this book.

50 Mannheim, *Ideology and Utopia*, p. 87.

51 Mannheim, *Ideology and Utopia*, p. 173.

52 Mannheim, *Ideology and Utopia*, p. 177. One may well ask who is to decide whether a utopia is relative or absolute. Again, the opinions will be divided between supporters and attackers of the *status quo*. Mannheim does not provide any objective criterion, but on the contrary, underlines the fact that 'every definition in historical thinking depends necessarily upon one's perspective'.

53 Mannheim, *Ideology and Utopia*, p. 183.

54 Mannheim, *Ideology and Utopia*, p. 184.

55 Mannheim, *Ideology and Utopia*, p. 87.

56 Mannheim, *Ideology and Utopia*, p. 94.
57 Mannheim, 'Competition as a cultural phenomenon', pp. 221–2.
58 Mannheim, 'Competition as a cultural phenomenon', p. 222.
59 Mannheim, *Ideology and Utopia*, pp. 135–6.
60 Mannheim, *Ideology and Utopia*, pp. 143–4.
61 Mannheim, *Ideology and Utopia*, p. 139.
62 Mannheim, *Ideology and Utopia*, p. 167.
63 As further evidence of Mannheim's problems on this issue one may quote him again: 'Nonetheless, though there is a *consensus ex post* or an increasingly broader stratum of knowledge which is valid for all parties, we should not allow ourselves to be misled by this or to overlook the fact that at every given historical point in time there is a substantial amount of knowledge which is accessible to us only seen in social perspective' (*Ideology and Utopia*, p. 168). So he constantly oscillates between the synthesis of the unattached intelligentsia and the socially determined perspective of intellectuals.
64 Mannheim, *Ideology and Utopia*, p. 227.
65 Mannheim, *Ideology and Utopia*, p. 225.
66 Mannheim, *Ideology and Utopia*, p. 236.
67 See note 42 to this chapter.
68 Mannheim, *Ideology and Utopia*, p. 249.
69 If, as Mannheim recognizes, the fact that all thought is related to a certain historical situation does not, however, rob it of all possibility of attaining the truth (*Ideology and Utopia*, p. 124), one wonders why it is that Marx should have recognized the ideological character of his own theory. Of course the answer is that Mannheim misunderstands Marx's concept of ideology, and makes it equivalent to the general social determination of knowledge.
70 Gurvitch criticizes Mannheim for this concession to epistemology. He thinks judgements of value have nothing to do with sociology. According to Gurvitch the difficulties which Marx, Durkheim and Mannheim came across stemmed from philosophical pre-conceptions. The evaluation of the validity of thought is a philosophical matter and therefore should be left outside. Consequently, Gurvitch propounds the idea that the sociology of knowledge cannot serve to invalidate false knowledge nor to demystify or 'disalienate' it; 'it is not its function to decide on the veracity of the content of knowledge'. See G. Gurvitch, *The Social Frameworks of Knowledge*, M. and K. Thompson (trans.), Basil Blackwell, 1971, pp. 10–13. If Mannheim succumbed to relativism, Gurvitch in his turn emasculates sociology of knowledge from any critical value, thus reducing it to a sort of inventory of classificatory schemes whose degree of abstraction makes it useless for the analysis of knowledge, let alone ideology.
71 Danto has rightly pointed out that we must not confuse the causes of a belief with the reasons for a belief (see A. C. Danto, *Analytical*

Philosophy of History, Cambridge University Press, 1965, p. 97). We can transpose this into the field of ideology by saying that the social sources of historical thought do not exhaust the validity of the content by themselves. The critical analysis of the content itself is required.

72 See T. Adorno, *Negative Dialectics*, E. Ashton (trans.), Routledge & Kegan Paul, 1973, p. 197.

73 A. Schaff, 'Marxisme et sociologie de la connaissance', *L'Homme et la société*, no. 10, October–December 1968, pp. 125–6.

74 Marx's theory of ideology is in this sense far more specific in determining the kinds of distortions which ideology entails. This is why, contrary to what Mannheim thinks, Marx does not dismiss all bourgeois thought as ideological, but rather sees a mixture of ideological and scientific aspects which varies along with the development of social contradictions.

75 See on this K. Lenk, 'Problemgeschichtliche Einleitung', in K. Lenk (ed.), *Ideologie, Ideologiekritik und Wissenssoziologie*, H. Luchterhand, Berlin, 1970, p. 54.

76 L. Goldmann, *Marxisme et sciences humaines*, Gallimard, Paris, 1970, p. 18.

77 Goldmann, p. 21.

78 L. Goldmann, 'Ideology and writing', *The Times Literary Supplement*, 28 September 1967, p. 904.

79 Goldmann, 'Ideology and writing', p. 904.

80 L. Goldmann, 'Introduction Generale', in M. de Gandillac, L. Goldmann, *et al.*, *Entretiens sur les notions de 'Genese' et de 'structure'*, Mouton & École Pratique des Hautes Études, Paris, 1965, p. 10.

81 Goldmann, acknowledges an important difference between Dilthey on the one hand and Lukács and Piaget on the other. Dilthey was indeed the first to emphasize the importance of comprehension, but he did it from a non-dialectical point of view and in such a vague manner that he was prevented from accomplishing any rigorously positive analysis. Lukács and Piaget, on the contrary, would have introduced a perfect methodological clarity upon the concept of genetic structure and would have defined with precision and rigour its positive use. See Goldmann, *The Hidden God*, P. Thody (trans.), Routledge & Kegan Paul, 1964, p. 14. Also Goldmann, *Marxisme et sciences humaines*, p. 28.

82 Goldmann, *The Hidden God*, p. 10.

83 Goldmann, *The Hidden God*, pp. 14–15.

84 Goldmann, 'Ideology and writing', p. 904.

85 Goldmann, *The Hidden God*, p. 17.

86 Likewise, the concept of world-view, according to Goldmann, enables one to distinguish between similar statements which have, nevertheless, entirely opposite meanings. As an example he mentions the theory of predestination of Jansenism and Calvinism; in their

statements they are not so different and yet they belong to utterly different world-views. See Goldmann, *The Hidden God*, p. 8.

87 Goldmann, *The Hidden God*, p. 17.

88 Goldmann, *Marxisme et sciences humaines*, pp. 125–6.

89 L. Goldmann, *The Human Sciences and Philosophy*, H. White and R. Anchor (trans.), Cape, 1973, p. 65.

90 See Goldmann, *The Hidden God*, chapter 6, p. 103 passim.

91 Goldmann, *The Human Sciences and Philosophy*, p. 64.

92 Goldmann, *The Human Sciences and Philosophy*, p. 51.

93 Goldmann, *The Human Sciences and Philosophy*, p. 52.

94 Goldmann, *The Human Sciences and Philosophy*, p. 56.

95 Goldmann, *The Human Sciences and Philosophy*, p. 103.

96 Goldmann, *The Human Sciences and Philosophy*, p. 57.

97 It is suggestive that Goldmann's otherwise brilliant analysis of Marx's *Theses on Feuerbach* has practically nothing to say about the second thesis. See Goldmann, *Marxisme et sciences humaines*, pp. 174–5.

98 Glucksmann's critique of Goldmann is less restrained in this respect. She accuses Goldmann of neo-Hegelianism and affirms that 'theory is denied any autonomy, and becomes an expression of class consciousness rather than a science capable of rigorous analysis and of providing a framework for political strategy'. See M. Glucksmann, 'Lucien Goldmann: humanist or Marxist?', *New Left Review*, no. 56, July–August, 1969, p. 49. However, one cannot but notice the strong structuralist overtones of Glucksmann's critique and her overrated valuation of science in the provision of a political strategy. It is true that science cannot be collapsed into class consciousness, yet it cannot substitute for class practice either. This is the problem of structuralist interpretations which understand theory quite separate from class struggle and make it the clue for liberation, disregarding the very practice of the liberating class. In this sense, Goldmann's insistence upon the connections between theory and class struggle are in the best Marxist tradition. The problem is that he accentuates their unity without insisting enough upon their distinction. Static structuralism falls at the other extreme by insisting only upon their distinction and disregarding their unity.

99 Goldmann, *The Hidden God*, p. 98.

5 Ideology and structural analysis

1 K. Marx and F. Engels, *The German Ideology*, C. Arthur (ed.), Lawrence & Wishart, 1970, pp. 50–1.

2 See on this E. Veron, 'Ideología y sociología: para una pragmática de las ciencias sociales', in R. Zuñiga (ed.), *Instinto, motivación, valores e ideología*, Ediciones Universitarias de Valparaiso, Valparaiso, 1971, p. 75. One must note though, that for Veron and other

structuralists, ideology is a level of meaning present in every discourse as a connotative dimension. It seems to me that connotation should not in itself be equated with ideology. Ideology is certainly a level of meaning in a discourse, but it may well be absent from it, even when this has several connotations.

3 F. de Saussure, *Cours de Linguistique générale*, Payot, Paris, 1949, pp. 43 and 124.

4 A good exposition of the basic tenets of structural linguistic can be found in R. Barthes, *Elements of Semiology*, A. Lavers and C. Smith (trans), Cape, 1967.

5 P. Ricoeur, 'Structure et herméneutique', *Esprit*, no. 322, vol. 2, November 1963, p. 599.

6 A. Schaff, *Structuralisme et Marxisme*, Anthropos, Paris, 1974, p. 23.

7 R. Barthes, *Mythologies,* A. Lavers (trans.), Cape, 1972, pp. 114–15. See also Barthes, *Elements of Semiology*, p. 89.

8 A. J. Greimas, *Sémantique structurale*, Larousse, Paris, 1966, pp. 123–6.

9 See Barthes, *Mythologies*, p. 115 and *Elements of Semiology*, p. 90. There is also another possibility of insertion of the first system into the second. This occurs when the system ERC becomes the *content* of a second system. According to Barthes, this is the case with all meta-languages, that is, those systems whose plane of content is itself constituted by a signifying system.

10 Barthes, *Mythologies*, pp. 117 and 123.

11 Barthes, *Mythologies*, p. 32. This kind of analysis can also be found with respect to wrestling, margarine, ornamental cookery, striptease and so forth. Barthes takes up almost every aspect of life, as described in magazines, and shows its connoted 'ideological' function.

12 R. Barthes, *Système de la mode*, Éditions du Seuil, Paris, 1967.

13 Barthes, *Système de la mode*, p. 231.

14 Culler maintains that Barthes's analysis of the rhetorical level of the fashion system is more pertinent and successful than his account of the vestimentary code. See J. Culler, *Structuralist Poetics*, Routledge & Kegan Paul, 1975, p. 38. From the methodological point of view, though, I think that the contrary is true. Barthes's ability in the study of the rhetorical level is beyond doubt. So is the interest of that section as compared with the description of the vestimentary code. Yet one wonders to what extent this analysis is really 'linguistic' and not, as it seems to me, a good traditional insight which can claim no methodological privilege.

15 Barthes, *Système de la mode*, p. 237 (my translation).

16 The methodology based upon structural linguistics claims to be more 'scientific' or more precise than a hermeneutical approach based upon a kind of intuition. Yet when the point is how to determine with accuracy the second-order structures, the methodology of structuralism does not seem much more developed. Nor indeed does

there appear to be a great deal of difference between the search for an underlying basic structure and the search for a world-view. In actual fact Barthes refers to the mythical level as contributing to form a 'general view of the world', a sphere where the linguistic analyst's task should stop to rejoin the historical world. See Barthes, *Système de la mode*, p. 238. Barthes will recognize later that semiology was originally based on 'a euphoric dream of scientificity'. See *Tel Quel*, no. 47, 1971, p. 97.

17 See Greimas.

18 Greimas, pp. 119–71. Greimas recognizes that semantics has been the poor relative within linguistics, but insists upon the importance of a scientific study of significance. According to Greimas, despite Lacan's, Barthes's and Lévi-Strauss's transpositions of 'epistemological attitudes' drawn from linguistics into other fields of reflection, there is still no 'methodological catalyst' truly based upon linguistics. He wants semantics to play its role in overcoming this deficiency.

19 A. J. Greimas, *Du sens*, Éditions du Seuil, Paris, 1970, p. 10.

20 Culler, p. 82.

21 Greimas roughly follows the scheme introduced by V. Propp in his *Morphology of the Russian Popular Tale*. Propp analyses the Russian popular tale by means of a model in which the actors are defined by their sphere of action, that is, by a number of functions that they always perform. Hence, each actor is reduced to a type or class of actor present in every tale. Propp arrives at seven basic actants: the villain; the donor; the helper; the sought-for person; the dispatcher; the hero; and the false hero. See Greimas, *Sémantique structurale*, pp. 174–5.

22 Greimas, *Sémantique structurale*, p. 181.

23 Culler, p. 75.

24 See on this, E. Veron and S. Fisher, 'Baranne est une crème', *Communications*, no. 20, 1973, p. 162. Culler has justly remarked that the difficulty is not only the fact that sentences have different meanings in different contexts, but also the fact that 'the context which determines the meaning of a sentence is more than the other sentences of the text; it is a complex of knowledge and expectations of varying degrees of specificity, a kind of interpretive competence which could in principle be described but which in practice proves exceedingly refractory'. See Culler, p. 95.

25 See for instance the attempt made by L. F. Ribeiro to interpret some political conflicts upon the basis of this model. L. F. Ribeiro *et al.*, *Sobre la justicia en Chile*, Ediciones Universitarias de Valparaiso, Valparaiso, 1973.

26 Culler, p. 91.

27 See on this K. Kosik, *Dialéctica de lo concreto*, A. Sanchez (trans.), Grijalbo, Mexico, 1967, p. 173.

28 U. Eco, *La struttura assente*, Bompiani, Milan, 1968, pp. 55–8.
29 P. Bourdieu, *Esquisse d'une théorie de la pratique*, Droz, Geneva, 1972, p. 186.
30 Culler remarks in this sense that 'the direct application of techniques for linguistic description does not in itself serve as a method of literary analysis. The reason is simply that both author and reader bring to the text more than a knowledge of language and this additional experience . . . is what guides one in the perception and construction of relevant patterns.' See Culler, p. 95.
31 E. Veron, 'Communicación de masas y producción de ideologias: acerca de la constitución del discurso burgues en la prensa semanal', *Revista Latinoamericana de Sociologia*, no. 1, 1974, p. 15.
32 Culler, p. 259.
33 In fact Lévi-Strauss claims to be the recipient of three major influences, namely, structural linguistics, geology and Marx, the latter particularly through the *Preface to a Contribution to the Critique of Political Economy* and *The Eighteenth Brumaire of Louis Bonaparte*.
34 K. Marx, *The Eighteenth Brumaire of Louis Bonaparte*, in K. Marx, and F. Engels, *Selected Works* in one volume, Lawrence & Wishart 1970, p. 96.
35 C. Lévi-Strauss, *Structural Anthropology*, C. Jacobson (trans.), Penguin, 1972, p. 23.
36 Lévi-Strauss, p. 33.
37 Lévi-Strauss, p. 47: 'The kinship system is a language; but it is not a universal language, and society may prefer other modes of expression and action.' Also, p. 62: 'the question may be raised whether the different aspects of social life (including even art and religion) . . . do not constitute phenomena whose inmost nature is the same as that of language'.
38 C. Lévi-Strauss, *Totemism*, R. Needham (trans.), Penguin, 1973, p. 84.
39 Lévi-Strauss, *Structural Anthropology*, p. 229.
40 C. Lévi-Strauss, *The Savage Mind*, Weidenfeld & Nicolson, 1974, p. 22. Lévi-Strauss, thus distinguishes between the scientist and the myth maker or '*bricoleur*'.
41 Lévi-Strauss, *Structural Anthropology*, p. 230.
42 See Lévi-Strauss, *The Savage Mind*, pp. 9–16.
43 Lévi-Strauss, *The Savage Mind*, p. 9.
44 In this sense one could assert that Lévi-Strauss is nearer Marx than Engels, Lenin and Mao insofar as the latter conceive of nature as contradictory in its very essence, independent of human practice.
45 Lévi-Strauss, *The Savage Mind*, p. 95.
46 Lévi-Strauss, *The Savage Mind*, p. 95.
47 Lévi-Strauss, *The Savage Mind*, p. 95.
48 Lévi-Strauss, *Structural Anthropology*, p. 209.

49 C. Lévi-Strauss, 'Réponses à quelques questions', *Esprit*, vol. 2, no. 322, November 1963, p. 640.

50 M. Glucksmann, *Structuralist Analysis in Contemporary Social Thought*, Routledge & Kegan Paul, 1974, p. 80.

51 Lévi-Strauss, *Structural Anthropology*, p. 211.

52 Lévi-Strauss, 'The story of Asdiwal', N. Mann (trans.), in E. Leach (ed.), *The Structural Study of Myth and Totemism*, Tavistock, 1973, p. 17.

53 Lévi-Strauss, *Structural Anthropology*, p. 214. Contrary to Greimas's semantic approach, Lévi-Strauss holds that sense results always from the combination of elements which are not themselves meaningful. See Lévi-Strauss, 'Réponses à quelques questions', p. 637. Ricoeur concludes in this respect that for Lévi-Strauss the savage thought is a thought of order. Yet it is a thought which does not think. So, in order to understand it there is no need to apprehend intentions, it suffices to grasp an unconscious arrangement. This could be described as a choice for syntax against semantics. See Ricoeur, p. 607.

54 M. Douglas, 'The meaning of myth, with special reference to "*La geste d'Asdiwal*",' in Leach, p. 64.

55 K. O. Burridge, 'Lévi-Strauss and myth', in Leach, p. 106.

56 Culler, p. 43.

57 C. Lévi-Strauss, *The Raw and the Cooked*, J. P. D. Weightman (trans.), Harper & Row, New York, 1975, p. 341.

58 N. Yalman, 'The raw: the cooked:: Nature: Culture – observations on *Le cru et le cuit*', in Leach, p. 82.

59 Culler, p. 48.

60 See Ricoeur, p. 607. Ricoeur's exposition and critique of Lévi-Strauss's theory is one of the best available.

61 Ricoeur, p. 608. Ricoeur maintains that temporality, the relationship between synchrony and diachrony, has a different meaning for each pattern. But these patterns are pure types only in the extreme poles. In the middle there are a series of combinations which vary according to whether synchrony is more important than diachrony or vice versa.

62 Lévi-Strauss, *Structural Anthropology*, p. 23.

63 Lévi-Strauss, *The Raw and the Cooked*, p. 12.

64 I. Rossi, 'Intellectual antecedents of Lévi-Strauss's notion of unconscious', in I. Rossi (ed.), *The Unconscious in Culture*, Dutton, New York, 1974, p. 17.

65 Ricoeur, p. 618.

66 Bourdieu, p. 178.

67 H. Lefebvre, *Au-delà du structuralisme*, Anthropos, Paris, 1971, pp. 272 and 277. Lefebvre's claim that structuralism contests movement in history is certainly excessive. Structuralism does not oppose synchrony to diachrony, at least certainly not Lévi-Strauss. As Ricoeur rightly points out, what structuralism claims is that dia-

chrony is only meaningful by its relation to synchrony, that is to say, there is no opposition but a relation of subordination. See Ricoeur, p. 599.

68 M. Godelier, *Horizon, trajets Marxistes en anthropologie*, Maspero, Paris, 1977, vol. 2, pp. 275–6.

69 K. Marx, *Capital*, F. Engels (ed.), Lawrence & Wishart, 1974, vol. 1, p. 77.

70 M. Godelier, 'Fétichisme, religion et théorie générale de l'idéologie chez Marx', *Annali*, Feltrinelli, Roma, 1970, pp. 30 and 35.

71 Godelier, 'Fétichisme . . . ', p. 23

72 Godelier, *Horizon . . .*, vol. 1, p. 14.

73 Godelier, *Horizon . . .*, vol. 1, p. 20.

74 See J. Mepham, 'The theory of ideology in capital', *Radical Philosophy*, no. 2, summer 1972, pp. 12–13.

75 N. Poulantzas, *Political Power and Social Classes*, T. O'Hagan (trans.), Sheed & Ward, 1973, p. 20.

76 L. Althusser, *Lenin and Philosophy and other Essays*, B. Brewster, (trans.), New Left Books, 1971, p. 151.

77 Althusser claims that the influence of structuralism upon him can be reduced to a simple 'flirtation' with structuralist terminology. See L. Althusser *Essays in Self-Criticism*, G. Lock (trans.), New Left Books, 1976, pp. 125–31. Despite this claim, I feel that structuralism affects him much more deeply than he is prepared to recognize.

78 This is abundantly shown by Schaff's analysis of Althusser's concept of ideology. See A. Schaff, *Structuralisme et marxisme*, C. Brendel (trans.), Anthropos, Paris, 1971, essay 2, p. 47. Schaff finds at least ten different definitions, not all of them compatible with one another. Another critique in this sense could be found in L. Kolakowski, 'Althusser's Marx', *The Socialist Register*, Merlin, 1971.

79 See the journal *Casa de las Americas*, no. 34, February 1966, La Habana, Cuba. The original French mimeo was entitled 'Théorie, pratique théorique et formation théorique. Idéologie et lutte idéologique' and is used by Rancière in his critique of Althusser's theory of ideology. See Rancière *La Leçon d'Althusser*, Gallimard, Paris, 1974, chapter 6. I am using a Spanish version which appeared under the title 'Práctica teórica y lucha ideologica', in L. Althusser, *La filosofia como arma de la revolución*, O. del Barco and E. Roman (trans.), Cuadernos del Pasado y Presente, Cordoba, 1970.

80 It was written in 1969, and appeared in Althusser, *Lenin and Philosophy . . .*

81 L. Althusser, *For Marx*, B. Brewster (trans.), New Left Books, 1977, p. 233.

82 Althusser, 'Práctica teórica . . .', p. 51.

83 See, for instance, P. Q. Hirst, 'Althusser and the theory of ideology', *Economy and Society*, vol. 5, no. 4, November 1976, p. 398. See also

G. McLennan, V. Molina and R. Peters, 'Althusser's theory of ideology', in Centre for Contemporary Cultural Studies (ed.), *On Ideology*, Hutchinson, 1978, p. 95.

84 Althusser, *For Marx*, p. 233.

85 Althusser, 'Práctica teórica . . .', p. 54–5.

86 Althusser, 'Práctica teórica . . .', p. 49.

87 Althusser, 'Práctica teórica . . .', p. 50.

88 Althusser, *For Marx*, p. 232.

89 Althusser, 'Práctica teórica . . .', p. 54.

90 Althusser, 'Práctica teórica . . .', p. 55. A similar explanation can be found in L. Althusser, *Reading Capital*, B. Brewster (trans.), New Left Books, 1975, p. 66: 'The mechanism of the production of this "society effect" is only complete when all the effects of the mechanism have been expounded, down to the point where they are produced in the form of the very effects that constitute the concrete, conscious or unconscious relation of the individuals to the society as a society, i.e., down to the effects of the fetishism of ideology . . . in which men consciously or unconsciously live their lives. . . .'

91 Althusser, 'Práctica teórica . . .', p. 48–9 and 56–7.

92 Althusser, *For Marx*, p. 184.

93 Althusser, *Reading Capital*, p. 52.

94 Althusser, *Lenin and Philosophy* . . ., pp. 151–2.

95 Althusser, *Lenin and Philosophy* . . ., p. 152.

96 Althusser, *Lenin and Philosophy* . . ., p. 150.

97 Althusser, *Lenin and Philosophy* . . ., p. 128.

98 Althusser, *Lenin and Philosophy* . . ., p. 141. Althusser makes a list of ideological state apparatuses such as education, family, legal system, trade unions, communications, politics, culture, religion (pp. 136–7). Perry Anderson has noted that, in adopting this terminology, Althusser assimilates one of Gramsci's formulae which abolishes all distinction between state and civil society. A consequence of this is the impossibility of distinguishing between bourgeois democracy and fascism. See P. Anderson, 'The antinomies of Antonio Gramsci', *New Left Review*, no. 100, November 1976–January 1977, p. 36.

99 Althusser, *Lenin and Philosophy* . . ., p. 147.

100 Althusser, *Lenin and Philosophy* . . ., p. 153.

101 Althusser, *Lenin and Philosophy* . . ., p. 156.

102 Althusser, *Lenin and Philosophy* . . ., p. 159.

103 K. Marx, *Grundrisse*, Penguin, 1973, p. 105.

104 Marx, *Capital*, vol. 1, p. 179.

105 K. Marx, letter to Annenkov, 28 December 1846, in K. Marx and F. Engels, *Selected Correspondence*, I. Lasher (trans.), Progress Publishers, Moscow, 1975, p. 36.

106 Althusser, *Lenin and Philosophy* . . ., p. 148.

107 The article on ISA published in Althusser, *Lenin and Philosophy* . . .

was written between January and April 1969. The Post-Scriptum (see pp. 170–3) was written in April 1970.

108 Hirst, p. 388.

109 Hirst, pp. 398–401.

110 Rancière, pp. 232–3. Rancière rightly argues that by following Althusser's conception one can easily arrive at the absurd proposition that the social totality in general entails the existence of a political superstructure and therefore, that, the general functions of the state can be defined prior to the appearance of class struggle (see p. 237). For some interesting comments on Rancière's critique, see Ted Benton, 'Rancière and ideology', *Radical Philosophy*, no. 9, winter 1974.

111 Hirst, p. 388.

112 Hirst, p. 390.

113 Althusser, *Essays in Self-Criticism*, p. 121. A discussion of Althusser's self-criticism concerning the relation between ideology and science can be found in the next chapter.

114 Hirst, 'Althusser's theory of ideology', p. 400.

115 It is in this sense that Marx accuses the utopian socialists of seeking a 'regenerating science' in their minds without understanding the connection of this science with the historical movement. See K. Marx, *The Poverty of Philosophy*, Martin Lawrence, 1966, p. 106.

116 Rancière, pp. 239–241.

117 See R. Coward and J. Ellis, *Language of Materialism*, Routledge & Kegan Paul, 1977. This text is a very good introduction to the thinking of *Tel Quel*.

118 J. Kristeva, 'L'engendrement de la formule', *Tel Quel*, no. 37, 1969, p. 35.

119 J. Kristeva, *Le Texte du roman*, Mouton, The Hague, 1970, pp. 67–9, quoted by Coward and Ellis, p. 52.

120 J. Kristeva, 'L'engendrement de la formule', p. 35.

121 R. Barthes, *S/Z*, Cape, 1974, p. 9.

122 J. L. Baudry, 'Écriture, fiction, idéologie', *Tel Quel*, no. 31, 1967, p. 22.

123 Coward and Ellis, p. 2.

124 Coward and Ellis, p. 61.

125 Coward and Ellis, p. 67.

126 Coward and Ellis, p. 73.

127 Coward and Ellis, p. 75.

128 Coward and Ellis, p. 91.

129 J. Kristeva, *La Révolution du langage poétique*, Seuil, Paris, 1974, p. 103, quoted by Coward and Ellis, p. 90.

130 P. Sollers, 'De quelques contradictions', *Tel Quel*, no. 38, 1969, p. III.

131 Sollers, p. III.

132 Coward and Ellis, p. 82.

133 Coward and Ellis, p. 82.

134 D. Adlam and A. Salfield, 'A matter of language', *Ideology and Consciousness*, no. 3, spring 1978.

135 Laplanche's and Leclaire's article can be found in *Yale French Studies*, no. 48, 1972, pp. 118–79. Lacan's repudiation is in the preface to A. Lemaire, *Jacques Lacan*, Routledge & Kegan Paul, 1977.

136 Adlam and Salfield, p. 108.

137 In this respect Adlam and Salfield's (p. 101) point seems quite pertinent in the sense that the correspondence between the subject in linguistics and the 'subject' in Marxism should be demonstrated, and that Coward and Ellis have just assumed their articulation to be unproblematic.

138 Marx and Engels, *The German Ideology*, p. 42.

139 Marx, *Capital*, vol. 1, p. 173.

140 Marx and Engels, *The German Ideology*, p. 58.

141 Sichère has accused *Tel Quel* of idealism disguised as materialism. In a sarcastic style he points to the last trick of idealism: to appear as materialism. He argues that 'today everybody would be more or less materialist. Writers, because they have to do with the materials of language. Painters, because they touch colours. Musicians because they manipulate notes. Psychoanalysts because they act on the pulsion. . . . We were within materialism without knowing it.' But of course, what Marx and Engels thought of materialism is never taken into account. See B. Sichère, 'Le faux matérialisme "tel quel", contre les interpreteurs', in *Marxisme-Leninisme et psychanalyse*, Maspero, Paris, 1975, p. 111–12.

142 Coward and Ellis, p. 91.

143 K. Marx, *Theses on Feuerbach*, in Marx and Engels, *The German Ideology*, p. 121, thesis III.

6   Ideology and science: Marx and the contemporary debate

1 See A. Schaff, 'Marxisme et sociologie de la connaissance', *L'Homme et la Société*, no. 10, October–December 1968, p. 141. Schaff argues that revolutionary classes have interests which coincide with the trend of social development so that their consciousness is a true reflection of reality. On the contrary, descendant or conservative classes, by opposing social development in defence of their interests, blind themselves to the truth. In a more recent book (*Structuralisme et Marxisme*, Anthropos, Paris, 1974), Schaff adopts a more cautious attitude by stating that the problem of scientificity of ideology has a 'relative autonomy'. Ideology, in this account, is conditioned not only by class interests but also by the 'intellectual materials' with which it is constructed. These two aspects are not identical, despite the fact that the latter is partially dependent upon the former. For another

distinction of this sort see L. Goldmann, *The Human Sciences and Philosophy*, H. White and R. Anchor (trans.), Cape, 1973, p. 103.

2 G. Stedman Jones, 'The Marxism of the early Lukács: an evaluation', *New Left Review*, no. 70, 1971, p. 40.

3 A. Schmidt, *The Concept of Nature in Marx*, B. Fawkes (trans.), New Left Books, 1971.

4 The construction and treatment of the first two positions, which represent different authors, is made only from the point of view of what is relevant for the clarification of the relationships between ideology and science. There is no doubt, for instance, that from other points of view Althusser and positivism are clearly antithetical and cannot be simply assimilated to one another. Similar considerations should be applied to authors like Lukács, Marcuse, Horkheimer, Habermas, etc.

5 I am indebted to R. Echeverría for drawing my attention to the stages of Marx's intellectual development. However, their description is entirely my responsibility. For a detailed analysis of his viewpoint see his unpublished doctoral thesis, *Marx's Concept of Science*, Birkbeck College, London, 1978.

6 K. Marx, *Economic and Philosophic Manuscripts*, in K. Marx, *Early Writings*, P. Livingstone and G. Benton (trans.), Penguin, 1974, p. 355.

7 Marx, p. 381.

8 Marx, p. 355.

9 Marx, p. 354.

10 Marx, p. 355.

11 K. Marx and F. Engels, *The German Ideology* (large version), Lawrence & Wishart, 1965, p. 28. Marx criticized Bauer's idea of an antithesis in nature and history 'as though they were two separate "things" and man did not always have before him a historical nature and a natural history' (pp. 62–3 of the student's edition).

12 Marx and Engels, p. 63.

13 K. Marx, *Theses on Feuerbach*, in K. Marx and F. Engels, *The German Ideology*, C. Arthur (ed.), Lawrence & Wishart, 1970, thesis VI, p. 122.

14 Marx, *Theses on Feuerbach*, thesis IV, p. 122.

15 K. Marx, *Capital*, F. Engels, (ed.) Lawrence & Wishart, 1974, vol. 1, p. 352, note.

16 Marx and Engels, *The German Ideology*, p. 48.

17 Marx and Engels, *The German Ideology*, p. 41.

18 K. Marx, *The Poverty of Philosophy*, Martin Lawrence, 1966, p. 117.

19 Marx and Engels, *The German Ideology*, pp. 58–9.

20 Marx, *The Poverty of Philosophy*, p. 106.

21 As we saw in chapter 2, some of Marx's expressions in this sense give the impression that he is an empiricist at this stage. However, one must understand them in the context of his critique of idealism which

had dissolved the material world in the idea. Marx is trying to convey the necessity of abandoning the world of ideas to look at material reality as it is. He is not making an empiricist claim about how this reality should be understood. The concept of practice with which he argues against the old materialism redresses the balance insofar as the external reality should not be understood as a mere given object. The problem at this stage is not so much empiricism as the fact that appearances are only seen as philosophical ideas. This is partly the result of the fact that Marx is criticizing philosophy and not yet political economy. (See note 23 to this chapter.)

22 See on this pages 54–5 of this book.

23 See note 21 to this chapter. In fact even before the *Grundrisse* Marx was aware of the distinction between essence and appearance. This is demonstrated by his comment on Feuerbach in *The German Ideology*, whose failure, he says was not that he subordinated 'the sensuous *appearance*' to the sensuous reality established by more accurate investigation of the sensuous facts. Feuerbach's failing was rather that he had a philosophical conception of essence. However, on the whole it is true that Marx's insistence is not on this distinction. See *The German Ideology* (large version), N.B., p. 56.

24 K. Marx, *Wages, Price and Profit*, in K. Marx and F. Engels *Selected Works* in one volume, Lawrence & Wishart, 1970, p. 207.

25 Marx, *Capital*, vol. 3, p. 817.

26 See on this Marx, *Grundrisse*, M. Nicolaus (trans.), Penguin, 1973, p. 164.

27 Marx never defined ideology in terms of the pair essence–appearance. In fact, even the name ideology is almost entirely absent from his mature economic writings. However, just as the apparent autonomy of ideas arises from material life itself, other deceptions arise from the appearances of that material life. It seems only logical to extend the concept of ideology to cover them.

28 Marx, *Capital*, vol. 1, p. 79.

29 Marx, *Grundrisse*, p. 700.

30 K. Marx, *Theories of Surplus-Value*, Lawrence & Wishart, 1969, vol. 1, p. 391. See also p. 176 and vol. 3, p. 443. Also Marx, *Capital*, vol. 1, p. 341 and *Grundrisse*, pp. 693–5, 699–700 and 704.

31 Marx, *Grundrisse*, p. 693. See also the 'First draft of "The civil war in France"', in Marx, *The First International and After*, D. Fernbach (ed.), Penguin, 1974, p. 259: 'Only the working class can . . . convert science from an instrument of class rule into a popular force, convert the men of science themselves from the panderers to class prejudice, place-hunting parasites, and allies of capital into free agents of thought! Science can only play its genuine part in the republic of labour.' In a speech at the Anniversary of the People's Paper in 1856 Marx affirms: 'All our invention and progress seem to result in

endowing material forces with intellectual life, and in stultifying human life into a material force. This antagonism between modern industry and science on the one hand, modern misery and dissolution on the other hand; this antagonism between the productive powers and the social relations of our epoch . . . is a fact, palpable, overwhelming and not to be controverted.' See Marx, *Surveys from Exile*, Penguin, 1973, p. 300.

32 Marx, *Grundrisse*, pp. 699–800.

33 Marx, *Capital*, vol. 1, p. 352, note.

34 Marx, *Grundrisse*, p. 410.

35 Marx and Engels, *The German Ideology*, p. 54. See also pp. 46–7: individuals work 'under definite material limits, presuppositions and conditions independent of their will'.

36 Marx, *Capital*, vol. 1, p. 166. See also *Grundrisse*, p. 222: 'The mania for possessions is possible without money; but greed itself is the product of a definite social development, not *natural*, as opposed to *historical*.'

37 K. Marx, letter to Kugelman, 27 June 1870, in K. Marx and F. Engels, *Selected Correspondence*, I. Lasher (trans.), Progress Publishers, Moscow, 1975, p. 225. Marx shows the same scorn for Townsend who affirms that 'it seems to be a law of nature that the poor should be to a certain degree improvident . . .'. See, Marx, *Grundrisse*, p. 845.

38 K. Marx, letter to Kugelman, 11 July, 1868, in Marx and Engels, *Selected Correspondence*, p. 196.

39 Marx, *Grundrisse*, pp. 831–2.

40 Marx, *Capital*, 'Afterword to the second German edition', vol. 1, p. 24.

41 Marx, *Theories of Surplus-Value*, vol. 3, p. 501.

42 Marx, *Theories of Surplus-Value*, vol. 2, p. 118.

43 Marx, *Theories of Surplus-Value*, vol. 2, pp. 497–8.

44 Marx, *Capital*, 'Afterword to the second German edition', vol. 1, p. 25.

45 Marx, *Capital*, vol. 1, p. 559.

46 Marx, *Capital*, 'Afterword to the second German edition', vol. 1, p. 24.

47 Marx, *The Poverty of Philosophy*, p. 43.

48 Marx, *Capital*, vol. 3, p. 830.

49 Marx, *Theories of Surplus-Value*, vol. 2, p. 106.

50 Marx, *Theories of Surplus-Value*, vol. 2, pp. 373, 399 and 173 passim, and vol. 3, p. 138 passim.

51 Marx, *Theories of Surplus-Value*, vol. 2, pp. 527–9.

52 Marx, letter to Annenkov, 28 December 1846, in Marx and Engels, *Selected Correspondence*, p. 34.

53 K. Marx, *Theories of Surplus-Value*, vol. 2, p. 164: 'The historical

justification of this method of procedure, its scientific necessity in the history of economics, are evident at first sight, but so is, at the same time, its scientific inadequacy.' See also pp. 165–9.

54 'Ricardo regards . . . capitalist production as the absolute form of production, whose specific forms of production relations can therefore never enter into contradiction with, or enfetter, the aim of production . . ., when contradictions appear . . . he denies the contradictions, or rather expresses the contradiction in another form. . . .' See Marx, *Theories of Surplus-Value*, vol. 3, p. 55.

55 Marx, *Theories of Surplus-Value*, vol. 3, p. 453.

56 Marx knew only the case of vulgar economy. After his death other forms made their appearance, specially under the guise of sociological theories. See on this N. Poulantzas, *Political Power and Social Classes*, New Left Books and Sheed & Ward, 1973, p. 195.

57 L. Kolakowski, *Positivist Philosophy*, Penguin, 1972, p. 18.

58 This terminology is derived from Horkheimer who opposes this instrumental or subjective reason to the objective reason which sees 'essences' in reality. See M. Horkheimer, *Eclipse of Reason*, Seabury, New York, 1974. Epistemologically speaking though, instrumental reason seeks to surpass the limitations of subjectivity in the objectivity of the scientific method. Adorno has called attention to the paradox that empirical methods in sociology, whose power of attraction lies in their claim to objectivity, favour nevertheless the subjectivity of what is investigated. Empirical methods in sociology have ignored societal objectivity while assuming that men's consciousness, statistically measured, possesses an immediate key role for the societal process. See T. Adorno, 'Sociology and empirical research', in T. Adorno *et al.*, *The Positivist Dispute in German Sociology*, Heinemann, p. 71.

59 F. Bacon, *The New Organon and related writings*, O. Piest (ed.), Liberal Arts, New York, 1960, p. 47. See also pages 19–22 of this book.

60 See pages 28–31 of this book.

61 See pages 91–9 of this book.

62 M. Schlick, 'Positivism and realism', in A. J. Ayer, *Logical Positivism*, Free Press, Glencoe, 1959, p. 88: 'a proposition has a statable meaning only if it makes a verifiable difference whether it is true or false'.

63 R. Carnap, 'The elimination of metaphysics through logical analysis of language', in Ayer, p. 79

64 J. Habermas, *Knowledge and Human Interests*, Heinemann, 1972, p. 68.

65 K. Popper, *Conjectures and Refutations*, Routledge & Kegan Paul, 1965, p. 256.

66 This means that Popper admits certain metaphysical statements as meaningful. However, this may well be due, as Carnap has pointed

out, to a fundamental misunderstanding. While logical positivists are concerned with the boundary between pseudo-statements on the one hand and scientific statements and pseudo-scientific statements on the other, Popper is concerned with the boundaries between the last two. Popper would classify metaphysics as a pseudo-scientific statement (like myth, magical beliefs or astrology) whereas Carnap would consider it to be a pseudo-statement which cannot be true or false but is simply nonsensical. See R. Carnap, 'Replies and systematic expositions', in P. A. Schilpp (ed.), *The Philosophy of Rudolf Carnap*, La Salle, 1963, pp. 878–81.

67 K. Popper, *The Open Society and Its Enemies*, Routledge & Kegan Paul, 1973, vol. 2, p. 218.
68 K. Popper, 'Reason or revolution?', in Adorno *et al.*, p. 299: to take an interest in natural science does not make one a positivist.
69 K. Popper, *The Open Society and Its Enemies*, vol. 2, p. 222.
70 K. Popper, 'The logic of the social sciences', in Adorno *et al.*, p. 95.
71 J. Habermas, *Theory and Practice*, Heinemann, 1974, p. 275. For a detailed analysis and critique of positivism see R. Keat and J. Urry, *Social Theory as Science*, Routledge & Kegan Paul, 1975, and T. Benton, *Philosophical Foundations of the Three Sociologies*, Routledge & Kegan Paul, 1977.
72 T. Kuhn, *The Structure of Scientific Revolutions*, University of Chicago Press, 1970, p. 2.
73 Kuhn, p. 138.
74 Popper accentuates this point when he argues that scientific knowledge may be regarded as subjectless! See Popper, 'Normal science and its dangers', in I. Lakatos and A. Musgrave (eds.), *Criticism and the Growth of Knowledge*, Cambridge University Press, 1970, p. 57.
75 See P. Feyerabend, *Against Method*, New Left Books, 1975, chapter 18.
76 This criterion of validity is not necessarily opposed to Popper's deductive approach. Kuhn's criterion shows how far from reality the conception of science is which relies on a pre-Kantian epistemology of adequacy to a seemingly objective reality. Popper would agree with this in general. Yet from a different viewpoint, he would disagree, for Popper does not accept 'normal science', except as a deviation. Popper thinks that most of the time science is critical or revolutionary. See Popper, 'Normal science and its dangers', pp. 54–5. For a critique of Kuhn see Benton, p. 185: the main criticism is that Kuhn's thesis of 'successive incommensurable "paradigms", make any conception of continuity through scientific revolutions unthinkable'.
77 In this sense Keat's and Urry's criticism that Kuhn fails 'to analyse the relations between the institutional features of the scientific community, and other elements of the societies in which these institutions exist', seems quite pertinent.

78 See H. Rose and S. Rose (eds.), *The Political Economy of Science*, Macmillan, London, 1976.

79 T. Adorno, 'Introduction' to Adorno *et al.*, p. 21.

80 L. Althusser, *La filosofía como arma de la revolución*, O. del Barco and E. Roman (trans.), Cuadernos del pasado y Presente, Cordoba, 1970, p. 57.

81 L. Althusser, *Reading Capital*, B. Brewster (trans.), New Left Books, 1975, pp. 84–5. For a detailed analysis of the first feature see J. Mepham, 'The theory of ideology in Capital', *Radical Philosophy*, no. 2, summer 1972, in which the relationships between phenomenal forms and real relations constitute the basis for the understanding of both Marxist theory and ideology.

82 Althusser, *Reading Capital*, pp. 41–2. A most peculiar reading of the 1857 Introduction makes Althusser think that Marx would have distinguished between the 'real object' (or the 'real concrete') and the 'object of knowledge', which 'appears in the process of thinking . . . as a process of concentration, as a result, not as a point of departure' (Marx, *Grundrisse*, p. 101).

83 G. Bachelard, *Le Materialisme rationnel*, PUF, Paris, 1953, p. 142, quoted by D. Lecourt, *Marxism and Epistemology*, New Left Books, 1975, p. 53.

84 L. Althusser, *For Marx*, B. Brewster (trans.), New Left Books, 1977, pp. 183–93.

85 Lecourt, p. 86.

86 Lecourt, p. 12.

87 G. Bachelard, *L'Activité rationaliste de la physique contemporaine*, PUF, Paris, 1951, p. 27, quoted by Lecourt, p. 13.

88 Given Lecourt's definition of positivism, it is not surprising that Kuhn should appear as a positivist.

89 Althusser's double object of knowledge resembles Hume's idealist positivism to which knowledge is limited to knowledge of the world of our impressions and our mental states. See K. Ajdukiewicz, *Problems and Theories of Philosophy*, Cambridge University Press, 1973, p. 64. The idealism of Althusser's position is also noticed by Benton, who finds that 'there is a remarkable homology between Althusser's insistence on the "constructed" character of the object of scientific knowledge and the Neo-Kantians' insistence on the same point'. See Benton, p. 185.

90 This peculiar name is used by Althusser in an effort to demonstrate that nobody made a consistent critique of his position before his self-criticism. Thus, as far as he is concerned, he is the first to come up with the real cause of his past mistakes. That his problem is less special than he likes to think is shown by the very fact that on one occasion he is obliged to describe this deviation as the *rationalist* opposition between science and non-science. See L. Althusser,

Essays in Self-Criticism, G. Lode (trans.), New Left Books, 1976, p. 119.

91 Althusser, *Essays in Self-Criticism*, p. 119.

92 Althusser, *Essays in Self-Criticism*, p. 66.

93 Althusser, *Essays in Self-Criticism*, p. 68.

94 Althusser, *Essays in Self-Criticism*, pp. 142–3.

95 See on this W. Outhwaite, *Understanding Social Life*, Allen & Unwin, 1975, and R. Aron, *La philosophie critique de l'histoire*, J. Vrin, Paris, 1969. For a critical exposition of Kant and historicism see Benton.

96 Stedman Jones, has emphasized this point. He also claims that Lukács did not clearly recognize the scientific character of Marxism. See G. Stedman Jones, 'The Marxism of the early Lukács: an evaluation', *New Left Review*, no. 70, 1971. I think a quick review of *History and Class Consciousness* would show that this latter contention is not exactly the case. Lukács repeatedly affirms the scientific character of Marxism although one may argue about the sense Lukács gave to these expressions.

97 G. Lukács, *History and Class Consciousness*, Merlin, 1971, p. 10.

98 Lukács, p. 104.

99 Lukács, p. 105.

100 Lukács, p. 10.

101 Lukács, p. 7.

102 Horkheimer.

103 Horkheimer, p. 24.

104 Horkheimer, p. 40.

105 Horkheimer, p. 93.

106 T. Adorno and M. Horkheimer, *Dialectic of Enlightenment*, Allen Lane, 1973, p. 26.

107 Lukács, p. 102.

108 M. Jay, *The Dialectical Imagination*, Heinemann, 1973, p. 259.

109 Horkheimer, p. 175.

110 H. Marcuse, *Negations*, Penguin, 1972, pp. 223–4.

111 H. Marcuse, *One Dimensional Man*, Abacus, 1972, p. 130.

112 Marcuse, *One Dimensional Man*, p. 23.

113 Marcuse, *One Dimensional Man*, p. 24.

114 Marcuse, *One Dimensional Man*, p. 138.

115 Marcuse, *One Dimensional Man*, p. 136.

116 J. Habermas, *Toward a Rational Society*, Heinemann, p. 87.

117 Habermas, p. 89.

118 I have restricted my analysis of Habermas's concept of ideology to his early elaborations on science and ideology. It has to be borne in mind that Habermas later introduced new elements to his conception of ideology which are related to his theory of 'systematically distorted communication'. For an analysis of these new elements see J. Larrain, *Marxism and Ideology*, Macmillan, 1983, chapters 3 and 6.

119 Habermas, p. 111. A similar, though even more extreme position is taken by Feyerabend. For him science is an ideology no better than religion which has succeeded in imposing itself by its power. Science as a neutral structure containing positive knowledge that is independent of culture, ideology and prejudice is a 'fairy tale'. Science is not only another ideology but also the objective measure of all ideologies. Feyerabend thinks that the fairy tale of scientific method assumes a decisive function in concealing the freedom of decision and protecting the 'big-shots' (Nobel prize-winners, heads of laboratories, etc.). See Feyerabend, chapter 18.

120 Habermas, p. 114.

121 See J. Habermas, *Legitimation Crisis*, Heinemann, 1976, p. 92.

122 E. Mandel, *Late Capitalism*, New Left Books, 1975, p. 501.

123 See Daniel Bell, *The End of Ideology*, Free Press, New York, 1965.

124 Mandel, pp. 506–7.

125 Mandel, p. 508.

126 See Marcuse, *Negations*, chapter 6.

127 Habermas, *Toward a Rational Society*, p. 111: 'For the leading productive force – controlled scientific-technical progress itself – has now become the basis of legitimation.'

128 Marx and Engels, *The German Ideology*, p. 41.

129 Lakatos proposes to understand the continuity in the growth of science upon the basis of 'research programmes'. This idea is conceived of as an alternative to Kuhn's conception of a 'normal science'. See 'Falsification and the methodology of scientific research programmes', in Lakatos and Musgrave.

130 Poulantzas, *Political Power. . . .*, p. 217.

Index